American State Politics:
An Introduction

American State Politics: An Introduction

BY *V. O. Key, Jr.*

LIBRARY
BRYAN COLLEGE
DAYTON, TENN. 37321

GREENWOOD PRESS, PUBLISHERS
WESTPORT, CONNECTICUT

Library of Congress Cataloging in Publication Data

Key, V. O. (Valdimer Orlando), 1908-1963.
   American state politics.

   Reprint. Originally published: New York : Knopf, 1956.
   Includes index.
   1. State governments.   I. Title.
JK2408.K4 1983   320.973   83-20498
ISBN 0-313-24246-1 (lib. bdg.)

Reprinted with the permission of Alfred A. Knopf, Inc.

Reprinted in 1983 by Greenwood Press
A division of Congressional Information Service, Inc.
88 Post Road West, Westport, Connecticut 06881

Printed in the United States of America

10 9 8 7 6 5 4 3 2 1

PREFACE

STUDENTS of American politics have concentrated their attention chiefly on the national scene to the neglect of the politics of the states of the Union. The size of their populations and the magnitude of their operations make many of our states quite as important political units as many of the independent nations of the world. State politics constitutes a field worthy of inquiry both for its intrinsic importance in our public affairs and because of the opportunities it affords for the study of the political process generally. The object here is not to present a comprehensive survey of the entire field of state politics. That endeavor must await the accumulation of a great deal more knowledge of a terrain both large in its extent and bewildering in its complexity. The purpose is the more modest one of opening up the discussion of some of the major problems, of suggesting modes of investigation, and of stimulating further inquiry. Within these limits the task has been reduced to more manageable size by the restriction of attention chiefly to the states with at least the rudiments of a two-party system. This definition of focus excludes, save for comparative reference, the states of the South, which possess their own peculiar political practices. Nor is there attempted the ambitious task of constructing broad descriptions of the political systems of each of the nonsouthern states. The approach is rather to develop systematic techniques for coping on a comparative basis with problems and questions common to many states. That approach, or so it is assumed, should permit findings of some generality.

The attribution to a single individual of the authorship of a volume resting on the kinds of data and the types of methods used here involves a degree of exaggeration. While the formulation of the argument is mine, I have relied heavily on several research assistants both for the analyses reported and for the many incidental unreported inquiries that led down blind alleys. In the final stage of manuscript preparation I had the invaluable aid of H. D. Price, now a fellow of the Social Science Research Council, and Frank James Munger, now an instructor at Syracuse University. Corinne Silverman made most of the analyses underlying Chapter III, which has been published elsewhere, in a somewhat different version, under joint authorship. Some chapters owe much to the work of Layman Allen and Stanley Hopper. For stenographic assistance and for a great deal of patient statistical work I am obliged to Aniela Lichtenstein. The Rockefeller Foundation, by a grant to Harvard University, enabled me to avail myself of all this assistance. While I am deeply grateful to the gentlemen of the Foundation staff, it should be absolutely clear that they have not indicated to me what I should or should not say. They have permitted me to make my own mistakes in my own way. Yet I do owe to them, as well as to others, the customary, although infrequently challenged, prefatory assertion of my full responsibility for all errors of fact and eccentricities of interpretation.

Several of my professional colleagues have reviewed the principal chapters and have given me the benefit of their advice and criticism. I am especially indebted to Oliver Garceau, of Bennington College, Avery Leiserson, of Vanderbilt University, M. Brewster Smith, of the Social Science Research Council, David B. Truman, of Columbia University, Angus Campbell, of the University of Michigan, and Alexander Heard, of the University of North Carolina. While scarcely a page remains unaffected by their critical observations, this acknowledgment does not mean that they concur with what I say. A most lively essay could be pieced together from their acid comments about passages that I have allowed to stand substantially unchanged. I must record also a different sort of obligation to Coleman B. Ransone, Jr., of the University of Alabama. Discussion with him, while he was in the early stages of his study, *The Office of Governor in the United States,* provided leads to data as well as to ideas that found their way into Chapter III. Whatever resemblance my analysis bears to his doubtless stems from his helpful suggestions to me. For permission to use, in a revised form, parts of the book that have appeared elsewhere I am indebted to the editors of the *American Political Science Review,* the *New Republic,* and *Public Policy.*

V. O. KEY, JR.

Littauer Center
Cambridge, Massachusetts

Contents

x   *Contents*

Figures

Tables

American State Politics:
An Introduction

Chapter 1

The American States:
Functional Growth and Political Atrophy

The American people are not boiling with concern about the workings of their state governments. In the competition for public interest and attention the governments of the American states come off a poor second-best against the performance of the finished professionals who operate in Washington. The salience of national issues, the magnitude of federal undertakings, and the stature of national leaders, creations of the arts of publicity though they may be, push into the far background the doings of the politicians in Springfield, in Sacramento, in Salem, in Bismarck, in Baton Rouge, and in Tallahassee.

This secondary position of the states diverges sharply from the pleasant fictions of American political mythology. The orators remind us on ceremonial occasions that the states of the federal union are close to the people; that local and state governments are the bedrock of popular government; that Washington must be held suspect and leaned upon only as a last resort; that states are sensitively responsive to local needs and sentiments; and that Washington is apt to be remote, unfeeling, arbitrary, capricious. In short, the virtues of the states rest in their qualities as both effective and sensitive instruments for popular government.

Another strain of commentary on our constitutional system, less given to sentiment but not invariably realistic, carries the view that the states have passed their zenith. A series of Supreme Court decisions, beginning with the validation of the National Labor Relations Act in 1937, in effect, transferred to the care of Congress all questions of importance that could have been handled by the states. The American states exist only as vestigial remnants left by the process of unification of separated entities into nationhood. They deserve what they get, viz., neglect.

Both these broad appraisals of the place and nature of the states in the American federal system merit abrupt dissent. Those who bemoan the passing of the states shed tears for the loss of power that had scarcely been exercised and probably, in the nature of things, never could have been activated to any major extent. In truth, the growth of federal power has served to liberate the states by making practicable state legislative action earlier estopped by the fear of loss of competitive position among the states. Furthermore, by its utilization of the states as agencies for the administration of such activities as old-age assistance and unemployment insurance, Congress during the past two decades has contributed to a remarkable growth in state activity. Instead of shrinking, state tax collections, expenditures, and activities have expanded at a rapid rate.

Similarly, the idyllic conventional view about the politics of the states does not stand up. Within the states, conditions have come to exist that make most difficult the organization of popular leadership. Instead of political sensitivity we often have political stalemate. Instead of ready and easy ways for the expression of popular will we have confusion and obstruction. Instead of the alertness and sensitivity described by the political orators, the actual situation discourages the maintenance of a party leadership and a party competition that might provide dynamic forces necessary for the fulfillment of the mission of the states. At times, in fact, obstructions to political initiative within the states divert to Washington activities that might as well be handled at state capitals.

1. The New Role of the States

Historically the comparatively cavalier public regard for the states found explanation, if not justification, in the fact that those matters of most importance were handled either by the federal government or by local governments. The flow of decision to Washington, the constitutional dialecticians made plain, reflected the indivisibility of modern political problems. What could be expected of the states on fiscal policy? On employment policy? On public works? On old-age security? On conservation? The restraints of fact, more obdurate than the restrictions of constitutions, made the states archaic survivals of institutional evolution—objects for scorn as well as neglect.

Perhaps the states should be written off as instrumentalities for the decision of many types of great questions that have grown beyond them. Yet, as their epitaph was being written, the states, by the unplanned processes of constitutional development, were taking on a new and different role. That role, whose character remains yet to be filled out in detail, will demand more adequate systems of political management and leadership within the states. Whether necessity will create its own remedy is problematic but the cost of neglect will certainly increase.

In one respect the new position of the states amounts only to an enormous expansion of their ancient role. Forty years ago the national and local governments were the centers of political action of genuine concern to the citizenry. The small-scale apparatus of state government did not make much of a dent on either the consciousness or the wallet of the taxpayer. Gradually the states have assumed a sharply altered position in the total governmental system. No longer can they be dismissed as a thin and insignificant governmental sliver layered between

Washington and the cities. Expenditure rates provide about as good a measure as can be had of the scale of governmental activity. In 1922 the activities of local governments—cities, counties, towns, school districts, and the like—almost dwarfed those of the governments of the 48 states. In that year local governments managed to spend about $3.25 for every dollar spent by the state authorities. Or, to reverse the arithmetic, the statehouses paid out about 30 cents while local governments were disbursing a dollar. By 1953 outlays by state governments, so rapid had been their growth, approached in size those of local governments. In that year the city fathers along with their other local government colleagues collectively managed to spend only $1.27 for every dollar spent at the statehouse. The differentials in growth of state and of local expenditures appear in another form in the chart in Figure 1. Nor do any of these

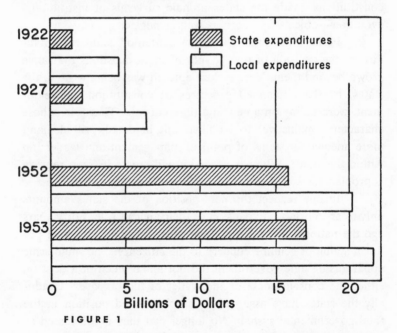

FIGURE 1

State Costs Grow More Rapidly than Local Outlays: State and Local Government Expenditures, 1922, 1927, 1952, and 1953

calculations take into account the fact that an increasing proportion of local government outlay is supported by funds raised by the state and doled out to its local governments.[1] In terms of dollars and cents extracted from the taxpayer, state governments collectively now outweigh their numerous local progeny.

From these broad trends the paradoxical conclusion emerges that, as the prophets of doom proclaimed the passing of the states during the ferment of the New Deal, state governments were expanding their staffs, enlarging the scope of their activities, spending more and more money, and in general enjoying a boom as such things go in governmental circles.

Along with the growth in the scale of its operations, the state has come to occupy a new and pivotal administrative and fiscal position in the governmental structure. One development contributing to its altered position has been the extension of the system of federal grants to states to cover more and more governmental activities. Under the grant system the states become, in effect, the agents of Congress to receive federal funds to aid in the support of governmental activities of national concern. In turn, the states often dispense federal funds—depending on the program and the particular state—to their local governments which actually administer the aided program. Thus a state government often serves as a conduit through which federal funds for old-age assistance reach a county welfare board.

In a parallel development state governments in greater and greater degree have come to the financial support of their local governments by collecting taxes and distributing the proceeds, either as subventions for particular purposes or as shared taxes, among the localities. The states tapped new sources of revenue, such as the income tax and the sales tax, to supplement the resources of local governments, which had exploited to the maximum the general property tax—historically their principal fiscal foundation.

[1] The data for Figures 1 and 2 are from Bureau of the Census, *Historical Statistics on State and Local Government Finances, 1902-1953* (Washington, 1955).

The seeds for the conversion of the states into governments that spend money they do not raise and raise money they do not spend existed, of course, even in 1920. Yet the change since that time has been so great as to be one of kind rather than of degree. The great boost in federal payments to the states came with the Social Security Act of 1935 and the subsequent enlargements of the programs financed under it. Similarly, the

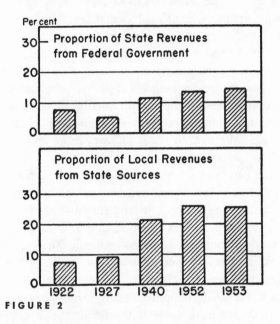

FIGURE 2

States as Financial Middlemen: Proportions of State Revenues from Federal Sources and Proportions of Local Revenues from State Sources, 1922, 1927, 1940, 1952, 1953

collapse of local revenue systems during the depression stimulated the growth in local reliance on state revenue sources. From 1922 to 1953 annual federal payments to states increased about 2500 per cent. In 1927 only one of twenty dollars of state revenues came from the federal government; by 1953 the ratio was about one of seven. In local government finance, funds from the statehouse similarly loom larger and larger. In 1922 less than 10 per cent of local revenues collectively came from state sources; by 1953 approximately one-fourth of all local revenues came from the state governments acting, in part, as channels for the distribution of federal funds. These ratios, of course, differ widely, with some states more dependent than others on federal funds and with some local governments more dependent than others on state funds.

As the states have gained a more prominent position in the governmental firmament, they have undergone another sort of growth that generates its problems in political leadership, organization, and education. The problems of democratic politics have some relation to the size of the population which attempts to govern itself. The larger the population, the greater becomes the task of organization of party machinery, the problem of campaigning, of educating the voter, and of getting out the vote.

The problems of state political leadership emerge strikingly by comparison of states with some of the full-fledged members of the family of nations. New York's population about equals that of the Dominion of Canada, and California's is substantially larger than that of Australia. The government of New Jersey serves about the same number of people as does that of Switzerland, and Portugal is not much more populous than Ohio. The Irish Free State and Minnesota have about the same population, as do Greece and Texas. Illinois politicians must cope with about as many people as do those of Belgium, while North Carolinians are about as numerous as Finns. Even the relatively small state of Colorado almost equals Paraguay in population. The people of Pennsylvania slightly outnumber those of the Netherlands, and the Virginia state machine should be able to man the government of Norway if the ratio of politicians to people is fairly uniform from culture to culture. Michigan has a little growing to do if it is to overtake Sweden, but the citizenry of Massachusetts slightly exceeds that of Denmark.[2]

2. Obstructions to Popular Government

The nature of the workings of government depends ultimately on the men who run it. The men we elect to office and the circumstances we create that affect their work determine the nature of popular government. Let there be emphasis on those we elect to office. Legislators, governors, and other such elective functionaries ultimately fix the basic tone and character of state government.

For fifty years the ills of state government have been a subject for diagnosis and prescription. The specialists on administrative organization have grouped and regrouped functions and defined and redefined lines of authority. The personnel experts have tinkered with civil service recruitment policies, and the fiscal analysts have surveyed financial practices and installed systems to plug the leaks. Little "Hoover Commissions" and countless other bodies, more or less expert, have labored and brought forth their reports, with consequences great and small.

Yet singularly little thought has been devoted to the corps of elective officers, the men who collectively compose the armature that turns the machinery of government. As the problems of the management of the state apparatus have grown in size and complexity the underlying political conditions and circumstances have made more difficult the development and recruitment of adequate popular leadership. Obviously the man-

[2] For reflective observations on the emergent problems of the states in the federal system, see Leonard D. White, *The States and the Nation* (Baton Rouge: Louisiana State University Press, 1953) and William Anderson, *The Nation and the States, Rivals or Partners?* (Minneapolis: University of Minnesota Press, 1955). The changes in the position of the states and the attendant problems receive extensive attention in the 1955 *Report* of the Commission on Intergovernmental Relations and in the studies prepared for the commission.

ner of ascent to public leadership and the mode of popular decision are rooted deeply in the social system and respond most grudgingly to proposals for change. The whole business might be dismissed as hopeless, with remarks about letting fools contest over forms of government. Yet that maxim of Pope's couplet may also be dismissed as an enduring half truth. Indubitably the arrangements of party organization, of governmental structure, and of electoral procedure influence not only the results of elections but also the behavior of officials once they are elected. Those forms that influence the determination of who is to do the administering and those factors that condition their work once they are chosen cannot be dismissed as of no importance.

Yet what is the bill of particulars for adequate popular leadership? How is one to judge whether the requisites have been met? Any set of standards must consist of more or less arbitrarily stated criteria, although a goodly number of such criteria might find widespread acceptance. Ultimately those criteria relate in one way or another to the system of political parties, for we have contrived no other instrument quite so suitable for the translation of democratic theory into working reality.

What functions should political parties perform in the governing process if our expectations about their performance as instruments of popular government are to be met? On the American scene a high priority would generally be given to the requirement that the parties compete for power. Although the struggle for position must avoid the threat of resort to the sword and must not be so intense as to disrupt the social system, competition itself rates a high value as a protector of liberty and as a means for assuring responsiveness of government. A belief in the corrective efficacy of competition permeates American political thought as well as other aspects of American life.

Most of the other criteria used to appraise party systems relate in one way or another to the competitive concept. A prime function in the achievement of party purpose consists of the recruitment, development, and support of candidates for public office. In the governance of large and complex societies, parties provide a means for sifting from the availables candidates behind whom support can be amassed in campaigns for office. Obviously, this operation of veto, of cajolery, of trial, of choice lies close to the heart of the governing process.

Our political lore makes it the function of the party system to create circumstances under which the electorate can act. The nomination of candidates, of course, facilitates electoral decision. The activity of the minority in criticism of the majority, and of the majority in defense of its position, contributes to public information basic for electoral decision. The party system may play a role of fundamental significance at times of crisis, at moments when novel questions of broad policy arise, and on those occasions when great issues agitate the electorate but leave unclear the nature of the dominant sentiment. At such times, the party system may facilitate a popular determination of the direction of the course of public action by offering, as it sometimes does, candidates with sufficient difference in policy orientation to make the choice between them something more than illusory.

These standards of political performance cumulate toward, but not necessarily all the way to, the notion of a party system in which parties with a relatively high degree of cohesion compete for power. Whether under American conditions that type of party system can be approximated on the national scene has been the subject of considerable debate.[3] One need not subscribe to the dogmas of responsible party government to employ this listing of functions of parties as a pattern against which to check the performance of the parties in the American states.

Perhaps a more general agreement exists on the proposi-

[3] See Committee on Political Parties, American Political Science Association, *Toward A More Responsible Two-Party System* (1950). For critiques of the committee report, see Julius Turner, "Responsible Parties: A Dissent from the Floor," *American Political Science Review,* 45 (1951), pp. 143-152; Austin Ranney, "Toward A More Responsible Two-Party System," *American Political Science Review,* 45 (1951), pp. 488-499; J. Roland Pennock, "Responsiveness, Responsibility and Majority Rule," *American Political Science Review,* 46 (1952), pp. 790-807.

tion that some such set of functions as those listed needs to be performed in a democratic polity than on the proposition that political parties must necessarily be the instrument for the performance of those functions. In the history of mankind popular government is a new art and practice. Undoubtedly variations in practice will develop and perhaps even fundamentally new modes of action will be contrived. In the present state of the art, however, systems of political parties seem indispensable to the practice of popular government. They may be discouraged, obstructed, and handicapped yet in one guise or another they make their way back into the political system. They are instruments for use; not objects for proscription in a democratic order.

How do the political systems of the American states stand up when they are tested against the stated pattern of functions? To cope with such a question in the absence of systematic description of the elements of the state political systems presents its hazards. Were our knowledge of state politics more complete, the diversity of practice would probably seem even more astonishing than it now appears. Yet probably a widespread, if not common, failing in practice—growing out of the weakness of political parties—consists of inadequate measures to recruit, develop, and advance candidates for popularly elective office. To be sure, many factors combine to make the business of running for office not highly magnetic in its attractiveness. And it may well be that the pulling power of elective office is not appreciably less than it was fifty years ago. Yet the decay of party organization has weakened an agency important in bestirring people to run for office. More commonly than may be supposed, even yet the office must seek the man. And those who devote themselves to the causes of political parties must either run for office themselves or induce some available but reluctant individual to make the sacrifice. To the extent that the party activists decline in number and energy, to that extent the supply of suitable candidates for public office is apt to decline.

Within a large proportion of the states only by the most generous characterization may it be said that political parties compete for power. In the pragmatic political doctrine of the United States great store is placed in party competition as a means of preventing wrongs, of keeping governments responsive to the general interest, and of keeping open to the electorate a choice between governing groups. Over a half century the vigor of competition between parties within the states has, on the whole, declined. Competition for power remains, to be sure, but the competitors tend generally to be different from those of fifty years ago. Less uniformly is the impression one of groups arrayed against each other under different party banners, although certainly in a few states that condition prevails. More commonly, competition for power takes the form of individual rivalry within the major party rather than group competition between parties. The measurement of the degree to which this shift has occurred is, of course, not a simple matter; the estimation of the broader consequences of the change is even more difficult. Yet the change patently alters greatly the problem of effective decision by the voters as a whole; and, with its precipitate of individual and independent centers of power within the government, it complicates the operation of government.

With the decay of the party system, the enforcement of accountability for the conduct of state government becomes more and more difficult. Even under the most favorable circumstances a sharp discrimination by the public between the rascals and others is difficult to achieve. Yet under less favorable circumstances the electorate can perform only less effectively. And circumstances have both developed and been created to handicap the electorate. The decline of party competition itself, by clogging the channels of information and by making the alternatives less clear, obstructs the enforcement of accountability. And, in truth, politicians, by some fundamental law of their behavior, tend to avoid responsibility; in the promotion of their own social security they have wrought structures of government honeycombed with havens where they may be secure from popular wrath. But apart from these artificial bulwarks, in the absence of a considerable degree of party solidarity the voter faces an impossible task in the enforcement of accountability save perhaps with respect to the most conspicuous offices. Given the length of the American ballot, and the basic complexity of American government, the simplest way for a voter to express satisfaction or dissatisfaction with the course of government is to vote a straight ticket. Yet few state party systems are sufficiently disciplined to present to the voter meaningful choices in these simple terms. Often the voter who marks a straight party ballot will be voting against himself at least part of the time.

The low priority of voter concern about state affairs affects the problems of political leadership in state politics. The character of the leadership may also in turn contribute to the low level of public interest. Ordinarily around one-fifth to one-fourth of the voters who express choices for governor in presidential years do not vote in the gubernatorial elections in the off years. For example, about 700,000 fewer persons voted in the Michigan gubernatorial elections in 1954 than in 1952. In Massachusetts about 450,000 fewer persons voted for governor in 1954 than in 1952. The same fall-off in turnout occurs regularly, as is shown in detail in the analysis in Table 1 of participation in gubernatorial elections in presidential years and in off years in a sample of states.

Although the movement of events may have developed extraordinarily complicated systems of popular government within the American states, the good old days do not provide a goal for the reconstruction of American state politics. The most limited investigation raises a serious doubt whether there ever were any good old days in state politics. The states have in fifty years progressed from orderly corruption to a condition of disorder probably less frequently tinged by corruption. The predicament of popular government within the states may be fundamentally the fruit of the consequences of reactions to the heroic political abuses of the good old days. Those reactions, in their long-run effects, have contributed, doubtless along with other factors, to a weakening of the party organizations of the states. That was precisely the objective of the muckrakers and reformers who flourished in our great age of corruption: they identified the political party as the culprit, as the source of political ills. By the elimination of the host of political parasites who had lodged themselves between the people and their government, the theory of the day went, politics would be purified and the righteous popular will would prevail.

TABLE 1

Weakness of Drawing Power of State Campaigns: Distribution of 176 Gubernatorial Elections in Selected States, 1926–1952, According to Proportion of Potential Electorate Voting, in Off Years and in Presidential Years[a]

PROPORTION VOTING FOR GOVERNOR	PER CENT OF OFF-YEAR ELECTIONS	PER CENT OF PRESIDENTIAL-YEAR ELECTIONS
25-29	2.4	0.0
30-39	16.7	1.1
40-49	26.2	3.3
50-59	32.1	10.8
60-69	17.8	37.0
70-79	4.8	42.3
80-89	0.0	5.4

[a] *The state coverage of the table is: Vermont, North Dakota, Maine, Wisconsin, Michigan, New Hampshire, Pennsylvania, Kansas, Massachusetts, Illinois, Wyoming, Ohio, Colorado, West Virginia, Missouri. The number of elections in off years was 84; in presidential years, 92.*

It is a fair question whether we did not burn the barn down to exterminate the mice. In any case the new and heavy responsibilities now borne by state governments will justify in the years ahead thoughtful and sustained attention to the art and practice of popular government within the states. That consideration must take into account the fact that the problems of the party system tend in most states to differ somewhat from those of the party system on the national scene. Doubtless within the states the element of new, broad policy bulks less large within the total governmental task than it does in the federal sphere. The work of state government consists in higher degree of the unglamorous chores of administration. State political processes have their role, to be sure, in the compromise of differences within the social order and in the performance of the grand functions of politics. Yet a major problem of the politics of the states is to provide administrative direction, powerful enough, honest enough, and stable enough to manage competently the very considerable services of the states. In the accomplishment of these ends the party system has no less a potentiality than it does in the solution of the greater and more dramatic issues of policy.

Questions of the capacity of leadership, of the degree and consequences of party competition, of the efficacy of popular accountability of public functionaries raise issues of fact almost impossible of assured answer. Nevertheless, in the chapters that follow, some systematic test-borings, comparing basic features of the political systems of the states, will provide a beginning toward an appraisal of the nature and workings of the party systems within the states.

Chapter 2

An Autonomous State Politics?

When considering the problem of organization for the conduct of state politics one fact of fundamental importance must be kept firmly in mind: the American states operate, not as independent and autonomous political entities, but as units of the nation. Within the states public attention cannot be focussed sharply on state affairs undistracted by extraneous factors; political divisions cannot occur freely on state questions alone: national issues, national campaigns, and national parties project themselves into the affairs of states. Political parties within the states become at times but the shadow of their national counterparts, and always the states' position in the federal system profoundly affects the form and character of their politics.[1]

Given the nature of the interconnections between national and state politics, the state candidates of a party at times become the undeserving beneficiaries of the exploits of their fellow partisans on the national scene. By the same token, either party, no matter how commendable its state record may be, is,

[1] In turn, of course, the position of the states in the federal system bears on the form and nature of the national parties. See David B. Truman, "Federalism and the Party System," *Federalism Mature and Emergent*, edited by A. W. Macmahon (Garden City: Doubleday, 1955).

from time to time, booted from office for the shortcomings of its national allies.

Both governmental reformers and professional politicians take note of the lack of autonomy of state politics and conduct themselves accordingly. Reformers, clergymen, editors, and good citizens in general, commonly urge that the tariff, farm policy, military problems, and other such national matters should have no bearing on the choice of governors and of state legislators. The admonition is to the effect that state questions should be considered separately, "on their merits," rather than handled in terms of party by straight-ticket voting. Professional politicians, perhaps more concerned with survival than with principle, contrive ways and means of offsetting or of capitalizing upon the relations between state and federal politics.

The practical yearning for a state politics uninfluenced by external forces does not diverge markedly from the theoretical presupposition about how a federal governmental arrangement ought to operate. Federal theory, at least tacitly, assumes the feasibility of a more or less autonomous politics within each unit of the system. Moreover, when the doctrine of popular government is superimposed over federal theory, the notion becomes implicit that each state of the federal system has the capacity to generate a party system adequate to perform the functions of recruitment of candidates, of competition for power, of conduct of the government, of criticism of public administration and public policy. In a word, federal theory, by its inner logic, must presuppose a political capacity congruent with the constitutional competence of each federated unit. Otherwise, political means do not exist for the exercise of the autonomous sphere of constitutional power held by the units of the system.

Yet the American states differ greatly in the degree to which they fit this pattern. In the organization and spirit of their politics the states vary markedly. Their oddities and variations may be accounted for in part by the fact that they are members of a federal system. The impact of national policies and parties powerfully influences the form and behavior of state political systems. The manner in which that impact strikes different states, differently constituted and situated, contributes to the variations in organization and conduct of state politics.

The narrow question to be examined here is the relationship of position in the federal system to the form, structure, and broad conduct of state politics. Such a focus of attention excludes, of course, many other ways in which state and federal politics are interwoven. In the polling booth one usually votes simultaneously for candidates for state and for national office. The bonds of party unite in common cause candidates for Congress and for state legislatures. Politicians often move from a governorship to the United States Senate, and occasionally the reverse occurs. States depend, in varying degrees, upon the actions of Congress for their revenues. Though these and many similar relationships have their relevance to the broad question of the interplay of state and federal politics, they are excluded from the present discussion by the choice of the narrower problem for analysis.

1. *Federalism, Sectionalism, and One-Partyism*

From the conditions associated with the formation of federations, a federal constitution by its nature obstructs to some extent in some states of the union the development of a full-blown party politics around state issues. The pursuit in national politics of ends of peculiar and overriding importance to a state or region demands a solidarity whose maintenance influences the workings of state politics. When the advancement of national objective requires that people within a state or region unite, that unity must affect the way in which they fight among themselves on state questions.

Although these propositions seem more or less self-evident, they need to be spelled out. The creation of a federal system implies the existence of territorial differences among the people of a nation. To some degree these geographical political cleavages solve themselves by the division of powers between national and state governments. So long as a sphere of action remains solely in the hands of the states, the people of New York cannot, through the national government, impose their views about a matter within that sphere upon the people of Texas or vice versa. Not all issues that set section off against section can be so nicely handled, or avoided, by the leaving of their settlement to the states. Some sectional questions fall to the jurisdiction of the central government. On such matters sectional differences will be projected into Congress and into the national political arena generally.

Political conflict on state issues may tend to be blurred or smothered to the extent that most of the people in a section place a high premium on a set of national policies of concern to the section. External defense of the sectional cause requires a degree of sectional unity internally. Essentially the argument is that the organizational tendencies and necessities of sectional solidarity nationally react back on state politics and induce a less complete mobilization of conflict over state questions than prevails in the absence of the conditions creative of regional unity on national questions.

The states of the South constitute, of course, the prime example of this phenomenon. Southern unity in national politics emerged from the complex of events climaxed by the Civil War. Hardened by Reconstruction, that unity persisted to defend, among other things, the view that the federal government should leave to the states the control of race relations. That defense did not, to be sure, require the maintenance of a steady fire. The issue was not continuously a live one. Yet it occasionally flared up, at least in symbolic form, which sufficed to keep sectional memories green and to maintain a posture of mobilization for defense. By the 1930's and 1940's the only type of issue on which southern Representatives and Senators held together in high degree against most Republicans and Democrats from the rest of the country were race measures, such as anti-lynching bills, anti-poll tax proposals, fair employment practices schemes, and the like.[2]

The maintenance of southern sectional unity in national affairs involved a drastic modification of the practice of politics locally. In view of the attitude of national Republican leaders toward the Negro, to support a Republican candidate for governor was in effect to give aid and comfort to the sectional enemy—the sectional enemy both in memory and in prospect. At least such was the view assiduously propagated by southern Democratic politicians. By a variety of means the Republican party was reduced locally to an innocuous position, and the party system of the region came to be oriented toward the fulfillment of sectional purpose in national affairs. So complete was Democratic control at home that during the first half of the twentieth century the rolls of governors of the 11 Confederate states were sullied by only two Republican names, both chief executives of Tennessee.

A set of special circumstances also affected the party system in the South, viz., the presence of large numbers of Negroes whose disenfranchisement was to be accomplished. The white primary came to provide a mechanism ideally designed to permit the maintenance of southern Democratic solidarity in national politics, with the simultaneous existence of quite warm political conflict among southern Democratic whites on state questions. Indeed, Democratic unity against the Negro locally perhaps was quite as important as the compulsion toward unity against the friends of the Negro elsewhere in the fixing of the form of the southern political system. For many decades the consensus on sectional interest in national affairs remained so complete that local differences could be fought out within the Democratic white primary with an extremely low probability that the local battle would spill over into the general election

[2] The question of southern congressional solidarity is analyzed in some detail in Key, *Southern Politics* (New York: Alfred A. Knopf, 1949), chaps. 16-17.

and become a cleavage between Republicans and Democrats threatening regional solidarity nationally.

The transfer of state politics in the southern states to the Democratic primaries was so complete that the consequence amounted more to an alteration in the form of state politics than in its substance. The fundamental change in form was from a conflict of parties to a conflict of personalities or of more or less amorphous factions within the Democratic party. While that alteration in the form was undoubtedly of significance for the substance of politics, the effects on substance remain extremely difficult of estimation and doubtless vary from time to time and from state to state within the South. In some circumstances non-party politics may place a premium on demagogic qualities. In others it may deprive of safeguards by its lack of institutionalized opposition to criticize, to harass, and to heckle. It may hinder mass movements by the ambiguity of the choices faced by the electorate. Those choices are in terms of candidates rather than of parties with divergent traditions and contrasting leadership cores. Yet in other instances party factions develop that appear to possess a coherence, a continuity, and a habit of competition not sharply at variance with the two-party model. That development, however, may be most apt to occur as sectional solidarity is in a state of erosion, at a stage when the primary battle is on the verge of spilling over into the general election and becoming a battle between Democrats and Republicans. In Louisiana, for example, the primary battle between the Long and anti-Long factions for years divided the people along lines similar to those that separated Republicans and Democrats outside the South. In 1952 the anti-Long voters crossed the line in large numbers to support General Eisenhower.[3]

Over the entire country the primacy of sectional purpose nationally has for considerable periods projected itself

[3] See Rudolf Heberle and P. H. Howard, "An Ecological Analysis of Political Tendencies in Louisiana: The Presidential Elections of 1952," *Social Forces*, 32 (1954), pp. 344-50.

back into state affairs. The party that functions as the sectional instrument becomes overwhelmingly dominant in state matters. The hopeless minority, although it may have a good cause locally, remains handicapped by the fact that it bears the name of the party that is the sectional enemy nationally. In the post-Civil War development of Republican dominance in the northeastern and midwestern states a sectional memory not unlike that of the South prevailed. Those who raised in this region the banner of the Democracy were not only serving illy the memory of the boys who fought at Bull Run but also were threatening the predominant sectional concern in national affairs. By the management of both sentiment and interest a party could gain a firm grasp of state affairs—a grasp that enabled it to resist or to minimize the effects of the great tides of national politics that wore upon its local hegemony.

Although in the older states of the Northeast and the Middle West the results for state politics were neither so spectacular nor so durable as in the South, the tendency was the same. The impact of sectionalism, in our peculiar historical and institutional setting, induced a fairly high degree of regional unity in national affairs which contributed to the entrenchment of Republicans in control of the state governments of the region. In these states Democrats made great gains in presidential politics in the 1930's yet their advances in state affairs were not proportionate. While only Vermont has a record of Republicanism in state elections that matches southern consistency in electing Democratic governors, some other states of the Northeast and of the Middle West only infrequently deviate from the straight and narrow and elect Democratic governors.[4]

The impact of national issues upon cleavages within state politics depends, to be sure, in part on the socio-economic

[4] Illustrative of the point are data on frequency of election of Democratic governors for the period 1920-1950. Over this period, in which the following states had fifteen gubernatorial elections each, the numbers of Democratic gubernatorial victories were: Vermont, 0; New Hampshire, 1; Maine, 2; North Dakota, 3; Iowa, 3; Kansas, 3; South Dakota, 4; Michigan, 5.

composition of each state. State boundaries may happen to encompass a population made virtually homogeneous politically by its response to the national political alternatives. A state consisting largely of active members of the CIO would probably harbor few Republicans. Or a state made up mainly of rural dwellers, not greatly diluted by in-migration since their ancestors wore the Blue in the Civil War, would not be a hotbed of the Democracy.

These relationships between population composition and party inclinations appear neatly in the upper New England states. Vermont, the least urbanized and the least affected by immigration, maintains the most impressive Republican record. In other states urbanization and immigration are associated with a lesser degree of Republican attachment. The relationships are suggested by the following figures:

	MEAN PERCENTAGE GUBERNATORIAL VOTE REPUBLICAN	PER CENT URBAN 1950	PER CENT FOREIGN-BORN 1930
Vermont	(1916-52) 69.5	36.4	3.6
Maine	(1912-52) 58.2	51.7	12.6
New Hampshire	(1910-52) 55.3	57.5	17.8
Massachusetts	(1913-52) 51.8	84.4	25.2

The question may well be raised whether the character of state parties is not determined by such factors of population composition rather than by the organizing impact of our federal history upon state electorates. Would predominantly rural Vermont, for example, have a lively two-party politics in state affairs if it were not pushed towards Republicanism by its historical national affinities? Perhaps both the impact of national politics and the social structure of the state operate to depress the minority party. For the gravitation of national issues to nudge a state towards one-partyism its population must possess a certain uniformity of response to those issues. Yet the people of the state might well divide otherwise on state issues if they were unaffected by their traditional national commitments.[5]

In recent decades the issues and forces of national politics have tended to wear down sectional groupings. The new issues push people, wherever they live, toward divisions different from the traditional sectional partisan cleavages, and the states gradually become more alike in the manner of their presidential voting. In the strongly Republican states the Republican majority has become a little less overwhelming than it once was. In the states of the South a more striking deterioration of the Democratic hold over the electorate has been taking place. Yet the data on presidential voting point to the conclusion that changes in sectional political attachments on the American scene occur slowly. The nature and rate of change are suggested by Figure 3, which indicates the deviations of the Republican percentages of the presidential vote in Florida and in Vermont from the Republican percentages of the national presidental vote. The division of the vote in Florida over half a century has approached more nearly the division of the nation as a whole. The Florida curve reflects the special effects of individual elections, such as 1928, but also shows a more gradual, secular movement upward in Republican strength. The forces driving toward a political realignment, of course, strike Florida more powerfully than they do most other southern states. The Florida trend, in fact, reflects more the influx of sun-seeking northern Republicans than a realignment of the natives. Figure 3 also presents the data for Vermont, whose divisions in presidential voting manifest a slight secular tendency toward greater similarity with the divisions within the country as a whole.[6]

[5] For a suggestive discussion somewhat related to the argument of these pages, see C. B. MacPherson, *Democracy in Alberta: The Theory and Practice of a Quasi-Party System* (Toronto: University of Toronto Press, 1953).

[6] The dispersion of the states according to the division of their presidential vote gives a crude measure of the tendency of states to become more alike in their presidential vote. In terms of the Republican percentage of the total state vote, the states fell within the following percentage-point ranges at the elections indicated: 1896, 73; 1920, 78; 1928,

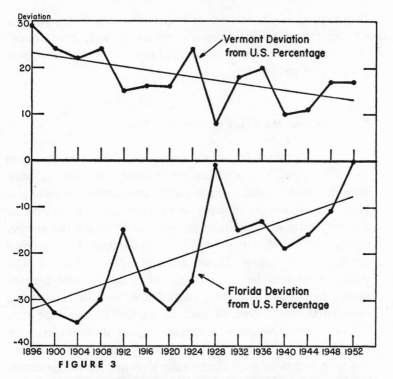

Erosion of Sectionalism: Deviation of Republican Percentages of Total Presidential Vote in Vermont and Florida from Republican Percentages of Total National Vote, 1896-1952

FIGURE 3

Sectionalism in national politics may very well be undergoing a decline, yet its effects on the organization of state politics will long survive its demise. From evidence to be presented later, it becomes clear that changes in the politics of a state government may lag considerably behind alterations in the presidential voting habits of the people of the state. The politicians

67; 1936, 55; 1952, 41. The semi-interquartile ranges for these elections were: 1896, 13.2; 1920, 7.3; 1928, 5.2; 1936, 6.5; 1952, 4.7. The use of these years as indicators probably exaggerates both the smoothness and extent of the trend. The similarity of the states apparently is greatest in years of presidential landslides.

in command of the statehouse may confidently be expected to demonstrate a fairly impressive staying power, even though there turns out to be a long-run trend toward a more competitive presidential politics.

2. States and the Tides of National Politics

The general drift of the argument to this point has been that the pursuit of particularistic regional, sectional, or state aims in national politics reacts on the organization of state politics. The imperative of unity in national affairs depresses the minority party in state affairs and profoundly affects the manner of organization of state politics in areas dominated by sectional concerns or traditions. In the extreme type of situation state politics comes to be the business of groupings and factions within the locally dominant party rather than a competition between the local arms of national parties. In any case state offices are monopolized with varying degrees of thoroughness by a single party. Vermont, thus, steadfastly clings to its Republican faith and turns back Democratic aspirants for the governorship for scores of years. And southern states maintain an equally imposing indifference to the blandishments of Republican candidates for governor. In other states the same broad influences contribute to one-party control only occasionally interrupted.

A different, and perhaps superficially contradictory, effect of national politics on the political process within the states now demands attention. Some states may be nudged toward one-partyism in local affairs by their position in the federal system but others tend to be carried along by the great swings of political cycle which mark the alternation in dominance of Democrats and Republicans on the national scene. The capacity of the state to act independently of national issues and with a focus on state questions withers as the affairs of states are swept along by the tides of national politics.

The great tides of national politics may not affect seriously the bastions of one-partyism but they engulf most of the states of the North and West and sweep them along in the same direction. The presidential candidate who leads his party to a landslide victory carries into office with him large numbers of gubernatorial candidates of his party, who win without much regard to their role or place in the state but because they float along with the national movement of sentiment. Similarly, those state candidates allied with the losing party on the national scene are caught up by the common misfortunes of their partisan allies over the nation.

A picture of the process emerges from Figure 4, which depicts the relation between simultaneous presidential and gubernatorial voting in states outside the South in the presidential years from 1920 through 1952.[7] The great upthrusts in the presidential strength of each party, as the chart graphically reveals, are paralleled by similar gains within the states. In the Republican sweep of 1920, Harding carried all the 28 states covered by the analysis as did his fellow Republicans in the races for governor. The election of 1936, the peak of Roosevelt's strength, saw also a peak in the proportion of states carried simultaneously by Democratic presidential and gubernatorial candidates. The pendulum swung in 1952 to an opposite extreme, when Republican aspirants for governorship found the company of General Eisenhower on the ticket most congenial.

Whether in these wide fluctuations in partisan strength the presidential candidate carries governors into office or the gubernatorial candidates give the presidential candidate a boost poses an interesting question, though one that is irrelevant to the main argument. Whatever the relation of mutual re-enforcement between national and state tickets, the states do not oper-

[7] The chart covers, for most of the period 1920-52, 28 states outside the South with gubernatorial elections falling in the years of presidential elections. Excluded are Alabama, Arkansas, California, Florida, Georgia, Kentucky, Louisiana, Maryland, Mississippi, Nevada, New Jersey, North Carolina, Tennessee, Texas, Virginia, and Wyoming. In the later years of the series several states that changed the timing of their gubernatorial elections to the off years were dropped: New York, Idaho, Connecticut.

Per cent of states

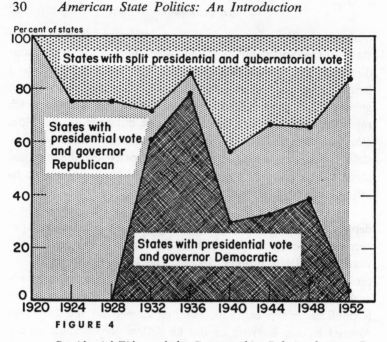

States with split presidential and gubernatorial vote

States with presidential vote and governor Republican

States with presidential vote and governor Democratic

FIGURE 4

Presidential Tides and the Governorship: Relation between Results of Presidential and Gubernatorial Voting in 28 Nonsouthern States, 1920-1952

ate independently of these broad national sweeps. Evidently in the public mind—at least in the framework of these great cycles of sentiment—no sharp differentiation between state and national affairs prevails. The electorate, on the whole, has no eye for fine distinctions but uses the only weapon it has or knows and elevates to power or relegates to oblivion according to party label—with exceptions, to be sure.[8] These exceptions are least

_____

[8] Instruction in American civics over the generations has had distressingly slight effect in drilling into the American voter a full comprehension of the complexities of the American governmental system. The Honorable Emanuel Celler, long a Member of Congress from Brooklyn reflects on his constituents' grasp of federalism: "The feeling of intimacy with the national government is much greater than that which people have for their own city or state. This, too, is unfortunate. My mail is heavy with letters from constituents who inform me that the traffic light

numerous at elections that mark the greatest party triumphs on the national scene. Note in Figure 4 that the states splitting their presidential and gubernatorial vote were fewest in 1920, 1936, and 1952. In 1952, Democrats Frank J. Lausche of Ohio, G. Mennen Williams of Michigan, Phil M. Donnelly of Missouri, and Dennis J. Roberts of Rhode Island survived the Eisenhower victories in their states and accounted for the states with split results shown in Figure 4. On the other hand, as the national political cycle moves away from landslide presidential peaks the number of states with split presidential and gubernatorial results increases. Perhaps the decline in forces driving toward unanimity nationally gives room for freer play of factors and circumstances peculiar to each state.

The great swings in the fortunes of the national parties are also associated with alternations in control of lesser state offices. A cyclical swing toward the Republicans on the national scene is accompanied, for example, by a similar movement in state legislative races in those states not almost completely immune to the fluctuations of national politics. Similarly, when Democratic candidates lead in the presidential sweepstakes, a considerable company of Democrats occupy seats in state legislatures that had been warmed by Republicans in the earlier stage of the cycle.

An illustration of the relation between presidential and state legislative politics appears in Figure 5, which shows the percentage of Missouri counties with popular pluralities for Democratic presidential candidates, along with the percentage of seats in the lower house of the state legislature won by Democrats over a period of a half century. While the two series do not march up and down in exact unison, their major movements manifest a remarkable similarity. It need scarcely be said

---

is broken on their street and would I please get it repaired? Or the policeman on the beat has been discourteous and would I have him reprimanded? Or there is no public library within walking distance from the constituent's home. Or the principal of the school is anti-Catholic, or anti-Semitic, or just 'anti'; would I please have him removed?"—*You Never Leave Brooklyn* (New York: John Day, 1953), p. 266.

that the fluctuations are not so closely aligned everywhere as in the competitive state of Missouri. A like analysis for all legislative districts and all counties over the nation as a whole would show a considerably wider fluctuation in the presidential series than in the state legislative series.[9]

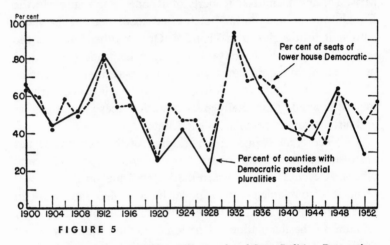

FIGURE 5

Interrelation of Cycles of National and State Politics: Proportions of Missouri Counties with Democratic Presidential Pluralities and Proportions of Missouri House Seats Won by Democrats, 1900-1954

The association between fluctuations in the presidential vote and in the results of legislative contests has effects that differ in consequence from state to state. In states strongly committed to one party or the other the only result is that the

[9] An analysis of county presidential pluralities and of the outcomes of legislative elections for 32 nonsouthern states lumped together, on the order of that of Missouri in Figure 5, shows the Democratic presidential curve at a considerably higher level than the curve for lower-house seats in 1932 and 1936. At another stage of the cycle, 1952, the proportion of counties carried by Eisenhower was substantially higher than the proportion of legislative districts won by Republican candidates. In states with parties less evenly matched than Missouri the legislative series has a narrower amplitude of variation than does the presidential series.

legislative minority, at the most minuscule, is a bit larger at some times than at others. For states not overwhelmingly Republican or Democratic—and not gerrymandered irrevocably to one party or the other—the consequence is sooner or later an overturn of the more or less normal legislative majority in harmony with shifts in presidential voting sentiment.

The association through time between national and state voting points to difficulties in the separation of state and national politics. The governmental system may be federal but the voter in the polling booth usually is not. Evidently great upsurges of sentiment are not often accompanied by widespread popular differentiation between state and federal politicians. Both tend to be the targets of the blasts of popular recrimination or the beneficiaries of movements of popular confidence or hope. Although this sort of behavior may not be regarded as rational, it may in truth make a good deal of sense, for, at least at times, the fulfillment of popular aspirations requires that the same crowd be thrown out of both Washington and the state capitals simultaneously.[10] That process may be both facilitated and made sensible by the tendency of state and national candidates of the outs to advocate similar or related lines of action. Certainly in times of deep and pervasive discontent few politicians saddled with the sins of the old order, no matter how cherubic their countenances, or whether they be state or federal officials, can expect to survive the anger of the multitude. And perhaps that is the way it should be.

[10] The impression develops that the states with parties powerfully enough entrenched to resist the national tides are not so immune to national movements of sentiment as might appear. Within the intraparty affairs of such states different types of individuals probably tend to rise to positions of leadership, depending on the tenor of the predominant national sentiments. That is, in Democratic states the fortunes of progressive and conservative leaders may depend somewhat on variations in the temper of the nation as a whole which is reflected in more competitive areas in shifts between parties.

3. Party: Solvent of Federalism

The common subjection of state and federal elections to the broad movements of sentiment that sweep the nation emerges sharply from the analysis just presented. Over the decades a gross correspondence prevails in the fluctuations of the fortunes of each party in both state and national politics—save in the areas of most dedicated one-partyism.

Another approach may demonstrate in another manner the tendency for common forces to gather up and virtually fuse the politics of state and nation. If, instead of examining the broad association of state and federal political movements through considerable periods of time, we concentrate on voting relationships at particular elections another aspect of the interweaving of state and national politics may be illuminated.

At individual elections powerful tendencies operate to induce voters to support both state and local candidates of the same party. Indeed, the electorate in large measure divides in the same manner in state and national politics, although not infrequently enough voters split their tickets to produce differing party majorities for President and for governor. While voter loyalty to party slates may well have declined during the past fifty years, to an impressive extent voters still cast ballots on the cue of party. The chances are that, by and large, the great issues of national politics drive the basic cleavages through the electorate and these divisions, in turn, project themselves into voting on state offices.

Despite the limited range of trustworthy knowledge about the extent and determinants of split-ticket voting and of straight-ticket voting, it may be quite simply established that on balance a high degree of net consistency in support of party slates ordinarily exists among voters.[11] Illustrative of this consistency in

[11] Of a national sample interviewed by the Survey Research Center in 1952, 66 per cent reported a straight-ticket vote. The remaining 34 per cent reported a split away from their presidential vote at the congressional level, the state or local level, or at both levels.—Angus Campbell, *The Voter Decides* (Evanston: Row, Peterson, 1954), p. 24. The

voting is the scatter-diagram in Figure 6, which could be dupli-
cated in many other elections in many other states. That figure
shows the relationship between the percentage of the vote polled
by Eisenhower, and the percentage polled by Herter, the Republican candidate for governor, in each of a sample of 76 towns
of Massachusetts in 1952. While in most of the towns the

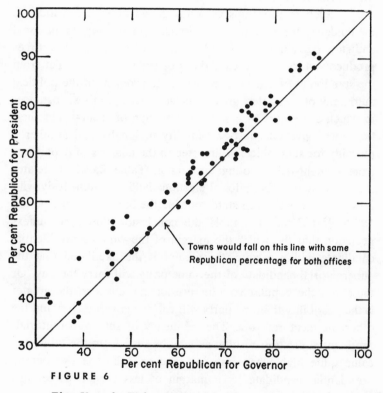

FIGURE 6

*They Vote the Ticket, National and State: Relationship between
Republican Percentage of Vote for President and of Vote for
Governor in 76 Massachusetts Towns, 1952*

chances are that the proportion of split tickets was unusually high in
1952. In any case the proportion probably varies from state to state and
to some extent the effects of splitting are offset in the total vote by movements in both directions.

General ran a few points ahead of Mr. Herter, a remarkably uniform tendency is revealed for the strength of the two candidates to vary similarly from town to town. In predominantly Republican towns both candidates ran quite strongly; in Democratic towns neither did very well. While their fortunes were inextricably intertwined, the chances are that the General pulled Mr. Herter to victory.

Such relationships as those shown in Figure 6 indicate the tendency for a common partisanship to envelop the national and state party apparatus. Indeed, most of the time these forces produce victory for the candidates of the same party. Yet from the standpoint of our main concern, the problem of the political autonomy of the states, great interest attaches to those instances in which the voters of a state—or enough of them—split their ticket and give one party a plurality nationally and another a plurality for state office. A first step in the analysis of departures from straight-ticket voting appears in Table 2, which relates the outcome of gubernatorial elections held simultaneously with presidential elections in states outside the South over the period 1932-1950. From the table the conclusion flows, not unexpectedly, that the wider the margin of the winning presidential candidate within a state, the greater is the likelihood that the gubernatorial candidate of the same party will carry the day. Or the closer the popular vote for presidential electors, the greater is the possibility that one party will win the governorship and the other the electoral vote. The frequency of split gubernatorial-presidential election results, as may be seen from the table, became quite high when states were carried by the Democratic presidential candidate by a margin of less than 5 percentage points. In these states almost half the governors elected simultaneously with the Democratic presidential victory were Republican.

How are the departures from straight-ticket voting revealed by Table 2 to be explained? Doubtless a variety of factors played a part. Probably the most general factor consisted in the capacity of entrenched state parties to mobilize the necessary narrow margin of strength behind their state ticket to offset the opposition presidential tide. The elections covered by the table occurred during an upsurge in Democratic presidential strength and mostly in states more or less normally Republican. State Republican organizations were able in some instances to stem the secondary effects of the presidential sweep and retain control of the state. This interpretation is nicely underpinned by the contrast between the results of gubernatorial elections in presidential years and those in the immediately following off-year elections, which also appear in the table. Many Democratic governors, pulled into office in the wake of their presidential candidate, fell prey to their Republican opponents two years later.

These observations point toward a more complete understanding of the nature of the simultaneous Republican and Democratic victories that appear in Table 2. The broad fluctuations in national politics sweep the states along in their presidential voting but the solidly entrenched local party, with its advantage in organization, in traditional loyalties, and often in leadership, can at least for a time maintain its local position. The greater the magnitude of the national fluctuation, the less able is the party historically dominant in state affairs to maintain its position against the national tide. To a considerable extent, then, Table 2 must be interpreted in the light of the earlier discussion of the nature of political movements through time.

Of course, not all split results are to be accounted for by the simple mechanical hypothesis of the friction offered by established state organizations to the trends of presidential politics. State political leaders often engage in positive action to take advantage of or to offset those trends. When states are closely contested, powerful strains may be placed on the relations of presidential and gubernatorial candidates on the same ticket. A gubernatorial candidate in a close state who judges the tide to be running against his presidential ally often succumbs to the temptation to wage an independent campaign that links him with the national ticket no more than is avoidable. In 1936,

for example, Republican gubernatorial candidates who thought
they had a fighting chance to win by a close margin were not
commonly among the most energetic in beating the bushes for
Mr. Alfred Landon, who, it may be recalled, was the Repub-

TABLE 2

*Two-Year Governors Outside the South, Chosen in Presidential
Years and in Off Years, 1932-1950, Related to Democratic Percentage of State Presidential Vote*[a]

DEMOCRATIC PRESIDENTIAL PERCENTAGE	NUMBER OF STATE ELECTIONS	PER CENT OF GOVERNORS DEMOCRATIC	
		PRESIDENTIAL YEARS	FOLLOWING OFF YEARS
Under 45	10	20.0[b]	20.0
45-49	17	29.4	17.6
50-54	20	55.0	25.0
55-59	21	90.5	57.1
60 or more	15	93.3[c]	80.0

[a] *States and elections analyzed: Arizona, Colorado, Connecticut, Idaho (through 1946), Iowa, Kansas, Maine, Massachusetts, Michigan, Minnesota, Nebraska, New Mexico, New
York (through 1938), North Dakota (except 1936-1938), Ohio,
Rhode Island, South Dakota, Wisconsin (except 1932-1942),
Wyoming (1932-1934).*
[b] *The deviate states in this cell were Maine in 1932 and
North Dakota in 1940.*
[c] *The deviate state in this cell was North Dakota which
elected Wm. Langer as its Republican governor in 1932. Langer,
a Non-Partisan Leaguer, was, of course, something less than an
orthodox Republican.*

lican presidential nominee in that year. Similarly, in 1952
some Democratic gubernatorial candidates in comparable pre-
dicaments were restrained in their exertions on behalf of Mr.
Stevenson.

The upshot of the analysis is that the issues, cleavages,
and loyalties of national politics push themselves powerfully
into the politics of states. Yet these factors do not invariably
determine the fortunes of parties in state affairs. A sufficient

degree of independence from national tendencies prevails in the states, more or less competitive between the two major parties, to produce split results with a fairly high frequency.[12] The incapacity of American parties to hold their communicants more completely in line in support of national and state tickets astonishes foreign observers who are accustomed to parties of some doctrinal purity and electoral discipline. Yet when they are viewed in their continental and historical setting, the potency of the major American parties in their absorption of state political systems may be their truly amazing characteristic. The battles of national politics may not incidentally settle in every instance the skirmishes within the states, but the national parties determine what parties will be permitted to contest for state office. In effect, they almost completely exclude from effective competition local parties organized solely for control of state governments. Of the hundreds of state governors elected in this century, only a handful did not claim at least a nominal affiliation with one or the other of the great national parties. And of these few, some had a real, although not a nominal, allegiance to such a party.

Parties organized for state purposes and unaffiliated with national organizations most infrequently attain power. If they gain power, their life is apt to be short. They soon dissolve or fuse with one of the major parties. The Progressive party of Wisconsin placed Philip La Follette in the governorship in 1934 and in 1936 but soon disappeared. Minnesota's Farmer-Labor party won several gubernatorial elections in the 1930's but eventually joined with the Democrats as the Democratic-Farmer-Labor party which functions as the local arm of the

[12] It may well be that on occasion the electorate, even though it may return split majorities for President and governor, acts with greater policy consistency than do the parties in making up their slates. In 1952, for example, Mr. Frank Lausche, a somewhat conservative Democrat, won in Ohio as General Eisenhower swept the state. Mr. Lausche's opponent, Charles P. Taft, had a reputation as something of a Republican New Dealer. In 1932, Roosevelt carried South Dakota by a wide margin but on the same day the voters returned the Republican agrarian radical, Peter Norbeck, to the United States Senate.

Democratic party.[13] Perhaps the most striking attempt of this century to found structures of political leadership around state issues was by the Non-Partisan League in North Dakota and neighboring states. Its difficulties were certainly not solely attributable to the party system; it did not have enough votes. Yet from time to time both major parties united against the League, which soon found it both necessary and expedient to work through one or the other of the major parties.[14] The local independent party that really threatens to gain power is almost certain to enjoy the enmity of both the established parties. For national purposes both must maintain state subsidiaries, which will, at least alternately, be supported by federal patronage. The independent state party can fuse with a major party, can perhaps swallow it up, or it may be absorbed by one of the major parties. The most serious obstacles exist to its long continuance independently as a principal contender for state control. And its existence with lesser ambitions—as the experience of the minor parties of New York indicates—is difficult enough.[15]

Not only do the nationalizing forces make the lot of the local third party a hard one; they make it most difficult for a state affiliate of a national party to differentiate itself in a marked fashion from the public image of the national party. In some of the states of the South, for example, the control of

[13] For an account of the relations between the Farmer-Labor party and the Democratic party before their consolidation, see George H. Mayer, *The Political Career of Floyd B. Olson* (Minneapolis: University of Minnesota Press, 1951).

[14] See S. P. Huntington, "The Election Tactics of the Non-Partisan League," *Mississippi Valley Historical Review,* 36 (1950), pp. 613-632.

[15] The general argument is re-enforced by mention of the rash of third parties, mainly agrarian parties, that ran gubernatorial candidates between 1880 and 1900. The sequence of events seemed to be, first, to back a third-party candidate for governor, usually without success, and then to nominate a fusion candidate with one of the major parties. Of the gubernatorial elections of all the states, 1880-1900, inclusive, 23 per cent involved minor party candidates or fusion candidates who polled 15 per cent or more of the total vote. So frequent an occurrence of minor party candidates polling so large a vote is, of course, in sharp contrast with the experience of recent decades.

the conservative Democrats is so thorough that the obvious strategy for the Republicans would be to cultivate the "liberal" vote. And, indeed, on occasion Republican candidates in such states turn up with an endorsement from the CIO. Yet the construction of a state Republican organization with an orientation diverging sharply from its national counterpart to contest for control of state government would present insuperable practical difficulties, even if it were desired by the state leaders. Consider, for example, the possibility of a Virginia state Republican party with a Trumanesque orientation created to do battle with the Byrd Democratic organization.

4. Isolation of State Politics

Framers of state constitutions have given thought to ways and means of diking off from state elections extraneous national influences on local decision. Their most common stratagem is to schedule gubernatorial elections in years when no presidential election is held. Usually this arrangement involves a four-year term for the governor with the election falling at the middle of the presidential term, a practice prevailing in 15 states. Kentucky, Mississippi, Virginia, and New Jersey achieve a more complete separation by scheduling the gubernatorial election in odd-numbered years, while Louisiana's state elections fall in April of presidential years.[16]

Though the separation of gubernatorial and presidential elections undoubtedly produces results that differ from what would occur with simultaneous state and federal elections, only in the most limited sense does such scheduling make for a state politics independent of national influences. The unlovely truth is that the manipulation of the gubernatorial election calendar is often merely a tactic in party warfare. Adjustments in the

[16] The broad conclusions and tabular material of this section appeared in the *New Republic,* November 23, 1953, under the title, "Now That 1954 Is Here."

timing of elections may be made, not to permit a freer choice, but to create circumstances that will tend to favor one party or the other.

The effects of the timing of gubernatorial elections upon party fortunes differ both from time to time and from state to state. The choice of governors only in the off years greatly handicaps the attempts of a weak minority party to build up its strength. If the governor is chosen in presidential years, the minority, despite the weakness of its local forces, gains advantage from the fact that in these years the voters are aroused by the issues and events of the national campaign. The minority candidate for governor may have little chance for victory but with politics in the air and with some help from the national ticket he may make a respectable showing. On the infrequent occasion when a presidential candidate wins by a landslide, his margin may be so wide that he carries into office the most improbable gubernatorial candidates in states where his party is ordinarily in the minority. An occasional victory, rare though it may be, helps mightily in building up a minority party. On the other hand, if a gubernatorial candidate of the weak minority must make his race in an off year on the slender local means of his party and without benefit of the presidential-year surge of popular political interest, his chances of even making a strong showing decline.

The record of Oklahoma illustrates how the separation of elections may handicap the minority and snatch from it the opportunity for a state victory in the wake of a national landslide. The Sooner State commonly rates as a Democratic stronghold yet it harbors a goodly number of Republicans who for almost fifty years have not managed to elect a governor. Their vicissitudes flow partly from the off-year election of governors. The state is by no means isolated from the great currents of national politics yet those tides run at the wrong time to benefit the Republicans of Tulsa and environs. The point is established by the graphs in Figure 7 which picture the voting performance of Oklahoma since statehood. Republican strength in the lower house of the state legislature, chosen once every two years, shot upward in the elections of 1920 and 1928, years of Republican sweeps. On the other hand, the state's Republican gubernatorial candidates, as the chart indicates, could not benefit from the great swells of the Republican national landslides as they undoubtedly would have under a different election schedule.

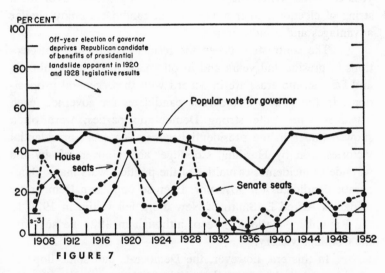

FIGURE 7

Insulation of Governorship from National Political Tides: Republican Percentages of Two-Party Vote for Governor and of Seats in Legislative Houses, Oklahoma, 1920-1952

In states with a traditionally one-sided division of strength between the parties, such as Oklahoma, four-year gubernatorial terms with elections in nonpresidential years clearly handicap a long-run build-up of minority strength. In other types of situations, however, other sorts of consequences follow. Where elections are normally more closely contested, the effects of the segregation of elections differ from time to time with changes in the balance of power in the national political arena.

In states in which the popular followings of parties are of about the same size—in which the parties are genuinely competitive —the simultaneous election of President and governor tends to tip the balance in favor of the gubernatorial candidates of the party winning the presidency. When the Republicans are riding high nationally, their gubernatorial candidates have brighter prospects for victory in presidential-year elections than in off-year elections. When the Democrats enjoy national favor for a string of elections, their gubernatorial candidates enjoy similar advantages and disadvantages.

The contrasts between the results of gubernatorial elections in presidential years and in off years, in both Republican and Democratic eras, are in accord with these general propositions. In the 1920's Democratic candidates for governor, even in states with quite strong Democratic parties, were often snowed under in the presidential years. The great presidential victories won by Harding, Coolidge, and Hoover left by the wayside as incidental casualties of the political wars many Democratic candidates for governor. Even so popular a Democratic leader as Alfred E. Smith of New York fell victim in 1920 to the Republican national sweep, although in 1924 he survived the Coolidge victory.

In this era, however, the Democrats had some hope of recouping their losses of the presidential year in those states whose governors served a two-year term. At the next polling when they did not have to struggle against the national Republican appeal, local Democrats could often recapture the state. The general rule prevailed that the narrower a state's Republican presidential margin in popular vote, the greater was the probability that the Democratic gubernatorial candidate would win at the next off-year election. With his opponent deprived of the momentum of the national campaign, the Democratic candidate could turn to his advantage both discontent with national Republican policy and dissatisfaction about matters of purely state concern. The nature of these relationships between the presidential voting and the outcome of gubernatorial elections in presidential and nonpresidential years appears from Table 3.

When the Democrats gain the upper hand in presidential politics, their state candidates enjoy advantages in presidential years but their Republican opponents often re-assert

TABLE 3

Two-Year Governors Outside the South, Chosen in Presidential Years and in Off Years, 1920-30, Related to Republican Percentage of State Presidential Vote[a]

REPUBLICAN PRESIDENTIAL PERCENTAGE	NUMBER OF STATES	PER CENT OF GOVERNORS REPUBLICAN	
		PRESIDENTIAL YEARS	OFF YEARS[b]
45-49	2	100.0[c]	50.0
50-59	11	63.6	36.3
60-69	22	90.9	45.5
70-79	16	87.5	68.7
80-89	6	100.0	100.0

[a] *The states included in the tabulation are Arizona, Colorado, Connecticut, Idaho, Iowa, Kansas, Maine, Massachusetts, Michigan, Minnesota, Nebraska, New Mexico, New York, North Dakota, Ohio, Rhode Island, South Dakota, Wisconsin, Wyoming.*
[b] *The off-year elections are classified according to the Republican presidential vote in the preceding presidential election. Thus the two columns, presidential and off years, compare the outcomes of gubernatorial elections in the same states in the two types of years.*
[c] *The two states with Republican governors but Democratic presidential pluralities were Massachusetts and Rhode Island in 1928. These instances, deviates in this tabulation, suggest that state political shifts may lag behind presidential shifts.*

their local strength in the nonpresidential years. In elections of the 1930's and 1940's Roosevelt carried many of his fellow Democrats into governorships which the Republicans retrieved in the off years. (These relationships were shown in Table 2.) By the same token, governors elected in presidential years for four-year terms were more likely to be Democratic than were governors elected in the nonpresidential years for four-year terms. The state Democratic disadvantage, in an era Democratic nationally, under a scheme that schedules gubernatorial elections in the off years appears plainly from Table 4.[17]

TABLE 4

Four-Year Governors Outside the South, Chosen in Presidential Years and in Off Years, 1932-1950, Related to Democratic Percentage of State Presidential Vote[a]

DEMOCRATIC	PRESIDENTIAL YEARS		OFF YEARS	
PRESIDENTIAL PERCENTAGE	GOVERNORS ELECTED	PER CENT DEMOCRATIC	GOVERNORS ELECTED	PER CENT DEMOCRATIC
45-49	5	40.0	6	33.3
50-54	10	40.0	13	23.1
55-59	15	80.0	4	50.0
60 and over	10	100.0	11	63.6

[a] *The states electing governors in presidential years covered by the table were Delaware, Illinois, Indiana, Missouri, Montana, Utah, Washington, West Virginia. The off-year states were California, Idaho, Maryland, Nevada, New York, Oregon, Pennsylvania, Wyoming. Some of these states elected in the off years only for a part of the period 1932-1950.*

[b] *The off-year states are grouped according to their presidential vote in the preceding presidential election. The two groups of gubernatorial elections compared are thus, of course, elections in different states with similar Democratic presidential margins. Apart from the fact that few cases are involved, it should be kept in mind that doubtless factors in addition to the presidential division affect the results of the gubernatorial elections.*

[17] With reference to Table 4, as elsewhere in this analysis, it needs to be kept in mind that at least a modicum of variety exists among the situations classified on the basis of the party label of the candidate. For example, one case hidden away in Table 4 is the election of Harry Nice as Republican governor of Maryland in 1934. Roosevelt had won Maryland in 1932 with 63 per cent of the two-party vote. The year 1934 probably marked the peak of Democratic strength generally. Yet Albert Ritchie in 1934 lost to Nice. Nice claimed that he would be a better New Dealer than Ritchie, a notable conservative of a states'-rights persuasion, and attacked Ritchie for his coolness toward the New Deal. The exaggerations of campaign fulminations perhaps did reflect the underlying realities. A partisan deviation by the electorate, within the limits of the alternatives available, may have been in reality an ideological consistency.

During the years of Democratic dominance of presidential politics, Republicans in various states contemplated the causes of their fate. In several states they initiated movements for a constitutional reform which might incidentally alleviate the sadness of their lot. In some instances they succeeded in bringing their states into that group which chooses governors for four-year terms in the off years. Thus their candidates for governor were relieved of the inconvenience of running, in effect, against Franklin D. Roosevelt; Democratic candidates would perforce be deprived of the advantages of being on the slate with him. Probably the advocates of these reforms did not weigh carefully the full consequences of their plan, for it was certain to rise up to plague them at a later date. Perhaps they worked on the assumption that Democrats would control the Presidency in perpetuity. Among the converts to the four-year term were Connecticut and New York. In the off year of 1954, Mr. Harriman in New York and Mr. Ribicoff in Connecticut eked out Democratic victories which would have doubtless been beyond their reach had they been running against a ticket with General Eisenhower at its head. In 1954 also the Democrats carried Pennsylvania, another four-year state, a feat which would have been most difficult of accomplishment had the General been on the ticket.[18]

The simple trick of election scheduling clearly affects the degree of integration of state and national politics. At one extreme the attempt at insulation of state politics apparently

[18] On occasion adjustments in ballot form are similar in motive to the tactic of election scheduling. Thus, in 1941, under Republican leadership, Delaware divided its ballot into two, one for voting for President and Vice-President and another on which candidates for other offices were listed. The supposition was that with this separation of choice Republican candidates for other offices would fare better in the immediate circumstances of Democratic dominance in presidential politics. Similarly in Michigan during the Roosevelt era the legislature made it impossible to vote a straight ticket with one mark or with the movement of one lever on the voting machine. In 1955, however, the legislature, still Republican, viewed the problem of ballot form differently, an alteration of opinion probably not unconnected with the probability that Mr. Eisenhower would be a candidate in 1956. The legislature acted to permit a straight-ticket vote with one mark.

retards long-term shifts in relative party strength by depriving a weak minority of the fillip that comes from the association of local candidates with presidential campaigns. In states with a more competitive party politics concentration of state politics in the off years evidently deprives the state associates of a popular President of the benefit of his pulling power and by the same token aids the other party. Competitive states with off-year elections are by no means untouched by the great fluctuations in party strength nationally; they are simply less closely artic- ulated with the national tides than are those close states whose local campaigns coincide with the commotion generated by a presidential election.[19]

Probably the preponderance of judgment among the architects and reformers of state government supports attempts to separate state and federal politics. A dissent from that view may be expressed, although the line of action promotive of the general weal in any particular state at any particular time is rarely patent. In terms of average long-run effects the case against attempts to isolate state politics hinges on the evident tendency of integration with national politics to strengthen party competition within the states on state matters. Competition may not invariably promote the public good but perhaps over the long term the maximization of competition among politicians turns out more happily than does the maximization of security for politicians.

Quite apart from the effects of separation of guber- natorial and presidential polling on the outcome of state elec- tions, it is evident that over the past 75 years a gradual decline has occurred in the capacity of parties to carry states simul- taneously for their candidates for President and for governor. In all the states with simultaneous presidential and gubernatorial elections—a group of states whose composition has changed

[19] The determinism of the election calendar also influences the extent to which governors confront legislatures controlled by opposition majorities. See Table 8 on p. 69 and the related discussion.

from time to time—the proportions of elections that produced pluralities for presidential and gubernatorial candidates of the same party by groups of presidential elections have been as follows: 1880-92, 93.1 per cent; 1896-08, 89.5 per cent; 1912-24, 81.2 per cent; 1928-40, 77.8 per cent; 1944-52, 75.5 per cent. This general trend in the absence of separation of elections suggests that perhaps some of the independence apparently achieved by segregation of choice through scheduling may have been the result of a long-run increase in the disposition of voters to view state and national affairs independently.

5. The States in the Nation

It becomes evident from this analysis that the balance between the confederative and nationalistic elements within our federal system conditions fundamentally the manner of conduct of politics within the states. To the extent that the confederative element has the upper hand, a state or a group of states maintains political unity in national affairs against the remainder of the country. To that extent, too, the internal politics of the state tend to be warped away from the competitive two-party pattern and find expression in forms and practices not well fitting the conventional concepts by which the instruments of popular government are described. Among the American states this phenomenon has been most marked in its connection with the heritage of the Civil War and it has been far more severe and more persistent in the states of the South than elsewhere. In the nonsouthern states, apart from the vestiges of party loyalties with the same historical foundation as those of the South, from time to time transient sectional drives for national action have reacted back on the politics of the states concerned.

It would, to be sure, be absurd to attribute the special qualities of the politics of the American states, in all their variety, entirely to the effects of their peculiar federal institutional setting.[20] Yet the functioning of the states as legally separate units in the federal system is conditioned by the fact that they are politically inseparable units of the nation. This interconnection of state and nation, commonly regarded as an indication of the disposition of the electorate to rely on its reflexes rather than on its intellect, may be, and often is, an entirely rational politics. Certainly at moments when great issues of domestic economic policy clamor for attention generally, similar divisions in state and federal voting may make good sense. Yet the looseness of the party system compounds the complexities of the politics of a federal system; it blurs and confuses the alternatives presented to the electorate simultaneously in national and state affairs. The electorate faces a formidable task in the discernment of the realities underlying the inevitably confused particular situation on which it must act. The pursuit of even a politics of the meanest interest becomes difficult in the institutional maze, and the notion of party responsibility for state affairs often becomes almost completely irrelevant.

The long-run social trends are wearing down sectionalism. Perhaps eventually the areas of one-partyism in state affairs will lose their special characteristics, although a forecast in terms of decades rather than years would be prudent. The disappearance of the one-party areas would, of course, have most profound consequences for national politics. The states of the respective sectional cores of the major parties have contributed significantly to the form of national politics. The one-party states

[20] The contention could well be made that federalism, as such, has little to do with the interaction between sectionalism nationally and the form or practice of state politics. In any polity, federal or non-federal, with fairly sharp geographical cleavages on issues of national policy a similar relationship might be expected to prevail, that is, if the non-federal polity had subordinate political units of considerable extent. Such an argument is plausible enough and perhaps correct. Yet it would be expected that federal regimes, by virtue of the circumstances of their emergence, would be especially marked by sectional or geographical concerns in national politics, with the consequent reactions on the forms of politics in those states sectionally oriented toward national questions. Yet one should be wary of extending the argument of this chapter to all federal systems; the argument here is explicitly limited to the peculiar features of the American federal system.

have sustained the minority party in the nation. Yet it should not be assumed that we must have one-party states to keep the national minority alive.

This discussion of the impact of the position of the state vis-à-vis the nation upon the internal structure of state politics should not obscure the fact that in various ways the form and pattern of state politics have their national effects. For example, the states, as substantial political entities in the federal system, develop party structures which must be founded on the cleavages peculiar to each state. Within the national party system, these peculiarities may project themselves upon the national leadership of the party. Thus, in a group of midwestern and plains states, the Democratic party, if it is to exist at all as a statewide party, must ordinarily exist as a party different from the Democratic party of an industrial state. In periods of Democratic triumph, as in the 1930's, these western state parties provided, on the whole, a relatively conservative bloc which had to be taken into account by the national leadership of the party. Other examples could readily be cited of the same general question as it applies to both of the major national parties.

Chapter 3

Frustration of Party:
The Perversion of Separation of Powers

Most American states have developed a wondrous damper on party government.[1] Their constitutional systems virtually foreclose full performance by political parties of their role in the democratic process. The states have uniformly adopted the system of separated powers, with the governor and the legislature independent each of the other and owing allegiance directly to the electorate. Onto the separation of powers have been grafted electoral arrangements which assure that at least one house of the legislature will at least some of the time be controlled by a political party in opposition to the party of the governor.

In such an institutional setting political parties suffer a double infirmity. The situation prevents the presentation of a choice between parties to the electorate. With one legislative house as safe for one party as the House of Lords, the voters often simply cannot exercise the democratic prerogative of overthrowing the government. In another way the institutional pattern obstructs the performance of party function. American

[1] A more extended version of this chapter was published jointly with Corinne Silverman in *Public Policy*, 5 (1954), pp. 382-412. Her assistance and collaboration are gratefully acknowledged, although it should be made clear that she bears no responsibility for the present reformulation.

tradition places a positive value on the jealousies between governors and legislators and at the same time takes comfort in the supposition that the party system makes workable the system of separated powers by keeping those jealousies in check. Party embraces the executive and the houses of the bicameral legislature and mitigates, if it does not remove, the obstacles to governance built into the constitutional system. Yet the realities are that the facts of political life, by producing partisan opposition between the major branches of government, make the performance of this function by the parties impossible in many states much of the time.

Our orthodox doctrines of constitutionalism justify a bit of friction between governors and legislators but the increasing divergencies between state systems of representation and the geographical distribution of the population leads from friction towards stalemate. A mixture of stubborn independence and statesmanlike collaboration between the branches of government works well only so long as the proportions of the ingredients are correct. The question is timely whether the ingredients have not come to be markedly out of balance in many states. In any case, control of legislative and executive branches of government by opposing political parties compounds the difficulties inherent in a system of separated powers.

The extent of division of party control of state governments differs among the states and with the stage of the political cycle. The major formal arrangement conducive to divided control is the system of representation, but other forms and procedures, such as the calendar of elections, have a bearing. These matters deserve exploration in some detail to build up a picture of the range and variety of practice in the states.

1. *Extent and Incidence of Division of Partisan Control*

A simple determination of the extent to which one party controls the governorship and another a majority of one or both of the houses of the legislature draws the line between the times and areas in which party government in the conventional sense can and cannot exist. If our institutional arrangements and electoral habits were perfectly adjusted to the doctrine of partisan integration of constitutionally independent organs of government, when a Democrat won the governorship his party would carry majorities of the seats in both houses of the legislature. The same parallelism of electoral preference would prevail when a Republican won the governorship. In fact, departures from common party control are common. Since the incidence of division of control differs markedly from time to time, a snapshot of the situation among the states at a given moment shows only one dimension of the interweaving of party system and constitutional structure. Their relations need to be traced through a political cycle to identify the bearing on divided party control in state governments of variations in balance between the parties in the nation as a whole.

A rough measure of the degree to which the states conform to and depart from the hornbook expectations about the relation of party and the separation of powers is provided by Table 5. That table classifies the states according to the proportion of the period 1931-1952 when one house or both houses of the legislature had a majority of members affiliated with the party opposite that of the governor. The ranking of the states reflects the peculiar character of the period, an upthrust in Democratic strength generated by economic catastrophe. Yet an examination of a period including wide swings in partisan strength provides an especially good test of the question whether the constitutional and party systems are geared together in a manner to create at least a nominal basis for party government.

The largest category in Table 5 consists of those 15 states in which at no time during the period 1931-52 was there partisan division between the governor and legislature. All states would, of course, fall into this class if shifts in party control of governor and legislature were synchronized. In fact, only South Dakota qualified for inclusion among the 15 states through simultaneous shifts in partisan control of both executive and legis-

TABLE 5

States According to Number of Years, 1931-1952, in which Governorship and One or Both of the Legislative Houses Were in Control of Opposite Parties[a]

DIVIDED CONTROL		STATES		
NO. OF YEARS	% OF 22-YR. PERIOD	NO.	%	NAMES OF STATES
0	0.0	15	32.6	Alabama, Arkansas, Florida, Georgia, Louisiana, Mississippi, North Carolina, Oklahoma, South Carolina, Tennessee, Texas, Virginia, New Hampshire, Vermont, South Dakota
2	9.1	4	8.7	Arizona, Iowa, West Virginia, Wisconsin[b]
4	18.2	6	13.0	New Mexico, Kansas, Maine, Oregon, Pennsylvania, Kentucky
6	27.3	5	10.9	California, Idaho, Illinois, Maryland, Michigan
8	36.4	3	6.5	North Dakota, Ohio, Utah
9	40.7	1	2.2	New Jersey
10	45.5	5	10.9	Colorado, Delaware, Montana, Washington, Missouri
12	54.5	4	8.7	Rhode Island, Wyoming, Indiana, New York
14	63.6	3	6.5	Massachusetts, Nevada, Connecticut[c]
Total		46[d]	100.0	

[a] *The basic data for this table and those that follow are from the* New York *Legislative Manual and George Gallup's* Political Almanac, 1952. *The computations for this table rest on a comparison of the political affiliation of legislators and governors from the election of 1930 through that of 1950. For states holding elections in odd years, the period 1929-1949 was used except for Kentucky, for which the elections of 1931-1947 were used.*

lature.[2] Nominal party harmony between governor and legislature in the other 14 states resulted from continuous control
of executive and legislature by the same party. In 12 states of
the South and in Vermont and New Hampshire the dominant
party held power continuously in little peril of displacement by
the opposition.

In about two-thirds of the states a sufficiently competitive political order existed to prevent consistent capture of governor and legislature by the same party at all elections during the
period. Yet the striking fact is that in all these states save South
Dakota, at one time or another, control of the executive and legislature was divided between the parties. Those states in which
divided control prevailed for only two or four years of the 22-
year period are readily recognizable as states in which the dominant party was strongly entrenched. In Arizona, West Virginia,
New Mexico, and Kentucky, the Republicans managed to cut
into the Democratic monopoly for a brief time, while in Iowa,
Wisconsin, Kansas, Maine, Oregon, and Pennsylvania the Democrats mustered enough strength to share power with the Republicans only for a brief interlude.

As one reads down Table 5, it becomes evident that the
proportion of the period in which a division of party control

---

[b] *Third-party and independent governors were excluded.
The exclusion includes the 1930 Oregon election, the 1936
North Dakota election, and the elections of 1934, 1936, 1940,
and 1942 in Wisconsin.*
[c] *The elections of 1934 and 1938 gave the Republicans
minorities in the state senate but by coalition with the handful
of Socialists they obtained working control. These elections were
considered as having resulted in Republican control. Throughout, in situations of a 50-50 division between Republicans and
Democrats, the assignment of party control was determined by
the party affiliation of the presiding officer and the party
affiliations of committee chairmen.*
[d] *Minnesota and Nebraska are excluded from this and
subsequent tabulations since their legislators are elected on a non-
partisan ballot.*

[a] In 1932 and again in 1934 Democrats won the governorship and
both houses of the legislature. During the remainder of the period Republicans controlled both executive and legislature.

prevailed increases roughly as states come to be characterized by fairly even party competition. States with the most evenly balanced party systems depart in highest degree from the nominal conditions essential for party performance of its supposed role as a solvent of separation of powers. In one-third of the states competing parties could joust with each other from opposite corners of the tripartite structure for more than a third of the period 1931-1952. The extreme situation prevailed in Rhode Island, Wyoming, Indiana, New York, Massachusetts, Nevada, and Connecticut where for more than one-half of the period the formal conditions existed for party warfare between organs of government rather than for their co-ordination by party.

2. Separation of Powers: Arbiter of Party Fortunes and Obstacle to Popular Decision

Perhaps the blending of party government and the separation of powers does not require that the conditions be such that at every election the same party will control both legislative and executive branches of the government. Yet in many American states, as has been shown, the constitutional and electoral system guarantees that executive and legislature will be controlled by opposing parties at least some of the time. In making good that guarantee the system shows a bias between the parties. It confronts Democratic governors with Republican legislative majorities far more frequently than it presents Republican governors with Democratic legislative houses. To analyze the bias of the system, let us exclude the 14 consistently one-party states identified in Table 5 on the ground that party has little bearing on their internal politics. With the additional exclusion of the two states with nonpartisan legislatures, there remain 32 states in which, except for South Dakota, at one time or another during the period under scrutiny a division in party control existed.

After one out of three elections held in the 32 states from 1930 to 1950 inclusive, the governor was faced by a legis-

lature with one or both of the houses controlled by the opposite
party. The term election, as used here, requires some definition.
It covers elections, such as those of Massachusetts, in which the
governor and both representatives and senators are elected simultaneously at two-year intervals. That state thus held 11 elections in the period 1930-1950. Another type of situation is
represented by New Jersey which, until its recent constitutional
revision, elected a governor triennially and both senators and representatives annually. New Jersey thus had 21 elections in the
period. An election in this analysis therefore represents a choice
of governor, house, senate, or any combination of them.[3] The
tabulation for the 32 states yields the results shown in Table
6.

Although the rain supposedly falls on the wicked and
the virtuous alike, Republican governors in our 32 states had
much less of whatever grief comes from dealing with an opposition legislature than did Democratic chief executives. The chances
for the period analyzed were about 50-50 that an election would
be followed by a period of divided control when the governor was
Democratic, although at times he might have one house with a
majority of his own party. When a Republican sat in the governor's chair, only about one out of six elections gave the Democrats a majority in one house or both houses. Table 6 must be
interpreted in the light of the fact that 1930-1950 marked a sharp
upward movement in Democratic strength followed by a reces-
sion. The characteristic situation accounting for the differences
appearing in Table 6 was one of a more or less traditionally
Republican state in which the Democratic sentiment did not
invariably have the depth or momentum to pull with it Democratic legislative majorities. At times the upsurge of Democratic
sentiment reflected itself in legislative majorities in opposition
to Republican governors, but more commonly the governor
functioned more accurately than the legislature as weather vane
for the political winds that swept the country. Almost four out of

[3] Elections that resulted in the victory of an independent or third-
party governor were excluded.

five elections resulting in divided control were those in which the gubernatorial victor was Democratic.

Nor do these partisan differences in the effects of the system result from narrower winning margins by Democratic governors. The proportion of legislative seats won by a governor's fellow partisans tends to increase with the percentage of the popular vote polled by the governor. On the average, however, a Democratic governor must poll a much higher proportion of the popular vote than must a Republican to carry into office with him legislative majorities of his own party. In our 32 states two-thirds of the elections won by Democratic governors by from 50 to 55 per cent of the two-party vote resulted in Republican majorities in one or both of the legislative houses, as may be seen in Table 6. Of the Republican governors winning by a similar margin, only 27 per cent had to cope with a Democratic legislative majority. Even when Democratic governors won by 60 per cent or more, the chances were about one out of three that Republicans would control one or both houses of the legislature. With that margin of popular victory Republican governors invariably had legislative majorities of their own party. Nevada accounted for three of the eleven elections, indicated in Table 6, in which a Democratic gubernatorial victory by 60 per cent or more of the two-party vote was associated with legislative opposition in at least one house. New York, Colorado, North Dakota, and Rhode Island were also represented by one or more elections in which this extreme disparity between gubernatorial and legislative votes occurred. Thus, in New York in 1930 Franklin D. Roosevelt rolled up more than 60 per cent of the two-party vote for governor as did Herbert Lehman in 1934 yet at both elections Republicans retained majorities in both the Senate and Assembly.

From these facts the blunt conclusion emerges that the constitutional systems really shut the door against a popular choice between political parties. At least the circumstances block a majority from expressing an effective preference for one crowd of politicians over another. In times of tranquillity this obstacle to popular decision may amount to no more than an amusing constitutional curiosity but at other times it may be akin to a sandbag on a safety valve. The party system may be regarded not so much as a mechanism for persistent and continuing competition in elections and in the conduct of government but as a

TABLE 6

Elections in 32 States, 1930-1950, Resulting in Majorities in One or Both of the Legislative Houses in Opposition to Republican and Democratic Governors, According to Percentage of Two-Party Vote Polled by Governor[a]

PER CENT OF TWO-PARTY VOTE FOR GOVERNOR	DEMOCRATIC GOVERNORS			REPUBLICAN GOVERNORS		
	NUMBER	NUMBER OPPOSED	PER CENT OPPOSED	NUMBER	NUMBER OPPOSED	PER CENT OPPOSED
50-54.9	90	58	64	78	21	27
55-59.9	70	28	40	52	8	15
60 and over	30	11	37	33	0	0
Total	190	97	51	163	29	18

[a] *In the classification of "elections," as defined in the text, those legislative elections held nonconcurrently with the election for governor were grouped according to percentage of the vote polled by the winning gubernatorial candidate at the preceding election. When those elections at which governor and both legislative houses are chosen simultaneously are analyzed separately, about the same percentage differentials appear as exist among the groups in this table.*

means for providing an alternative set of political leaders that can be voted into office at rather widely separated intervals when the normally dominant leadership becomes discredited. From such a temporal view of the party system, institutional checks to the expression of majority sentiment take on a special significance in their relation to popular government at times of widespread public exasperation. When the arrangements are such that one set of politicians cannot be simultaneously thrown out of both executive and legislative posts without a virtual popular uprising, something short of popular government in the conventional sense of the term exists.

How the party system and the constitutional system do or do not mesh together over the period of a political cycle may

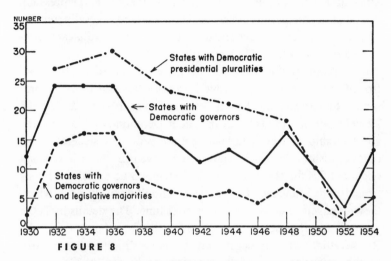

FIGURE 8

Elections in 31 States, 1930-1950: Number of States with Demo-cratic Presidential Pluralities, Number with Democratic Gov-ernors, and Number with Democratic Governors and Democratic Majorities in Both Legislative Houses[a]

[a] *The figure includes those states covered by the immedi-ately preceding tabulations except Kentucky which holds its gub-ernatorial elections in odd-numbered years.*

be discerned from Figure 8, which analyzes the 32 states, exclu-sive of Kentucky, from 1930-1950.[4] Even with the aid of the Great Depression, Democrats were able in 1934 and 1936 to capture both executive and legislature in only 16 of the 31 states.

[4] Let it be remembered that our 32-state group excludes 12 con-sistently Democratic states of the South, the two consistently Republican states of Vermont, and New Hampshire, and the two states with non-partisan legislatures, Nebraska and Minnesota.

As depression anxieties subsided, the number of states under complete Democratic control dropped sharply. If the record in the chart has any predictive value, it would be concluded that to control the governorship and both houses of the legislature in more than 10 of the 31 states, the Democrats must be beneficiaries of a catastrophe on the order of the Great Depression. Throughout the period, however, Democrats in a goodly number of states won the governorship although the Republicans controlled one or both of the legislative houses.

Another dimension of the phenomenon of divided control of executive and legislative appears when our data are presented to indicate the length of time for each state during the 22-year period, 1931-1952, in which Democrats controlled the governorship and both legislative chambers. The general Democratic position in the 32 states seems even more parlous when one identifies the states in which the Democratic party never controlled both branches of government simultaneously or in which they managed to do so for only a brief time. The details in Table 7 speak for themselves, but consider the fact that even in the Rooseveltian era Democrats did not have simultaneous control of the governorship and both legislative houses in California, Connecticut, Massachusetts, and New Jersey. In New York and Pennsylvania they controlled the governorship and both legislative chambers for only two of the 22 years and in Michigan for only four years. Republicans failed to gain simultaneous control in a group of smaller states including Arizona, Kentucky, Maryland, New Mexico, Utah, West Virginia, and Missouri. The states in which the Democrats never gained complete control contained within their borders 28 per cent of the 1950 national population.

Institutions that deny victory to heavy majorities in times of stress—not snap majorities of the moment but solid majorities —scarcely accord with the spirit of popular government. It is, of course, at such times that the consequences of the bickering and paralysis induced by divided control are most grave. And it is at such times that the will to constitutional obedience is most apt to be strained to the breaking point. That strain can only be aggravated by practices on their face calculated to obstruct popular choice.[5]

Yet the different impacts of the swings of the political cycle on Democrats and Republicans should not be regarded

TABLE 7

Thirty-two States According to Number of Years, 1931-1952, Democrats Controlled Governorship and Both Legislative Houses

YEARS	STATES
0	California, Connecticut, Delaware, Kansas, Maine, Massachusetts, New Jersey, North Dakota, Oregon, Wisconsin
2	Pennsylvania, New York
4	Iowa, Michigan, Nevada, South Dakota, Wyoming
6	Colorado, Illinois, Indiana, Montana, Ohio, Rhode Island
8	Idaho
10	Washington
12	Missouri
14	Utah
16	Kentucky, Maryland
20	Arizona, New Mexico, West Virginia

[5] The timing of Rhode Island's so-called "revolution" of 1935 illustrates the point. The Democrats in 1934 elected the governor, the lieutenant-governor, a majority in the lower house, and, at the peak of the Democratic tide of the 1930's, apparently only 20 of the 42 senate seats. When the legislature convened, the lieutenant-governor ordered all senators sworn in save two Republicans. A committee dominated by Democrats recounted the ballots from the two districts in question, threw out "defective" ballots, and recommended seating the Democratic contestants. The committee's report won acceptance from the Democratic majority of a quorum which included two Republicans brought in by state troopers. The new Democratic senate majority then, in less than 15 minutes, declared vacant the state Supreme Court seats, none of which had been filled by a non-Republican for 63 years, abolished several state boards that controlled activities in Democratic areas of the state, strengthened the powers of the governor, and passed a reorganization act grouping 80 units of government into 11 departments, an action not without effect on Republican incumbents. See Zechariah Chaffee, Jr., *The Constitutional Convention That Never Met* (Providence: The Book Shop, 1938).

solely as the result of partisan manipulation of the conditions under which the political battle is fought. Probably an element of wider generality is involved. The data suggest that under American circumstances the weaker party—not simply the Democratic party—may be unable to build up its legislative strength as rapidly as its gubernatorial vote increases either in secular movement or through a stage of the political cycle. If the Republican party were to begin to gain strength in gubernatorial politics in the South, the chances are that in legislative races it would enjoy the same handicap that the Democrats face elsewhere in the country. Indeed, that disadvantage has appeared in instances of Republican gubernatorial victories and legislative defeats in such border states as Maryland, Tennessee, and Kentucky.

3. *Factors Contributing to Divided Party Control*

Some commentators on American state politics take satisfaction from the thought that the division of partisan control of the governorship and the legislature reflects a preference of the people. On rare occasions elections with divided results certainly reflect such a preference. By and large, however, the governmental system is so arranged that the voters on election day can express no such choice; whatever the majority does and however large the majority may be the election will result in split control. The conditions of popular choice permit no other result. Perhaps a more accurate way to put it would be to say that in some states if the voters want a Democratic governor they are sure to have at least one Republican legislative house; in other, and fewer states, if the voters prefer a Republican governor, they are quite certain to have a Democratic legislature. By far the most important element producing these results is the malapportionment of representation in the legislature, but other institutional and procedural factors also contribute.

The varieties of legislative malapportionment reflect the

range of human ingenuity in adapting political geography to partisan advantage. The old-fashioned gerrymander consists in the creation of legislative districts of grotesque form to produce a maximum number of districts with majorities for the party in charge of the districting. The "silent gerrymander" results from inaction. Without a reallocation of legislative seats the number of representatives of areas of growing population remains constant as does the representation of areas of relative decline in population. In some instances constitutions prescribe that either counties or towns shall be represented more or less equally in one house of the legislature. Other constitutions adhere to the doctrine of representation according to population with the exception that specified populous counties or cities shall not be entitled to more than fixed numbers of representatives.[6]

Whatever the legal or constitutional pattern may be, the interaction between the apportionment system and the party system produces several characteristic types of consequences. In one recurring type of situation the apportionment arrangements are such that even repeated Democratic gubernatorial victories leave Republicans in control of one or both of the legislative houses. Only the most extraordinary popular Democratic gubernatorial majority brings with it legislative control. In those states in which this condition prevails the parties are competitive in gubernatorial politics but a majority of the membership of one or both of the houses is, in effect, allocated to the Republicans by constitution or statute. Massachusetts exemplifies this type of polity. As Figure 9 indicates, in seven of 17 elections, 1920-1952, Democratic candidates won the governorship but in no instance did they gain a majority of the concurrently chosen senate.[7] Only in

[6] For surveys of formal rules of representation, see Lashley G. Harvey, "Reapportionment of State Legislatures—Legal Requirements," *Law and Contemporary Problems,* 17 (1952), pp. 364-376; K. C. Sears, *Methods of Reapportionment* (Chicago: University of Chicago Law School, 1952); Belle Zeller (ed.), *American State Legislatures* (New York: Crowell, 1954), chap. 3.

[7] A part of the Democratic difficulty flows from one of the more or less inevitable frailties of geographical representation. Although Suffolk County (Boston) is not discriminated against in the allocation of

1948 and 1950 did a Democratic governor go into office with Democratic majorities of the lower house.

In several other states the politico-constitutional system resembles, in its effects, that of Massachusetts. The New York

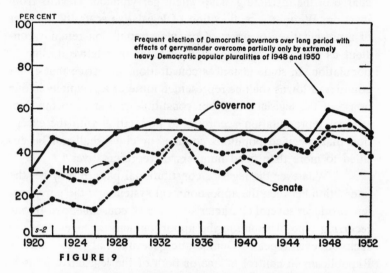

PER CENT

Frequent election of Democratic governors over long period with effects of gerrymander overcome partially only by extremely heavy Democratic popular pluralities of 1948 and 1950

Governor

House

Senate

FIGURE 9

Gerrymander and Separation of Powers: Democratic Percentage of Two-Party Vote for Governor and Democratic Percentage of Seats in the Legislative Houses, Massachusetts, 1920-1952

Constitution virtually assigns control of both houses of the legislature to the Republican party. In 1910 and 1912 the family troubles of the Republicans gave the Democrats majorities in both houses as well as the governorship. In 1922 Alfred E. Smith won along with a Democratic senate majority, but usually Democratic governors have had to deal with Republican majorities in both houses. Connecticut's lower house follows the Massachusetts

---

legislative seats, the heavy concentration of Democratic voters in the county "wastes" a good many votes in legislative races. Democrats there elect legislators by overwhelming majorities. The same number of popular votes distributed more widely over the state would yield a larger number of Democratic senators.

and New York pattern; it has been consistently Republican since 1876.[8] On the other hand, Connecticut Democrats have a better chance to win a senatorial majority when they carry the governorship. They may even put into office a senate majority as the Republicans are winning the executive post. The New Jersey pattern follows that of New York. In no instance since 1913 has a Democratic governor carried into office with himself a majority of either house. If California should elect a series of Democratic governors, its senate would probably remain Republican. Los Angeles County, with its four million people, is entitled to one of 80 senators, as is the smallest rural district with a population of 14,000.

In addition to simple malapportionment of representation, other formal practices contribute to party division between legislature and executive. These practices often produce divided control seemingly by chance or by caprice rather than by any considered choice of the sovereign voters. One type of situation with such results develops from the existence of nonconcurrent terms for governor and legislature. A common arrangement is a gubernatorial term of four years and a term of two years for the members of the lower chamber. Under certain political conditions, such nonconcurrent terms give the governor a lower house controlled by the opposition during the second half of his term. To isolate those conditions an analysis was made of those gubernatorial elections in our 32 states in which governors, chosen for four-year terms, went into office with a lower house controlled by their own party (thus are excluded those elections in which the governor's party could not command a majority of the house even in the flush hour of gubernatorial victory). By the restriction of attention to legislative chambers elected simulta-

[8] In 1950, about 11 per cent of the state's population resided in towns of 5,000 or less. These towns elected 52 per cent of the house members, and eight out of ten of their representatives were Republicans. An apportionment on the basis of population would have resulted in an overwhelming Democratic majority. In a survey of all the states Gus Tyler finds that in 21 states less than one-third of the population elects at least a majority in one house of the legislature.—"The Majority Don't Count," *New Republic*, August 22, 1955.

neously in their entirety with the governors, the analysis excludes the effects of staggered terms and other such practices contributory to executive-legislative division.

In one out of five such instances, in the period analyzed, a governor with a four-year term could expect the opposition to gain a house majority at the election in the middle of his term, as is indicated by Table 8. This type of partisan divergence of executive and legislature, however, rested not so much on non-concurrence of terms as on the relation of those terms to the national election calendar. All those Democratic governors who drew a Republican house at the middle of their term had been themselves elected in presidential years; the Republican legislative victories were an incidental product of the sharp slumps in the Democratic vote in 1938, 1946, and 1950. On the other hand, all those Republican governors whose fellow partisans fell by the wayside at midterm had been elected in nonpresidential years; Republican state legislators became casualties of the presidential campaign. Such embarrassments of Republican governors chosen in the off years would be expected to disappear in an era of national Republicanism, while Democratic governors elected in off years at such a time might expect a Republican legislature to be chosen in presidential years.

Another procedure deliberately designed to check popular surges of sentiment accounts for extremely few instances of divided control. Some state constitutions stagger senate terms so that only a part of this chamber must seek a new mandate at two-year intervals. Under an appropriate apportionment and a correct rate and range of fluctuation in popular sentiment, shift in party control of the upper house would lag behind that of the lower house both in the upswing and downturn of a party's fortunes. In fact, this exact sequence rarely occurs. Only two such instances of lag on both the up- and down-sides of the cycle could be identified in the period examined. Democrats won a majority of the Colorado house seats in 1930; in 1932 the senate came under their control. In 1938 the Republicans won the house but Democrats held the senate until the election of 1942. In Indiana, Democrats captured the house in 1930; the staggered senate term delayed an upper-house majority for them until 1932. On the downswing, Democrats retained a senate majority for a

TABLE 8

Nonconcurrent Terms and Party Control of Executive and Legislature, 1930-1950: Governors Elected for Four-Year Term with Simultaneous Election of House Majority of Their Party, Related to Results of House Elections Two Years Later[a]

| CATEGORY OF GOVERNORS | GOVERNORS ELECTED WITH HOUSE MAJORITY OF THEIR PARTY | PARTY CONTROL OF HOUSE TWO YEARS LATER | | | |
| | | GOVERNOR'S PARTY | | OPPOSITION PARTY | |
		NO.	%	NO.	%
Total	64	51	80	13	20
Democratic	37	29	78	8	22
Republican	27	22	82	5	18
Elected in Presidential Years—					
Democratic	25	17	68	8	32
Republican	6	6	100	0	0
Elected in Off Years—					
Democratic	8	8	100	0	0
Republican	21	16	76	5[b]	24
Kentucky: Democratic[c]	4	4	100	0	0

[a] *States included in the analysis are California, Delaware, Idaho, Illinois, Indiana, Kentucky, Missouri, Montana, Nevada, New York, Oregon, Pennsylvania, Utah, Washington, West Virginia, Wyoming.*

[b] *Includes Idaho Senate (then chosen for a two-year term), which was Democratic in 1948.*

[c] *The Kentucky governor is chosen for a four-year term in 1947, 1951, etc.*

couple of years after their loss of the house in 1938. In a few other instances partial renewal of the senate accounted for party divergence between upper and lower house on either the upswing or the downswing of the cycle but not both. Usually the amplitude of electoral shifts is so great that the winning party captures both houses simultaneously; or one house is so apportioned that the Democrats seem never to be able to muster enough of a popular vote to carry a majority of its seats. The staggered term, however, affects the size of party majorities and often causes changes in party strength in the senate to lag behind those in the house without affecting partisan control.

The institutions and electoral procedures described have been more or less deliberately designed to frustrate popular majorities. They account for a large proportion of the instances of partisan division between state executives and legislatures. Yet not all elections that result in partisan divisions are products of rigged rules of the game. Some credit must be accorded to the nature of the organization of parties, to popular capacity to manage the electoral mechanism, as well as to an occasional instance of deliberate, perhaps amply justified, differentiation by the electorate—or by enough of the electorate—to create a condition of governmental schizophrenia.

A type situation that recurs is that of a state that ordinarily elects Republican governors and only a corporal's guard of Democratic legislators. The high visibility of the gubernatorial office permits social tension, such as existed in the 'thirties, to be discharged by the election of a Democratic governor and the temporary banishment of the Republican contender. Yet the Democratic party, often virtually dormant in the constituencies, is unable to carry majorities of the legislative districts. Long nourished only by the prospect of defeat, it has neither the candidates nor the campaign resources—to say nothing of a frequent lack of will—to command support at the grass roots commensurate with its gubernatorial vote. In this type of situation the gubernatorial vote seems to be far more sensitive to the movement of mass sentiment than is the vote for legislative candidates. The occasional winning of a governorship, in time of crisis or mass discontent, represents an achievement of a rather different order than that of building a support sufficiently rooted

in the legislative districts to make a consistently respectable
showing in legislative elections.

Precise measurement of the factor of party weakness at
the grass roots as it bears on our problem would be quite difficult.
Yet evident instances may be cited. In 1930 and 1936, Democratic candidates Harry H. Woodring and Walter Huxman,
respectively, won the Kansas governorship, through a combination of agrarian disillusionment with Republicanism generally,
Republican indiscipline and ineptitude, the national swing to the
Democrats, and a variety of other factors. Similarly, in Maine an
occasional Democratic candidate makes his way into the governor's office. In both states, the distribution of legislative seats
handicaps the Democrats but beyond this a fundamental weakness in party organization in the constituencies assures legislative
victories less than commensurate with the gubernatorial vote.
Similar legislative-gubernatorial disparities appear in states
dominated by the Democratic party. In those southern states in
which Republicans poll a substantial popular vote for governor,
the Republican legislative contingent is usually minute.

Another type of gubernatorial-legislative division flows,
not so much from systems of apportionment or other formal institutional causes, as from the success of a popular gubernatorial
candidate in differentiating himself so effectively from his party
that he survives the tides that inundate his fellow partisans. Only
infrequently does the electorate deliberately choose to place the
executive and legislature in the hands of opposing parties, despite the prevailing impression to the contrary. By sifting through
the records of our 32 states over a period of 22 years, only a
half dozen or so instances can be isolated in which such was apparently the case. In screening out these instances there had to
be excluded first those states so gerrymandered that if the voters
chose to elect a governor of one party the legislature was certain
to be controlled by the opposition. The electorates of these
states really had no alternative. This exclusion left those states in
which both parties had shown a capacity to capture both the
governorship and the legislature. From the records of these

states there could then be sorted out those elections at which
divergent trends in the movement of a party's gubernatorial and
legislative strength or especially wide disparities in a party's gubernatorial and legislative strength suggested deliberate electoral
choice as a significant factor in the party division of legislative
and gubernatorial control.

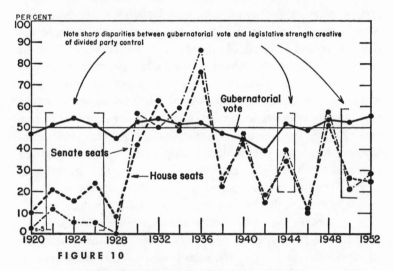

FIGURE 10

*Independence of Gubernatorial Vote from Party Trends in Legis-
lative Strength: Democratic Percentage of Two-Party Vote for
Governor and Democratic Percentage of Legislative Seats, Ohio,
1920-1952*

The type of election isolated by the screening process is
illustrated by the Ohio record shown in Figure 10. That state
manifests an unusual disposition to choose governors independently of the prevailing party trend. Note in the graphs that in
the 1920's the state's Democratic legislative representation remained at an extremely low level in harmony with the state's
Republican presidential attachments. Despite Ohio's preference
for Republican presidential and state legislative candidates, Vic

Donahey, a Democrat, managed to get himself elected governor in 1922, 1924, and 1926. In more recent times another Democratic governor overcame the Republican tide. Frank J. Lausche went into office in 1944 as the state went Republican for President and as the Democratic legislative representation declined from its 1940 level. He repeated the performance in 1950, when Taft won the Senate race, and in 1952 when Eisenhower swept the state. Although the disparity between Democratic gubernatorial and legislative strength comes in part from gerrymandering, it evidently also rests in considerable measure on electoral differentiation.

Although the Ohio record is unusual in the frequency of gubernatorial voting that diverges significantly from the apparent general balance of party strength, scattered instances have occurred in other states. In Delaware in 1948, for example, Mr. Dewey carried the state's electoral vote, his fellow Republicans won majorities in both houses of the legislature, but Democrat Elbert M. Carvel made his way to the governorship. Carvel, who was completing a four-year term as lieutenant-governor, opposed Hyland P. George, a contractor who was making his first political campaign. In Washington in 1940 Senator C. C. Dill, a liberal Democrat, lost the governorship as his party won majorities of the seats of both legislative houses, the United States Senate seat, the various minor state offices, and the electoral vote of the state. A bitter left-right battle in the Democratic primary perhaps aided the Republicans in selling Arthur B. Langlie, twice mayor of Seattle, to enough voters to split the results.[9]

The instances in which—under the conditions as they have been defined—the electorate apparently deliberately chooses a governor of one party and a legislature of another are quite few. Division of executive-legislative control stems in far higher degree from factors of institutional design.

---

[9] See C. O. Johnson, "The Washington Blanket Primary," *Pacific Northwest Quarterly,* January, 1942, pp. 27-39; D. M. Ogden, Jr., "The Blanket Primary and Party Regularity in Washington," *Pacific Northwest Quarterly,* 39 (1948), pp. 33-38.

4. Interaction of Institutional Structure and Party System

This inquiry began with a curiosity about the role of party in overcoming the hindrances to governance inherent in the state systems of separated powers and about the bearing of electoral and constitutional system on the opportunity for clear-cut choice by the electorate between the parties. On these two points the evidence does not allow much leeway in interpretation. The minimum condition essential for parties to perform their supposed function of meshing the independent organs of government is that electoral procedures and representative systems be so constructed that candidates of either party may capture both executive and legislature. That condition is not met in substantial degree in many of the American commonwealths. The combination of party system, separated powers, and over-representation of the nonmetropolitan estate often makes irrelevant any conception of party collaboration in the operation of government or any theory of party accountability for its conduct. In the states with a semblance of a party system, however, the Republican party manages more often to gain complete control of the state apparatus than does the Democratic party.

The evidence on the question of the relation of the combination of separation of powers and the system of representation on popular decision points toward a less obvious sort of interpretation. The institutional ensemble suffuses the process of electoral choice with an illusory quality, but an appreciation of the full significance of that consequence requires that it be related to the variations in the processes of politics as they move through time. In its literary form at least, the biparty system provides the electorate with a choice between alternative sets of officials, a choice basic to popular government. In the pure form of the literary theory each campaign involves a contest between two more or less evenly matched sets of contenders, with the outcome in some doubt. That sustained struggle for power at so high a level of tension is a necessary feature of a going democratic order may well be doubted.

Attention to the facts of state politics suggests another conception that assigns to parties a role other than the maintenance of fierce competition from election to election and that places a different interpretation on the nature of basic electoral decision than that of the literary theory. Such a conception provides a different standard for gauging the efficacy of the party system as an instrument of popular government. The facts, as they may be seen in the various charts indicative of long-term fluctuations in electoral sentiment, suggest that tension builds up or that great events occur to demand far-reaching electoral decision at points more widely spaced in time than the two- or four-year election intervals. At these times the party system in conjunction with the constitutional procedures may or may not permit a choice between alternative sets of candidates. The facts suggest that at these dispersed moments of critical decision the state politico-constitutional systems often deny to the electorate a choice between competing sets of candidates. In at least one house of the legislature the old crowd simply cannot be ousted.[10] From another viewpoint the general arrangement might be likened to an institutional shock-absorber that snubs down those violent upthrusts of mass anxiety and unreason that occur at times of great stress or of popular commotion and confusion. Whatever the viewpoint may be, the function and effect of the system remain the same. All this argument does not deny that state governments can and do manage under conditions of relative calm to cope with routine questions and with some problems of considerable import despite a party division between executive and legislature. Yet even under such circumstances party divisions, by narrowing the range of the feasible, may limit the scope of initiative and of action.

[10] It is from failure to take into account the dimension of time and the factor of broad electoral decision that many assessments of the role of party in state government are not completely persuasive. An analysis of a legislative session or so reveals fairly few roll calls on which party lines are drawn. Ergo, party is insignificant. A look at elections and legislatures through time indicates whether party facilitates electoral choice and at critical moments perhaps brings shifts in policy broadly responsive to that choice.

On these two major points the evidence speaks clearly enough, but reflection on the condition of affairs outlined in the foregoing pages suggests another set of more subtle, and also more conjectural, conclusions. The question is whether the institutional system to which the parties must accommodate themselves may not mold in basic ways the nature of the party system as well as limit the range and character of electoral decision. In turn, the interaction between constitutional forms and informal organisms of party may influence the character of the constitutional system of the states. Since the total system affects the range of state activity, the chain reaction may influence the place of states in the federal system as a whole.

Perhaps as useful a way as any of thinking about these questions is to regard the formal organs of government as operating in a field of influences which may react on them and condition, even alter, their roles in the formally ordained constitutional system. The governor who must more or less regularly face an opposition legislature tends to be thrown with special force into a role of representation of those sectors of the electorate upon which he depends most obviously for popular majorities. Often in such a situation he must depend on urban majorities while the legislature looks countryward for its support. The governor has thrust upon himself the function of majority representation. He thereby gains the moral authority of a role to which he is more or less inexorably pushed by contextual circumstances.[11]

Further, the relations between the formal governmental structure and its matrix of influences may both mold behavior and fix the status of the legislative body. Many factors have conspired to produce the low status of the American state legislature. Yet, among these factors, its unrepresentative character must be assigned a high rank. A body that often acts reluctantly

[11] The contrasting case of Georgia re-enforces the broad theoretical point. By a county-unit system of nominations, which places determinative power in the small rural counties, the governor is put into a field of influence that minimizes metropolitan pressures and tends to make the governor as well as the legislature a spokesman for the "wool-hat" boys.

under executive pressure and whose chief purpose often seems to be one only of negation cannot but in the long run lose prestige. A body that is condemned by its constitution to the defense of a partial interest in the state becomes, if not a council of censors, something other than a representative body in the conventional sense.[12]

The constitution of the American state represents, in its extreme form, an odd melange to which none of the descriptive terms we use really apply. In one of its various forms a tribune of the people rallies a majority of the people to his banner. He has, typically, but not always, allied with himself more than one-half of the members of the lesser legislative chamber; he negotiates, bullies, or buys, with varying success, action from another chamber, chosen, in effect, by a system of weighted voting to serve as the guardians of a minority of the population defined by the accidents of residence and of history. Such a description may differ only in degree from the condition that exists when a loosely organized party controls all; yet that difference accentuates the difficulties of governance by the introduction of different party groups into the process and, negatively, by the obstruction of whatever impulse to party government there may exist. Our technical vocabulary for describing the sorts of government that exist within the states is inadequate. "At Westminster," says Holcombe, "party government is the essence of constitutional government, but at Washington there is both party government and constitutional government." [13] The mixture of party government and constitutional government prevails also at the state capitols but the proportions of the two ingredients vary so greatly from place to place as to produce not only differences of degree but different species for which we have no suitable nomenclature.

[12] The long-term trends in the position of the legislature have undoubtedly generated compensatory changes in the formal constitutional power of the governor as well as the inflation of his informal political position. On the growth of the veto power, for example, see Frank W. Prescott, "The Executive Veto in American States," *Western Political Quarterly*, 3 (1950), pp. 92-112, especially at p. 100.

[13] "The Changing Outlook for a Realignment of Parties," *Public Opinion Quarterly*, 10 (1946-1947), pp. 455-469.

At times the ingredients are proportioned to produce government of the metropolis, by the country, for the suburbs. At other times the governor performs the function of mediation among the great interests of the state, a representative function denied to the legislature by the divergent composition of its two houses.

The specific consequences in the kinds of actions taken and not taken because of the politico-constitutional systems of the states differ, of course, from time to time and from state to state. Each reader from the observation of his own state government could fill in relevant illustrative detail. Yet it is evident that quite generally divided control encourages a good deal of maneuver for short-term partisan advantage. At times this takes the form of irresponsible grandstand actions, as when one legislative house appropriates with great generosity secure in the knowledge that the governor and other legislative house will be compelled to redress the balance in the absence of revenues. The arrangement provides ready and easy means for legislative extortion from the governor and the executive departments. Perhaps, most important of all, the scheme delays or forecloses certain types of policy actions. Thus, in 1955 the Republican chairman of the Connecticut House Finance Committee could say: "As long as Republicans control either branch of the General Assembly there will be no income tax." [14] The Republicans have controlled the house without a break since long before 1900.

The pattern of linkage of party forces to the organs of government may over the long run significantly shape the role and status of executive and legislature in the American state. The relationship of influence may well be operative also in the other direction. The constitutional forms may constitute something of a system of sluices and dikes that impart their shape to the party structure. May not, for example, the institutional structure in its long-run effects have an important bearing on the nature and form of party competition? What is the consequence for the long-term build-up of minority strength in circumstances that make victory most improbable? It might be supposed that partic-

[14] New York *Times*, April 3, 1955.

ular interests, groups, sources of party finance would have to be extremely dissatisfied with the majority to be driven to cast their lot with a seemingly permanent minority. Scattered cases of the CIO-PAC diligently supporting a candidate for nomination in a Republican primary illuminate the point. Perhaps to attract and retain strength a party must have enough of a chance to win so that its supporters need not expect serious reprisals, if a particular election is lost. A minority may be a minority because for historical or other reasons it does not have the votes. The question is whether in their effects in the channeling of the activists the institutional form may not help keep the minority in its minority status.

By the same token, if the activists, moved by short-run considerations, are channeled into the dominant party, it continually renews its strength. The dominant party retains and tightens its nominal grasp of the apparatus of state government, although in the process the inner coherence of the majority may be reduced and a vague sort of factionalism develop. By the destruction of alternative routes to power, the party is apt to make impracticable any measure to maintain its own policy integrity. If such tendencies are operative in the formation and maintenance of party groupings, their effects cumulate over long periods and deposit a residue in customs of action not to be quickly altered.[15]

Insofar as the patterns of relationships described contribute to the weakness of the Democratic party in state politics, they share in the determination of the nature of the national party system. If a national party derives strength and builds its inner core of professionals by control of state governments, it is disadvantaged to the extent that the rules of the game, directly or indirectly, put states beyond its grasp. Would the Democratic

---

[15] An additional possibility is that the institutional forms, at least under some circumstances, encourage a limitation of competition between the professionals of the two parties. With victory beyond their reach, minority professionals may be especially open to understandings to limit their efforts to specified offices or areas or to accept appointments that carry with them an acquiescence in the party status quo.

party, for example, have a larger group of professionals tied to it by interest of ambition and career if conditions were more favorable for its operation in state affairs outside the South? The fact of the matter is that in a goodly number of urbanized, industrialized states the Democratic party lacks a foundation of strong and well-led state subsidiaries or affiliates. To that condition a variety of factors contribute, but probably not the least of them consists of the constitutional bars to the dislodgment of Republicans from state governments.

The institutional depressants of minority endeavor in state politics may also tend to divert the efforts of such minority leadership as there is from state to national politics. The extreme situation is represented by southern Republican leadership which has not for many decades exerted itself to win state office. Its energies have been absorbed in the politics of national conventions and, in days of Republican national rule, in the politics of patronage. Outside the South the Democrats often occupy a position in state politics almost as hopeless as do the Republicans in the southern states. During the years of Democratic national dominance the easy rewards of national politics did not always intensify efforts by the professionals to capture state governments.

In another respect, the pattern of relations between the institutions of state government and the parties has an important bearing on the broad constitutional problem of centralization, of the allocation of governmental functions between the national and state governments. The essence of the situation is that the Democratic party can from time to time capture control of the national government while it has been virtually precluded from gaining for any substantial time complete control of many of the states from which it has drawn heavy popular support. On the other hand, Republicans can capture both national government and state governments outside the South. Excluded from control of some states and able to win others for only brief intervals, the major forces allied with the Democratic party during the 'thirties and 'forties could win elections only by winning national elections. Hence, in considerable measure, the ends of the Democratic party became ends to be achieved through national action or not at all.

In its effects over the long run the politico-constitutional system described must be regarded as a centralizing factor in the federal system. Institutional gadgets that wear down, discourage, or defeat local majorities can only drive them to the alternative route to action through federal power. Given alternative paths to their objectives, political movements tend to follow the route of least resistance. When the dominant mood of an era encounters institutional blockages at the state level, the flow of effective political power is apt to result in accretions to federal functions. Over broad functional areas of government the doctrine of states' rights tends to be equivalent in its effect to a doctrine of political dual federalism: a decision against federal action coupled with the politico-constitutional system of the states amounts to a decision against any action. Those persons concerned in good faith about federal centralization might well give their attention to the effectiveness of state political systems as instruments of popular government.

As the discussion has been cast, the broad problem of governmental design appears as a question of partisan advantage or disadvantage. There can be no blinking the fact that this element looms large but the system as a whole has a quite important bearing on the relative position of shades of opinion within the Republican party, a matter less easily identifiable for analysis and presentation. Republican governors of states with considerable metropolitan populations have their own difficulties with the rural wing of their party which may be dominant in one or both legislative houses. Probably in the long run the Republican party would benefit substantially from constitutional corrections, for it would be compelled to carry the fight into districts now conceded to the Democrats. Those Republican governors who develop strength in the metropolitan centers would tend to gain support from Republican legislators more similar to themselves in outlook than the prevalent types of Republican legislative majorities. Further, given present trends in population redistribution, suburbanites can be relied upon soon to cry to the high heavens about the iniquities of the system of representation.

The general position of this analysis has been that politico-constitutional situations into which the states have drifted weaken the governing capacities of the states. This is paralleled, however, by the view that no uniform sort of corrective action can very well be prescribed; circumstances differ from state to state. Yet this discussion should not be closed without mention of the justifications that have been developed for the present state constitutional systems. These justifications have not attained a high plane of political speculation. Commonly they justify particular interests or rationalize positions taken in particular situations. One broad view, which probably gains potency from the pastoral nostalgia of a newly urbanized people, rests on the proposition that metropolitan peoples are really incompetent in self-government. Their legislators tend to be, so the argument goes, small men not given to statesmanship but adept in the arts of sandbagging. Hence, the greater the number of rural legislators, the better governed will be the commonwealth. Whether, as a question of fact, these differentials in corruptibility actually prevail is not really known.[16] The belief that they exist, however, probably continues to carry considerable weight.

Another position is antimajoritarian, sometimes openly, sometimes not. A more or less typical pattern of political action on state constitutional questions involves a combination of metropolitan business and rural elements to maintain the prevailing system. The implicit, but rarely the explicit, position is that these minorities require for their protection some special position in the constitutional system. The explicit argument often takes the form of an analogy between geographical representation in state legislatures and the equal representation of states

---

[16] Another widely held belief is that rural legislators are more corrupt because they are less costly to buy. Given the relatively small size of rural constituencies, the expense involved in electing a rural legislator is ordinarily much less than the outlay required to elect an urban representative.

in the federal Senate. While the comparison doubtless has persuasive qualities, its scientific utility is slight. The federal Senate, given the total formal and informal context within which it operates, differs greatly in its workings from a similarly constituted house of a state legislature.

The antimajoritarian position at times takes the form of the contention that a democratic order should equip its minorities with instruments for self-defense. The opposing position would place no limitation on the will of the majority. When one settles this abstract issue, or so the argument goes, the issue of constitutional form is solved. This intellectual technique of moving from general principle to specific action substitutes the seductive certainties of logic for the difficult task of estimating the actual consequences of particular arrangements. Even if the broad antimajoritarian position is conceded, the questions remain: What minority is to possess a veto? Over what range of action should that veto be allowed? Would the particular arrangements have the desired result? Is the permanent assignment of control of one legislative house to a particular party requisite to the end sought? Might not the checks built into the formal system, such as the governor's veto, and the informal obstacles to action inherent in the party system and in ordinary legislative procedure serve adequately to protect minority concerns at less cost to the general interest?

Another line of defense of the system runs to the effect that by a process of trial and error an illogical but workable sort of system has evolved which copes with the circumstances of actual American political life. Moreover, the antimajoritarian features of the system enjoy the toleration and perhaps the positive support of the American people. The system certainly represents the precipitate of an evolutionary process and it works after a fashion.[17] Certainly, too, majorities of those voting on

[17] These remarks suggest some observations on the occasional side effects of the functional interpretation of political institutions. Those who employ this tool of interpretation tend to seek the explanation of institutions in the function they perform within their total social context. Often the oddest sorts of arrangements make a good deal of sense when

issues of legislative apportionment have from time to time ratified schemes involving gross malrepresentation. When they have had a chance to vote on the question, state voters have sometimes approved, sometimes disapproved. In 1948, for example, California voters declined to alter their "federal" system. The proposal became sharply identified with the cause of its chief sponsor, the State Federation of Labor, while San Francisco did not relish the prospect of a Los Angeles represented according to population in the state senate.[18] On the other hand, in 1950 Oregon voters turned down a proposal under which each of the counties would have been entitled to one, and only one, representative.[19] In 1954, Utah voted on a similar proposal. Rural majorities for the "federal system" did not suffice to offset the urban opposition.[20] In fact, the people of most states do not get an opportunity to express a view on the matter one way or another. Only by a mystical procedure may their long toleration be used to elevate the systems that have been described into an element of the American political faith.

---

they are examined in the spirit of an anthropologist looking at the rituals of a primitive tribe. But it is easy to creep from this analytical position to the view that whatever is, is correct. Often closely associated is the notion that institutions are the product of a more or less non-conscious groping for workable arrangements—rather than of rational prevision— and that what emerges must be correct for the time and place. These approaches, it must be recognized, have a genuine utility in the analysis of political phenomena. To convert them into universal prescriptions for acton—or, principally, inaction—could only lead to stagnation.

[18] See T. S. Barclay, "The Reapportionment Struggle in California in 1948," *Western Political Quarterly,* 4 (1951), pp. 313-324.

[19] See Hugh A. Bone, "States Attempting to Comply with Reapportionment Requirements," *Law and Contemporary Problems,* 17 (1952), pp. 387-416.

[20] M. Judd Harmon, "The 1954 Election in Utah," *Western Political Quarterly,* 7 (1954), pp. 625-629.

Chapter 4

Nonparty Politics:
The Governor and the Direct Primary

From the preceding comparative analyses, an impression begins to emerge of the range of variety in the forms of organization and in the modes of operation of state political systems. In a few states the party system, although obstructed in its workings by the institutional structure to which it must adapt itself, resembles closely the classic model of two-party competition. Most states, however, in varying degrees and for varying reasons, deviate from that pattern. These common and persistent deviations reflect the existence of systems and instruments of popular government which are not well described by the ordinary vocabulary of political analysis.

Another test-boring into the confused mass of the American state political systems will reveal another dimension of their variety. Characteristically the formal contest, one-sided though it may be, for the control of the American state is fought out in the two-party pattern between candidates of the Republican and Democratic parties. Often this contest is but shadow-boxing. Behind the formal façade of party competition, the rites of which are duly and regularly observed at the November general elections, another political ceremony determines, with a varying probability of finality, the victor in the general election. The outcome of the direct primary nominating procedure, a peculiarly American political invention, anticipates and often forecloses the results of the general election.[1]

The controlling decisions in the American states flow quite as often from the processes of intraparty politics as from those of interparty politics. Yet the degree to which the decisions of intraparty politics prevail differs from state to state as well as from time to time within any particular state. All of which creates formidable impediments to the description and understanding of the political systems of the states. If a fix is taken on the formal two-party façade, the states may be arrayed according to the degree to which they approximate or diverge from the pattern of two-party competition. A state in which the division of the popular vote for Democratic and Republican candidates for governor hovered around the 50-50 point over a long period might clearly be regarded as a two-party state. A state with a division tending around a point of 80-20 would be an indubitable case of one-partyism. Other states might range themselves between these extremes in the degree of their deviation from the pattern of dual competition.

Such a study of the patterns of competition between parties, it could be contended, is of little avail in the understanding of state political systems. The competition between parties may amount only to an empty formality; one should examine the internal politics of the dominant party, principally its nominating activities. In fact, of course, both aspects of state political systems must be examined; each represents an aspect of state politics. The operations of the direct primary occur within the framework fixed by the two-party division, and the nature and function of the party primaries vary roughly with the degree to which the formal party system diverges from the pattern of dual competition. The state systems in a sense

[1] Parts of this chapter appeared under the title, "Party Systems in the States," *Public Policy*, VI (1955), pp. 3-24.

arrange themselves along a scale from the extreme point at which intraparty politics is dominant to the other extreme at which the political battle occurs between parties.

An examination of the nomination of gubernatorial candidates through the direct primary will provide an impression of the variations among the state political systems along this scale. Yet before digging into the workings of the primary, some background should be set out to suggest the logic and place of the direct primary in the American party system and in American democratic thought. In truth, the development of a full comprehension of the primary nominating process would carry one a long way toward an understanding of the basic differentiating characteristics of American democratic practice. Here an inquiry more modest in aspiration—some etiology and a little ecology of the primary system—may serve to underpin the later detailed analysis.

1. Direct Primary: Escape from One-Partyism?

If the direct primary embodies a good deal of the peculiar essence of the American spirit and practice of self-government, some understanding of how and why that procedure of nomination came into being ought to be illuminating. In the evolution of American state political institutions the direct primary system replaced the delegate convention for the nomination of candidates for governor and other statewide offices chiefly during the period from 1896 to 1915. Convention nominations had been indirect nominations. Delegates chosen in various ways —by mass meeting, caucuses, conventions—in counties or other local areas met in a state party convention to nominate candidates to vie in the general election campaign with opposition candidates who had been designated in a similar manner. The adoption of the direct primary struck down the intermediate links between the rank and file of the party and would-be candidates and permitted a direct expression by the voter of his preferences for party nominations.

An explanation of why the direct primary developed ought to aid in an understanding of its place in the political system, but the contrivance of a plausible theory of so complex a process presents its own problems. One could proceed by recapitulating the arguments of the advocates of the new system. That attack would summarize an impressive volume of oratory concerning democracy, government by the people, the abuses of machines, the indefensible privileges of the special interests, the purity of the popular will when undefiled by percolation through the labyrinth of delegate convention process, and other related matters. What people say about what they do may not go far toward explaining why they do what they do. Perhaps a better explanation, or at least a less proximate explanation, may come from inspection of the general situation in which people say what they say. The broad political circumstances in which the advocates of the direct primary found themselves may point toward the more basic reasons why they took the position they did.

The direct primary method of nomination apparently constituted at bottom an escape from one-partyism. A major heritage of the Civil War in many states was a party system unable to implement the doctrine of popular government by presenting the electorate with genuine alternatives. The impact of the federal system—itself newly molded by the war—on the politics of the states, as has been suggested in an earlier chapter, contributed to the unworkability of the party system. With the states of the South irrevocably tied to the Democratic party and with many of the states of the North and West almost equally attached to the Republican party, oligarchical control of party —of which the nominating convention became the symbol and often the reality—amounted to a denial of popular government. Unable to find expression through the channels offered by the party system, the impulses to political conflict in a society with a faith in popular government were bound, as social tensions built up, to break the hold of party oligarchies on the dominant party and to develop an intraparty politics.

If this broad theory of the genesis of the direct primary system holds water, those states most obstinately attached to a single party would presumably be the points of first appearance of the system. And, perhaps, the states most nearly competitive between the major parties would never adopt the primary or would, in the pattern of imitation common to the American states, be quite late in adopting the new pattern. Although all the steps in the adoption of the direct primary do not fit neatly into these expectations, a panoramic view of the origin and spread of the primary conforms to the general theory. The primary system of nomination first came into general use in the southern states; in those states at the time of the germination of the primary far fewer gubernatorial races were closely contested than in the other states of the Union. The Civil War and Reconstruction made Democrats of most southerners. Scarcely had federal troops been withdrawn when it became apparent that one-party dominance demanded a new type of nominating procedure. The Atlanta *Daily Constitution,* in defending in 1876 the use of the direct primary in Fulton County, Georgia, put the rationale of the system in this way:

> The system of primary elections is admirably adapted to our city and county. If parties were evenly divided perhaps the old caucus plan would do. Then there would be two good tickets for local officers in the field. The knot of worthies who, under that plan would gather in a room just large enough to hold them, would be on their good behavior. They would remember their constituents, and would confine their log rolling within prudent bounds. But when as in our local politics, they have nothing to fear from the opposition, there is very little guarantee that the delegate system would give the voters a square chance. For maneuvering and wire pulling, the delegate plan is entitled to the blue ribbon in local contests.

We have no desire to return to it. We prefer the easier
simpler plan of direct voting.[2]

Locality after locality in Georgia introduced the direct primary,
and gradually delegates to state nominating conventions came to
be chosen by local direct primaries rather than by caucuses or
mass meetings. Presently aspirants for the gubernatorial nomination began to appeal to the people for their vote in these primaries through their choice of delegates. The gubernatorial nomination of the 1886 Democratic state convention was, in effect,
made before the convention met by the voters in these local
primaries. In 1898, under party rule, Democratic candidates for
statewide office were chosen directly by the party voters.

In other states of the South the direct primary also
evolved to permit popular government under circumstances that
precluded party government. In Mississippi in the 1870's some
counties inaugurated the system for nominations to county office.
Experimentation with the local primary and criticism of the state
convention system continued for a couple of decades. The state
convention came to function as an instrument of the Delta counties and, therefore, as a stifler of the agrarian unrest centered
in the poorer, hill counties. In 1902 the legislature enacted a
direct primary law.[3] Probably the course of development in each
state resembled somewhat the gradual permeation of the entire
electoral process by the new system in Georgia and Mississippi, although the detailed stories have not been assembled.[4]

[2] Quoted by L. M. Holland, *The Direct Primary in Georgia* (Urbana: University of Illinois Press, 1949), p. 21.

[3] See Albert D. Kirwan, *Revolt of the Rednecks* (Lexington:
University of Kentucky Press, 1951)'. On South Carolina, which abolished
the convention system in 1896, see Francis B. Simkins, *The Tillman
Movement in South Carolina* (Durham: Duke University Press, 1926),
pp. 87-88, 239-243.

[4] Although the possibility of excluding the Negro from the primary may have had something to do with its attractiveness, the significance of that factor in the adoption of the primary has never been in-
vestigated and weighed carefully. The primary, in effect, superseded a
Democratic nominating process from which Negroes were already excluded partially by the fact that they were mostly Republicans. The movement of whites into the Democratic party and the taboo against general

The early adoption of the primary in the southern states was correlated with a far lower degree of interparty competition for the governorship than prevailed in the other states of the Union. During the period 1880-1899, in 18 per cent of the gubernatorial elections in the southern states the Democratic candidate polled between 45 and 55 per cent of the vote of the two high candidates. In the other states of the Union 54 per cent of the gubernatorial elections fell within this relatively closely competitive range. In the southern states 95 per cent of the elections were won by Democrats; in the other states, 33 per cent. The two southern states that held out against the primary system the longest—Virginia and North Carolina—were states with a fairly lively party competition for the governorship during the 1880's and 1890's. In this respect they resembled more the states of the North than the other states of the South.

Outside the South the statewide direct primary first took hold in the West and then spread to the eastern seaboard. Wisconsin enacted the first more or less comprehensive act in 1903 and Oregon followed the next year. Before 1910 complete, mandatory, statewide primary laws were enacted in Illinois, Michigan (complete save for the omission of minor state office nominations), South Dakota, Iowa, Nebraska, Missouri, North Dakota, Washington, Kansas, Oklahoma, Arizona, California, Idaho, Nevada, and New Hampshire. The fact that there remained a semblance of an opposition party in these states may explain in part why they embraced the primary procedure somewhat later than did the southern states. Yet the order in which states adopted the primary does not neatly correspond with a ranking according to degree of one-party domination. A measure is, of course, lacking for such a ranking, but it is evident that factors in addition to one-partyism contributed to the primary movement.

---

election challenge of the nominees had the effect of removing the threat of a Negro balance of power between whites in the general election. Yet even that threat had been taken care of fairly generally by other means before the statewide direct primary came into use. See Paul Lewinson, *Race, Class, and Party* (New York: Oxford University Press, 1932).

The selective manner of the infiltration of the East by the primary system re-enforces the supposition that states with powerful one-party attachments tended to be especially vulnerable to the primary movement. States with old and well-established party systems, more or less competitive, were less fertile fields for primary agitation. New York adopted the system but it never took root and the legislation in its application to statewide offices was repealed. Delaware has never become a wide-open primary state. New Jersey took on the forms of the primary system but the dominant voice in statewide nominations still tends to be the caucus of county leaders. Connecticut and Rhode Island did not respond to the early wave of agitation. On the other hand, Maine, New Hampshire, Vermont, and Massachusetts joined the primary parade.[5] As the movement for the primary took on an evangelical tone, the procedure spread into states with a competitive party politics although it often never really took root in such states. In truth, the lot of the opponent of the primary was not a happy one. He was made to appear to be, ipso facto, an enemy of democracy.

The argument has been that one-partyism more or less compelled resort to the direct primary to maintain something of the reality of popular government. Some appreciation of the character of the one-partyism prevalent at the time of the birth of the primary idea may be essential to understand why the alternative of a competitive party politics did not develop instead of the direct primary. The predominance of the Democratic faith in the South requires no labored explanation. The combination of defeat in war, a military occupation, the problem of race relations, and the necessity for regional unity in national politics made the Republican party an unappealing alternative to whatever group happened to control the Democratic party machinery. If there were to be political contests, they

---

[5] On the history of the primary movement, see C. E. Merriam and Louise Overacker, *Primary Elections* (Chicago: University of Chicago Press, 1928); E. C. Meyer, *Nominating Systems: Direct Primaries Versus Conventions in the United States* (Madison: The Author, 1902).

had to occur within the Democratic party and the direct primary was the logical means for their conduct.[6]

The one-partyism of the West and the Northwest, although less thoroughgoing than that of the South, partook of the same spirit. The Republican party proclaimed itself the party of the Union and of freedom, and the waving of the "bloody shirt" from campaign to campaign renewed the loyalties of the faithful. Wisconsin, the home of Robert M. La Follette, famous as an advocate of the primary, in 1890 elected its first Democratic governor since 1873. Even the 1890 deviation from regularity required the combination of a statute, enacted by a Republican legislature, to compel, in a land of many German-speaking people, attendance at schools teaching in the English language, and the nationwide disaster that struck the Grand Old Party as a consequence of the McKinley tariff.[7]

La Follette, in his battle against the Republican machine, could have presumably turned Democrat and fought the organization from without. Yet the firm Republican loyalties of the mass of the voters made this an unpromising alternative. Party competition is illusory in an electorate with frozen party loyalties. La Follette and the voters who followed him perhaps wanted to go to heaven but they insisted on traveling under Republican auspices. In fact, the frozen party loyalties of political leaders may very well have been more important in blocking the workings of the party system than the viscosity of voter attitudes. La Follette himself, in his younger days, was not above waving a bloody shirt. The ranks of the Republican leadership in the agrarian states harbored many Union veterans and sons of

---

[6] The alternative of action through a third party or through a third party fused with the Republicans had been tried and found wanting. An extremely high incidence of attempts to win the governorship by such means occurred in the former Confederate states in the 1890's. Of the gubernatorial elections in those states, 1890-1900, both inclusive, 45 per cent involved third-party or fusion candidates who polled at least 15 per cent of the vote.

[7] R. N. Current, *Pine Logs and Politics: A Life of Philetus Sawyer* (Madison: The State Historical Society of Wisconsin, 1950), pp. 240-241.

Union veterans not disposed to settle Republican family quarrels by bolting to the Democrats.

The rigidities of the Republican-Democratic division were compounded in their effects by the nature of Democratic leadership cliques in northern and western states. They were generally not of a sort to take advantage of the stirrings of discontent with Republican leadership. As the great Progressive movement developed, its publicists disseminated a stereotyped picture of the Republican party as dominated by lumbermen, bankers, railroads, and an unsavory assortment of the seekers of privilege who flourished in the mighty economic growth of the country after the Civil War.[8] The indictment had within it no little truth. Yet the Democratic party in these states tended to be controlled, if not by the same individuals, by leadership cliques similarly constituted and motivated.[9] Although openly the warmest hostility existed between Democrats in Wisconsin there prevailed, says Current, "a fine spirit of camaraderie at the top levels of command."[10]

The impressive structure of the power of privilege erected upon the idealistic popular foundations of the Republican party and the subjection of the controllers of the Democratic organizations to the same influences made the party system an unpromising mechanism through which to fight out the great issues that came to a head around the turn of the century. Third parties had been tried and found wanting in the 1880's and 1890's. In the North and West the Republican party turned out to be the arena in which the Progressives battled the standpatters. In the process the convention system, the critical point of conservative control, fell before the movement for the direct primary. In the South also the regular Democratic organizations often came under the control of conservative

[8] See Russel B. Nye, *Midwestern Progressive Politics* (East Lansing: Michigan State College Press, 1951); B. P. De Witt, *The Progressive Movement* (New York: Macmillan, 1915).

[9] See H. S. Merrill, *Bourbon Democracy in the Middle West 1865-1896* (Baton Rouge: Louisiana State University Press, 1953).

[10] *Op. cit.,* p. 241.

Democrats and ex-Whigs, the so-called Bourbons, which fact placed the agrarian radical leaders in the forefront of agitation for the direct primary.[11]

This broad situational explanation does not make allowance for another factor in the process. The shape of a maze may fix the path which a rat travels but it does not explain why he bothers to travel at all. In the situation in which they found themselves those who advocated the direct primary had little other alternative. Yet they were driven by the articles of democratic faith. They were moved by a desire to limit the privileges of the interests of the day—which were not simply figments of imaginative political oratory. Many of them were inspired by personal ambitions which had been rudely blocked or retarded by the ruling oligarchies. A curious strain of utopianism also ran through the primary movement. The prominent northern and western advocates of the primary, such as La Follette of Wisconsin and Hiram Johnson of California, attained power through the convention system, which established that their brand of politics was not completely blocked off by that procedure. The primary would, according to one line of reasoning, simplify the perpetuation of control by such forward-looking leaders who had an eye out for the people rather than for special interest.

Robert M. La Follette put the essence of the democratic argument in a speech in 1898:

Under our form of government the entire structure rests upon the nomination of candidates for office. This is the foundation of the representative system. If bad men control the nominations we cannot have good government. Let us start right. The life principle of representative government is that those chosen to govern shall faithfully represent the governed. To insure this the representative

[11] See, for example, Francis B. Simkins, *Pitchfork Ben Tillman* (Baton Rouge: Louisiana State University Press, 1944). Also C. Vann Woodward, *Origins of the New South, 1876-1913* (Baton Rouge: Louisiana State University Press, 1951).

must be chosen by those whom he is to represent. This is fundamental. . . .

To accomplish this we must abolish the caucus and convention by law, place the nomination of all candidates in the hands of the people, adopt the Australian ballot and make all nominations by direct vote at a primary election.

With the nominations of all candidates absolutely in the control of the people, under a system that gives every member of a party equal voice in making that nomination, the public official who desires re-nomination will not dare to seek it, if he has served the machine and the lobby and betrayed the public trust; if he has violated the pledges of his party and swapped its declared principles to special interests for special favors.

But under a primary election the public official who has kept faith with the public can appeal to that public for its approval with confidence. He will then have every incentive to keep his official record clean. . . .[12]

La Follette and his fellow advocates of the primary system could point to widespread, if not universal, abuses under the convention procedure. Bribery, disorder, boss domination, and picturesque manipulations occurred with great frequency and were believed to be inherent in the convention system. "The defects of the caucus, convention and delegate system are fatal because organic," La Follette asserted. "It cannot be amended, reconstructed or reorganized and its perpetuation secured. Its end is decreed by the enlightened moral sentiment of the entire country." [13] The convention, a contemporary concluded, was a place "where the youth of the Nation instead of learning their first lessons in the great science of government are trained in the ways of professional politicians, are taught the most debasing practices of corrupt politics, have their polit-

[12] *The Political Philosophy of Robert M. La Follette As Revealed in His Speeches and Writings* (Madison, 1920), pp. 29-31.
[13] La Follette, *op. cit.,* p. 40.

ical morals debauched, and their political ideals prostituted." [14]

Whether the indictments of the convention system were correct in all particulars, the primary advocates had hold of a fundamental problem in popular government. The process of popular government tends to be a sequence of clashes to check the accretion of privilege in the hands of those who manage to grasp public power. In the circumstances of the time the enemies of privilege had to try to bust the political machines, as well as the trusts, and the attack against the machines became in part an attack against the convention system, an instrument for the monopolization of political power, given the nature of the party system at the time.

2. The Bipartisan Framework of Intraparty Politics

The introduction in most of the states of the direct primary led to a substitution in considerable degree of intraparty politics for interparty politics. Earlier cliques of Democratic and Republican leaders, operating through their respective state conventions, designated candidates for governor who pleaded their causes before the electorate. Under the direct primary, centers of informal leadership—often but not always a new system of cliques—developed within the stronger party to plead the causes of aspirants for the nomination before the electorate —or at least before that part of the electorate entitled to vote in the primary. The variations among the states both in the extent of reliance on intraparty politics and the forms that intraparty struggles take contribute to the great complexity of the American political system.

If the analysis of the factors influential in the development of the direct primary system is substantially correct, the presumption would be that the intensity of intraparty politics would depend largely upon the balance of strength between the parties within the electorate. As the customary popular mar-

[14] Meyer, *op. cit.*, p. 64.

gin of the stronger party in the general elections becomes wider, the greater would be the tendency for forces concerned with the issues of state politics to bring their influence to bear at the point of real decision, viz., the direct primary of the dominant party. On the other hand, with the most frequent general election division around the 50-50 point, a different disposition of political forces would be expected to occur.

To differentiate the operation of the direct primary in one-party states, in two-party states, and in the states with intermediate forms of politics requires a measure of the balance of electoral strength of the parties. The average percentage division of the general election vote between the Republican and Democratic gubernatorial votes provides a crude measure of relative party position. Twenty-one nonsouthern states are arranged roughly according to their ranking by this measure in Table 9.[15] Vermont, with an average Democratic percentage of 30.5 per cent places as the most Republican state, while at the other extreme of the states listed Nevada leans Democratic with an average Democratic percentage of 52.9. These averages are not, of course, refined measures. Among other things, the average takes no account of the frequency with which elections result in alternations of power between parties. One state may, for example, divide around an average of 46-54 for a long period with no shifts in power while another state with the same average division may experience occasional periods of governance by the lesser party.[16]

The ranking of states in Table 9 also reflects the differences in popular interest in the gubernatorial primaries of the parties. If primary participation is not governed by caprice, it

[15] The same technique has been used by Austin Ranney and Willmore Kendall in "The American Party Systems," *American Political Science Review*, 48 (1954), pp. 477-485. They include in their averages votes for presidential electors and certain other officials and thereby arrange the states somewhat differently than does Table 9.

[16] A measure of party competition that takes this element into account is reported by Joseph A. Schlesinger, "A Two-Dimensional Scheme for Classifying States According to Degree of Inter-Party Competition," *American Political Science Review*, December, 1955.

TABLE 9

Selected States According to Relative Strength of Gubernatorial Candidates in General Elections and Relative Total Vote in Nominating Primaries

STATE	MEAN DEMO-CRATIC PER-CENTAGE OF GENERAL ELECTION VOTE	DEMOCRATIC PRIMARY VOTE AS PERCENT-AGE OF REPUB-LICAN PRIMARY VOTE, AVERAGE	PERIOD
Strong Republican			
Vermont	30.5	6.3	1916-52[a]
North Dakota	39.9	13.7	1914-52
Maine	41.8	23.6	1912-52
South Dakota	41.3	28.4	1908-52
Wisconsin	42.0	23.7	1906-52
Michigan	44.7	26.0	1908-52
Iowa	42.4	31.1	1908-52
New Hampshire	44.7	33.7	1910-52
Less-Strong Republican			
Minnesota[b]	41.5	39.6	1912-52
Pennsylvania	42.6	36.1	1918-50
Kansas	43.1	38.8	1910-52
Competitive			
Massachusetts	48.2	76.7	1913-52
Illinois	49.1	60.0	1908-52
New Jersey	49.9	55.2	1913-53
Wyoming	49.7	61.4	1922-50
Ohio	50.1	70.9	1914-52
Leaning Democratic			
Colorado	51.8	103.4	1912-52
West Virginia	52.1	104.5	1920-52
Idaho	52.3	128.4	1932-50
Missouri	52.6	146.5	1908-52
Nevada	52.9	150.3	1910-50

[a] *Democratic primary figures available only since 1926.*
[b] *In Minnesota and Wisconsin when a "third" party became in fact one of the two major parties, data relating to it were substituted in the appropriate major party series. Thus,*

would be expected that popular interest would tend to center in the primary of the stronger party. The more imbalanced the relation between the two parties, the more marked would be this concentration of voter interest in the primary of the more powerful party.

The data of Table 9 show, in a striking manner, the tendency for popular interest to concentrate in the primary of the stronger party. From that table it is quite evident that as the average Democratic proportion of the general election vote for governor declines, the proportion of all primary voters who vote in Democratic primaries declines but at a more rapid rate. Examination of the column showing the Democratic primary vote as a percentage of the Republican primary vote suggests that this ratio reflects an aspect of the balance between the parties not so clearly revealed by the division of the general election vote. The fact that six persons, on the average, in Vermont vote in Democratic gubernatorial primaries while 100 are marking their ballots for Republican aspirants for nomination suggests a dimension of the party balance in that state not indicated by the fact that Democratic candidates poll an average of about 30 per cent of the general election vote. Moreover, the primary ratios differentiate the states more sharply than do the general election percentages. Thus, the average Democratic general election percentages in Kansas and Massachusetts appear in the table as 43 and 48, respectively, figures which suggest that no great difference exists between these states. The primary participation ratios are 38 and 76, a spread of sufficient magnitude to be congruent with common knowledge about the contrasts between the party systems of these two states.[17]

---

when the Farmer-Labor group in Minnesota outstripped the Democratic party, figures on it were substituted in the Democratic series.

[17] The obvious point ought to be made explicit that the qualities of the primary participation ratio as a separator come in part from the method of its computation. Thus, a 60-40 division of total primary vote between Republican and Democratic primaries becomes 150 on the scale used.

Table 9 categorizes the 21 states selected for analysis as Strong Republican, Less-Strong Republican, Competitive, and Leaning Democratic. In drawing the lines between these categories the wider gaps between the primary participation ratios were principally controlling. Yet not too great weight should be given to names attached to these groupings, for the lines separating the classes of states could have been drawn at other points. Nevertheless the groupings will serve adequately as a basis for later analyses.

Although the technique applied in Table 9 groups the states roughly according to their degree of conformity to or departure from the two-party pattern, one of the weaknesses of the measures of relative party strength should be noted in particular. Eyebrows may be elevated by the classification of Michigan as strong Republican. The characterization of Massachusetts as competitive similarly raises doubt. Early in the period covered by the table this state was overwhelmingly Republican; in the later part of the period it became definitely competitive. The averaging of votes spread over several decades, as was done in the table, inevitably conceals any long-term shift in the balance of power within a state. One series of elections might cluster between a 45-55 and a 55-45 division and yield an average of 50-50. Another series might through time gradually move from a 25-75 division to a 75-25 division and also result in an average of 50-50. This inherent defect in the measure does not invalidate the yardstick for our immediate purposes as subsequent tests will indicate. Of the states in the table, Michigan and Massachusetts have undergone the most marked secular change in party strength. The trends in the division of primary voters between the two parties in these states appear in Figure 11, which shows the percentages of the potential electorates of these states voting in each of the major party primaries, 1914-1952. Apart from its indication of one of the limitations of our measure of relative party strength, the figure suggests a useful way to get at the process of party realignment. Wide changes in the ratios of primary participation between the parties probably reflect fairly durable changes in the relative sizes of the groups of strong partisans, a matter perhaps of more significance than momentary shifts in voting strength in response to the appeals of particular campaigns.

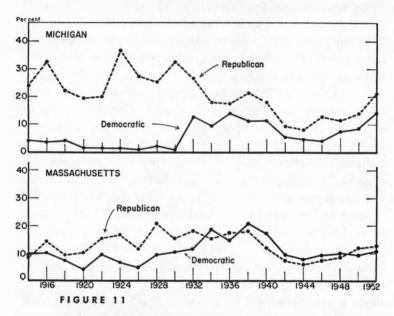

FIGURE 11

Long-Term Partisan Realignment: Percentages of Total Potential Electorate Voting in Republican and in Democratic Gubernatorial Primaries in Michigan and Massachusetts, 1914-1952

Table 9 differentiates 21 selected states, on which the subsequent discussion will be mainly centered, according to the balance of strength between the parties within each state. The ratios shown for each state provide rough measures of the framework of bipartisan balance within which the politics of the state takes place. Another analysis may be useful to indicate for all the 48 states the frequency of closely contested gubernatorial elections as well as the frequency of elections settled by wide popular margins. A distribution of all gubernatorial elections in all the states during the years 1940-49 appears in Figure 12. In 36 per cent of the elections during this decade, the Democratic candidate polled between 45 and 55 per cent of the total vote of the two high candidates. Thus about one-third of the gubernatorial elections in the states were fairly closely contested. In 57 per cent of the elections Democratic candidates attracted between 40 and 60 per cent of the vote for the two

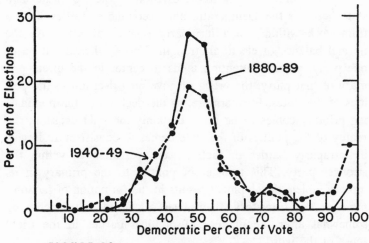

FIGURE 12

Declining Frequency of Close Gubernatorial Elections: Distribution of all Gubernatorial Elections, 1880-1889 and 1940-1949, According to Democratic Percentage of Vote for Two High Candidates

high candidates. Thus over 40 per cent of all gubernatorial elections were decided by quite wide popular margins, a fact that points to the very considerable significance of intraparty politics within the states. Figure 12 also shows for comparative purposes the distribution of gubernatorial elections in the period 1880-89 according to the Democratic percentage of the vote for the two high candidates. Over the long run a marked decline has occurred, as will be noted from the figure, in the proportion of gubernatorial contests settled by small margins in the popular vote.

3. Primary Competition in the Framework of Bipartisanism

The more or less stable division of the electorate of a state between the Democratic and Republican parties fixes a framework within which intraparty politics operates. As the normal balance of electoral strength shifts to the advantage of one party, popular attention tends to center in the direct primary of that party, the arena of governing decision in the politics of the states. Furthermore, as the decision of the nominating primary comes to be more certainly the final decision, the reality of the politics of the state comes to consist more largely in intraparty battles of factions and personalities within the stronger party. This transfer of politics to the primary in its most complete development results in the formation of factions, more or less transitory, themselves organized and functioning somewhat after the manner of political parties in the usual sense of the word.[18]

All these propositions, however plausible they may seem, require checking against the facts of state politics. Popular interest, it has been suggested, tends to organize itself around the points of actual decision rather than the points of *pro forma* action. The direct primary system, as the bipartisan balance becomes more uneven, heightens interest in the primary of the dominant party. Perhaps, more specifically, the primary system maximizes the interest of the followers of the majority in the

---

[18] Although most of these propositions have been a staple of political science for a long time, the first systematic validation of the presumed relationship between party strength and primary competition was made by Julius Turner, "Primary Elections as the Alternative to Party Competition in 'Safe' Districts," *Journal of Politics,* 15 (1953), pp. 197-210. The technique of analysis employed here is a variation on that developed by Turner.

primary of their party while the adherents of the minority, reconciled to defeat in the general election, infrequently bother to vote in their party primary, which serves only to nominate some willing soul to make the sacrifice in the general election.

Roughly what the primary system does is to organize the electorate of a state into groups. One of these groups consists of those voters who participate in the stronger primary and thereby make the decisions that control in the general elections. The other group participates as an act of faith or habit in the primary of the lesser party. Yet as the parties come to compete on more nearly even terms in the general election, popular concern tends to be centered less on the nominating primaries and more largely upon the general election itself. Popular attention moves toward the alternative point of controlling decision.

These propositions find general support from an inspection of the record of participation in the gubernatorial primaries of the states under analysis here. In the strong Republican states, as appears in Table 10, one-fourth of the Republican primaries attracted more voters than did the Republican candidates in the general election. The Democratic primaries of the same states had much weaker drawing power. Almost one-half (44 per cent) of these primaries drew less than one-fifth as many voters as did the Democratic candidate in the general election. These types of behavior manifest themselves at the extremes of Republican strength and Democratic weakness appearing in Tables 10 and 11. Inspection of the tables will make clear the tendency for the structure of popular interest to change as the parties become more closely competitive in the general election. The primary action becomes less surely the controlling decision and the politics of the electorate becomes in higher degree a party politics and less an intraparty politics.

Varieties of Democratic Intraparty Politics. The internal characteristics, as well as the functions, of the Democratic parties of the states tend to differ with the position of the party vis-à-vis the Republican party. The workings of the guber-

TABLE 10

Republican Gubernatorial Primaries According to Relation of Total Primary Vote to Vote of Republican Candidate in General Election[a]

STATE GROUP	TOTAL PRIMARY VOTE AS PERCENTAGE OF CANDIDATE'S ELECTION VOTE						N
	0-19	20-39	40-59	60-79	80-99	100+	
	PERCENTAGE OF PRIMARIES IN EACH STATE GROUP						
Strong Repub.	0	2	26	30	16	26	165
Less Strong	0	8	32	31	6	23	52
Competitive	1	23	38	26	8	4	78
Leaning Dem.	2	25	50	19	2	2	56

[a] *The state groupings and the coverage are identical with Table 9.*

natorial primaries serve as a rough index of these varying characteristics. Extremely weak Democratic parties may have their internal factional differences, but these differences infrequently manifest themselves in stiff battles in the primaries for the gubernatorial nomination. In fact, most often the leaders of such parties contrive in advance of the primary to agree upon —or to draft—a candidate who becomes the unchallenged contender for the nomination.

As the cause of the Democratic party within the state becomes less hopeless its internal structure changes. Within the party competing centers of leadership arise. They may rest on a foundation neither more nor less substantial than the ambitions of political personalities for positions of leadership. They may be founded on quite real social, economic, geographic, or other cleavages within the membership of the party. They may be embodied in more or less formalized subparty organizations with long traditions and perceptibly contrasting policy colorations. As these characteristics develop they are paralleled by more frequent and more intense competition within the party among the continuing or transient centers of leadership. And,

TABLE 11

Democratic Gubernatorial Primaries According to Relation of Total Primary Vote to Vote of Democratic Candidate in General Election[a]

	TOTAL PRIMARY VOTE AS PERCENTAGE OF NOMINEE'S ELECTION VOTE						
	0-19	20-39	40-59	60-79	80-99	100+	
	PERCENTAGE OF PRIMARIES IN EACH STATE						N
STATE GROUP				GROUP			
Strong Repub.	44	46	9	1	0	0	154
Less Strong	12	55	27	4	0	2	51
Competitive	5	54	32	7	2	0	88
Leaning Dem.	3	17	43	26	9	2	58

[a] *The state groups and the coverage are identical with Table 9.*

as these circumstances come about the politics of the state becomes more an intraparty politics and less an interparty politics.

These broad propositions about the internal characteristics of Democratic parties in different types of states are reflected in the records of their direct primaries which are analyzed in Table 12. One hesitates to utter the admonition—so general is the aversion to figures unless preceded by a dollar sign or enveloped in a bikini—but Table 12 needs to be given careful examination if the analysis is to be understood. The table shows the frequency of different types of contests in Democratic gubernatorial primaries. Nominations made by from 90 to 100 per cent of the primary vote obviously do not involve much of a fight. On the other hand, when the nominee receives less than 50 per cent of the primary vote the probabilities are that he has had to exert himself against strong opposition. The table relates the frequency of these sorts of contests to the position of the Democratic parties in relation to opposition. In other words, the table puts intraparty politics into its bipartisan framework.

Few Democratic nominations, the table indicates, were

closely contested in the strong Republican states. Over one-half of them were made without primary opposition; over three-fourths, by a primary vote of two to one or better. Only rarely is there a stubbornly fought contest in such states for the Democratic nomination which has mainly an honorific value. The function of the Democratic party in these states is to be understood only in the context of time. Widely spaced outbursts of public exasperation drive out the majority; the minority Democrats happen to be on hand to harvest the fruits of unearned victory. It may be doubted that these social convulsions often represent solely dissatisfaction with Republican management of state matters for in these states Democratic gubernatorial victories are bunched at moments of Republican tribulation on the national scene.[19]

As one moves down Table 12 it appears that the proportion of Democratic primary nominations won with only nominal opposition or with none decreases as the states move toward a Democratic commitment. Similarly, the proportion of nominations made after a sharp contest increases as the degree of Democratic commitment increases. (The states classed as Less-strong Republican states mar the regularity of the relation, a point to which we shall return.) In the strongest Democratic states nomination through ordeal on the hustings becomes most common and few get to run for governor in the general election without overcoming real primary opposition. The table, it should be noted, includes no primaries in which incumbent governors were candidates for renomination. The purpose of this exclusion was to remove from the data those primaries in which incumbents are renominated unopposed more or less as a matter of custom.

Apparently differentiations both in internal party structure and in the function of party in the governing process roughly parallel these variations in the incidence of competition

---

[19] One-half of the Democratic gubernatorial victories in the strong Republican states (first line of Table 12), occurred in the years 1932, 1934, and 1936; another 15 per cent, in 1912 and 1914.

TABLE 12

Distribution of Democratic Gubernatorial Primaries Involving No Incumbents, by Percentage of Primary Vote Polled by Nominee, in Relation to Political Complexion of State Groups[a]

STATE GROUPS	PERCENTAGE OF PRIMARIES ACCORDING TO PROPORTION OF VOTE TO NOMINEE IN PRIMARY				TOTAL NUMBER OF PRIMARIES	PER CENT OF GOVERNORS DEMOCRATIC[b]
	UNDER 50	50-59	60-89	90-100		
Strong Republican[c]	6	15	23	56	151	15
Less-strong Rep.	32	28	34	6	47	21
Competitive	17	25	21	37	57	49
Leaning Democratic	44	22	27	7	45	60
Strong Democratic[d]	61	18	21	0	28	98

[a] *The primaries included in the tabulation are those of the states listed in Table 9 for the periods there indicated.*
[b] *These percentages are of all governors elected at all elections for the periods indicated in Table 9, not simply those elected after the primaries included in this table.*
[c] *The first four groups of states are identical with those in Table 9.*
[d] *The states included in this group are Louisiana (1920-48), South Carolina (1922-46), Tennessee (1920-50), Texas (1920-52). The basis for classification was the first primary vote. These plurality primaries were, of course, followed by run-off primaries between the two high candidates in the first primary. The proportion of primaries in which the high man received less than 50 per cent of the vote in the first primary may, of course, be affected by the existence of the run-off procedure.*

for party nomination. At one extreme—in the strong Republican states—the Democratic group wins through no virtue of its own at infrequent intervals and performs national functions, such as the designation of national convention delegates and, perchance, the distribution of patronage. At the other extreme—in the strong Democratic states—the party becomes, for state purposes at least, no party at all but a holding company for factions that contend for control of the state. With respect to internal party structure, the primary competition data point to a more continuous intraparty battle as the Democratic predilections of the state increase. That is, the party tends toward a dual or multifactionalism as the certainty of general election victory increases.[20]

On this matter of variations in internal factionalism within the Democratic party in relation to its power position, the data of Table 12 are paralleled by variations in the average number of candidates polling 5 per cent or more of the total Democratic primary vote. These averages for the states and periods covered by Table 12 are as follows:

Strong Republican	1.58
Less-strong Republican	2.86
Competitive	2.17
Leaning Democratic	3.00
Strong Democratic	3.71

Here again the small group of states classified as Less-strong Republican deviates from the general relationships, an arithmetical aberration which raises another question to be touched upon later.

While the facts on primary competition and on average numbers of candidates point toward a sharper and more persistent factionalism as party strength increases, emphasis on that formulation may obscure the components of the proposition. As one moves up the table from the strong Democratic states to the more competitive states, the presence of Republican opposition may provide a compulsion toward the suppression of

[20] By this statement of the relationship it is not asserted that as the percentage of the election vote polled by the Democrats increases, these other variables increase, without a time lag, more or less on a one-to-one basis. The power position of a party vis-à-vis the opposition changes very little by a movement of the average general election vote from 25 to 30 per cent; the 5 point movement from 50 to 55 represents a much greater change.

internal Democratic strife. All this may be a special case of the general theory that the internal structure of a group depends somewhat on the nature of its environment of other groups. Then, as one moves to the sure Republican states the expectation of defeat depresses competition for Democratic nominations.

This analysis develops an index that parallels broad differentials in the factional structure of Democratic parties under different sets of circumstances, yet it leaves to be filled in the details of the nature of party factions. These patterns of faction are almost as numerous as are the states, at times amorphous and transient, at times relatively durable, at times economically based, on occasion ideologically oriented.[21] The hypothesis may be suggested that when a party gains complete domination of a state its factions are more likely to be durable groupings of voters bound together by some common interest or to be constituted of persons mainly similar in some politically significant social characteristic. As a state becomes competitive between parties the cleavages within the party (as manifested in primary voting rather than leadership divisions) are likely to be changeable, non-recurring, and not so clearly associated with social differences within the electorate. Under such circumstances the social differences tend to be wider between the parties than within the parties.

In supplementation of the observations to this point, Table 13 presents the data on competition within Democratic primaries in which gubernatorial incumbents were seeking nomination. Although the cases in the table are few, the striking differentials shown may be regarded as a further illustration of the radically different nature of "party" in different sorts of states. While in the strong Democratic states incumbents may look forward to renomination, they ordinarily encounter more than token opposition in the primary, reflective of the fact that

[21] An extended analysis of the factional systems of the Democratic party in the southern Democratic states appears in Key, *Southern Politics*, chaps. 2-12.

the real popular plebiscite occurs there. The full electoral strength of competing factions tends to be mobilized at each primary just as party strength is mobilized at general elections under conditions of party competition. On the other hand, in the more competitive states party unity is adequate to assure renomination without contest in a substantial proportion of the

TABLE 13

Distribution of Democratic Gubernatorial Primaries Involving Incumbents, by Percentage of Primary Vote Polled by Nominee, in Relation to Political Complexion of State

CHARACTER OF STATE	PERCENTAGE OF PRIMARIES ACCORDING TO PROPORTION OF VOTE POLLED BY NOMINEE IN PRIMARY				TOTAL NUMBER OF PRIMARIES
	UNDER 50	50-59	60-89	90-100	
Strong Rep.[a]	6	0	18	76	16
Competitive	0	9	45	46	22
Leaning Dem.	13	13	20	54	15
Strong Dem.	10	58	32	0	19

[a] *The state groups and coverage are the same as in Table 12 except that the strong Democratic group here consists of Texas and Tennessee and the less strong Republican category has been omitted since it included only four cases.*

primaries. It may well be supposed that in those rare instances in which a Democrat managed to get himself elected in the strong Republican states, the patronage of office, the lack of a tradition of intraparty conflict, as well as the improbability of re-election combined to keep down competition for renomination.

Attention was directed earlier to the fact that the group of states labelled "Less-strong Republican" diverged from the expected on the basis of the presumed relationship between Democratic general election position and incidence of primary competition. Evidently factors other than party position in relation to the opposition also bear on the nature of internal party structure and operation. The three states in the less-strong Republican group, Minnesota, Pennsylvania, and Kansas, were set off from the strong Republican states by somewhat higher rate of participation in Democratic primaries. As a group they also went Democratic in presidential elections far more frequently than did the strong Republican states. The proportions of governors Republican and the proportions of elections resulting in Republican electoral votes for the different categories of states were as follows:

	GOVERNORS	PRESIDENTIAL ELECTIONS
Strong Republican States	85%	74%
Less-strong Republican	79	58
Competitive	51	49
Leaning Democratic	40	39

In the less-strong Republican states the frequency of their success in presidential voting may have given Democrats hope for victory in state affairs and stimulated competition within their primaries. Yet the chances are that other factors peculiar to each state were also contributory.

The aggregate figures for each group of states conceal individual states that diverge from the norm of their group. Thus, New Jersey is ranked among the competitive states and would be expected to have frequent contests within its Democratic primaries. Yet it does not have.[22] The ready answer might be in terms of the long hegemony of Frank Hague, but the practice both antedated and survived him. Such deviations suggest a point of considerable theoretical interest about the nature of party structures. While a good deal of the variation among state practices may be explained in terms of the relation of internal party structure to its power position, other elements

[22] Both Jersey party organizations strive to avoid primary contests, the Democratic with greater success. For an account of a relevant case on the Republican side, see Walter E. Edge, *A Jerseyman's Journal* (Princeton: Princeton University Press, 1948), chap. 14.

cause particular cases to deviate from the general relation. Apparently patterns of behavior within even large, complex, and informal party structures have considerable durability. These patterns could be called, after both the terminology and spirit of the anthropologist, elements of political culture, although it cannot be asserted with assurance that so denominating them contributes materially to enlightenment.

Varieties of Republican Intraparty Politics. An analysis of Republican gubernatorial primaries would be expected to reveal a gradation among Republican parties of the states similar to that already shown to exist for the Democratic parties. In the strong Republican states, the Republican primaries would presumably be characterized by warm and frequent battles between personalities and factions while in the strong Democratic states the primary would be a quiet affair infrequently contested.

While these differences exist in Republican intraparty politics, the differences that appear in Table 14 are not nearly so wide as those shown earlier to exist among state Democratic parties. The explanations for the relative narrowness of the differences among the groups of states analyzed in Table 14—which also requires careful examination—are several. Wider differences would appear if data on Republican nominations in the strong Democratic states were available. Such data would add another line to the table for a group of states in which serious dispute over the Republican nomination is most rare. In the strong Democratic states, however, Republican primaries occur infrequently; conventions usually nominate. Further, the Democratic party, since it is more widely established over the country than the Republican, has representation in more bands of the spectrum of relative party strength than does the Republican. In all the states covered by Table 14, moreover, Republicans can look forward with some hope for victory, a factor that generates interest in primary politics. Despite the narrowness of the differences among the Republican parties of the different groups of states, the broad relationship between intensity of internal party competition and power position of the party prevails.[23] Incidentally, the pattern of competition in Republican primaries involving incumbents resembles that shown to exist in Democratic primaries in Table 13.

TABLE 14

Distribution of Republican Gubernatorial Primaries Not Involving Incumbents, According to Percentage of Primary Vote Polled by Nominee, in Relation to Political Complexion of State[a]

| | PERCENTAGE OF PRIMARIES BY PROPORTION OF VOTE POLLED BY NOMINEE | | | | PER CENT OF GOV- | |
| | | | | | TOTAL NUMBER OF PRI- | ERNORS REPUB- |
STATE GROUP	UNDER 50	50-59	60-89	90-100	MARIES	LICAN[b]
Strong Rep.	38	30	21	11	97	85
Less-strong Rep.	41	18	35	6	34	79
Competitive	32	29	18	21	56	51
Leaning Democratic	28	28	23	21	53	40

[a] *The table covers the states for the periods indicated in Table 9 as grouped there.*
[b] *All gubernatorial elections for the period covered; not simply those preceded by primaries involving incumbents.*

The inquisitive technical reader may surmise that Table 14 conceals differences occurring over time within our groups of states. To illustrate: Within the group of states classified as leaning Democratic, the Republican party may have been far stronger before 1932 than after. The level of competition shown

[23] By breaking the strong Republican category of Table 14 into two groups (dividing into halves the states so listed in Table 9) and by re-arranging the classes a bit, one sees a more marked sort of relationship than is revealed by Table 14. In these two subgroups of the strong Republican group and in the other classes of states in Table 14, listed according to declining degree of Republican commitment, the proportions of nominations made by under 60 per cent of the primary vote were: 77, 64, 59, 61, 56.

to exist within the primaries of this group of states may average an intense and frequent primary competition of the victorious days of party with a disinterest in primaries in times of party doldrums. While the figures are affected slightly by these variations, the fact of the matter seems to be that the patterns of behavior—or perhaps the factional structure within a party—does not seem to adjust itself quickly to changes in the general power position of the party. For the entire group of states covered by Table 14 the differences from time to time in the frequency of warmly contested nominations are not marked for either Democratic or Republican primaries. The proportions of nominations (in primaries involving no incumbents) by less than 60 per cent of the primary vote were:

	REPUBLICAN	DEMOCRATIC
through 1930	70%	40%
1932-1952	59	36

The rough similarity of primary competition in the two periods suggests that the internal structure of party and the habitual modes of action may have considerable momentum. A sharp and prolonged change in the power position of the party may be necessary to bring about much of a change in the patterns of intraparty politics.

The Spectrum of State Political Systems. Although the foregoing analysis carries its own conclusions distilled about to the irreducible point, a few comments may be in order by way of attempt at even further summarization and toward an indication of the inferences suggested by the data. What does the analysis suggest about the nature of the organization of politics of the American state?

The concept of party has a rather limited applicability in the description of the politics of the American state governorship. No single concept or set of categories can well describe the varieties of political structure that exist among the states. The descriptive problem is more one of delineating gradation than of categorization. Instead of classes of one-party states, or two-party states, or states leaning this way or that the data suggest the existence of various sorts of multigroup structures operating through the primary system. The character of these structures rests to a considerable extent on the degree to which final gubernatorial choices are made in the primaries.

Gradations exist among these multigroup structures within formal parties both in the number of intraparty groups and in the intensity of competition among them. The frequency of nominations contested with varying degrees of closeness has been used as an indicator of these characteristics of intraparty structure. The assumption is that differentiations both in internal party structure and in the function of party in the governing process roughly parallel these variations in the incidence of competition for party nomination.

The evidence suggests that, in the absence of disturbing factors, as states deviate from equality of strength between parties, the frequency of sharp competition within the stronger party increases. Primary competition tends to be substituted for general election competition; competition within parties for competition between parties. It is the character of the competitors and in the considerations at stake in this intraparty process that one must seek the nature of state politics in many states. It is not suggested that this competition within parties necessarily possesses the same characteristics as a competition between parties, although at times it may do so. The issues, the electoral groupings, the process of advancement to roles of leadership may well be on the whole quite different.[24]

[24] While this analysis in terms of group structure highlights one aspect of state political systems, there seeps from the data the notion that another dimension would be revealed by appropriate attention to the time dimension especially with respect to states with competitive parties. The usual notions of two-party competition carry connotations of evenness of strength, of struggles determined by superior strategy and wit, of uncertainty of outcome, of great groups locked in recurring struggle. If one attends to the time dimension and regards the process of acquisition of power as the natural history of a sequence of connected events rather than as a matching of strength at a moment in time between continuing groups, the process may look different. Shifts in power may re-

The focus of popular attention on the primaries of the dominant party may over the long run attract to that party men with political ambitions who see the minority candidates regularly defeated in the general elections. Though the evidence on this point is limited, Figure 13 is worth some reflection. It charts the distribution of gubernatorial elections in the South according to the percentage division of the vote for three periods: 1880-89, 1910-19, 1940-49. The shape of the distribution changed drastically over this 70 years principally because of the decline in the numbers of candidates who bothered to make the hopeless race against the Democrats. Many factors were, of course, at work to produce the changes reflected in the figure but perhaps not the least of these was a gradual shrinkage of Republican and other opposition leadership. The potential opposition leadership corps probably made its way largely into the Democratic ranks.

4. Signs of Party Revival

While the preceding analysis reveals some notable variations in the general characteristics of the party systems of the states under varying conditions, some of the significance of the complicated tables of figures has to be read into them. From the analysis, it became plain enough that in many of the states, even reputedly two-party states, the battles of state politics are fought out within the primary by intraparty groups. Even in the more competitive states, to speak of a corporate party leader-

---

sult from a cumulation of effects: The disappearance from the scene of a leader with a hold on the people, the decay of zeal as a ruling clique grows old, the infiltration of discordant elements into a group that once captured popular loyalties, the rise of a new leader, the fierce strivings of politicians long out of power who sense victory in the air, the activation of new elements in the electorate, the effects of a national landslide or other events outside and beyond control of state government. The semantics of such an approach tends to put the discussion in terms of a process which, through time, produces party fortune and misfortune rather than in terms of a series of engagements between a seemingly identical pair of combatants.

ship is often pure fiction. At worst the party's business is no-body's business and the choice of candidates is a choice by those who happen to vote in the primary between random self-starters with an itch for office. In a word, the figures reflect in an abstract way what the old-time politician has in his mind when he speaks with tears in his eyes of the destruction of party organization, the disappearance of party responsibility, and the evil days that have befallen the party system.

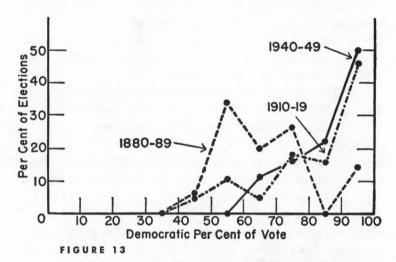

FIGURE 13

Republican Gubernatorial Candidates Become Scarcer in the South: Distribution of Gubernatorial Elections in 11 Southern States, According to Democratic Percentage of Total Vote for Two High Candidates, 1880-1889, 1910-1919, 1940-1949

A half century's experience with the direct primary has brought some second thought about the political party as an in-strument of popular government. The direct primary mode of nomination came into general use on a wave of widespread pop-ular disillusionment about parties and politicians. In a sense, an objective of the primary movement was to destroy the party or-ganizations which had, indeed, acquired a well-deserved bad name. The perceptiveness of hindsight makes it clear that the primary reformers had not generally thought through the nature of the problem of popular government. They had—or at any rate the bulk of them had—a sort of a theory of perpetual motion of political systems. They seemed to think—or at least most of them—that party organizations amounted to no more than an excrescence on the body politic and served no purpose. They apparently expected that with the destruction of the party organizations some sort of process would be set in motion by which leaders would more or less spontaneously emerge. They did not see that if party machines were reduced to impotence, other cliques and groups would have to pick up and carry their burden to keep the political system going.[25]

The consequences of the adoption of the direct primary for state party organizations varied, of course, enormously from state to state. In some states, principally closely competitive states, inner cores of party leadership continued to function largely as of old and designated slates of candidates which were often routinely nominated in the direct primaries. Indeed, in some of the most closely competitive states—New York, Indiana, Connecticut, Delaware—the primary has never gained much acceptance or importance. In other states, party organization—save on paper—tended to disintegrate in varying degrees. There rose up to replace the party organization in its role in the grooming and promotion of candidates the bewildering variety of patterns of initiative and leadership whose shadows are reflected in the tables in the earlier section of this chapter. The responsibility for initiative was taken up by cliques surrounding more or less charismatic individuals, by the remaining urban machines, by the spokesmen for ethnic and religious groups, occasionally by a manufacturers' association, by news-

[25] Some of the advocates of the direct primary had, of course, a clear appreciation of the role of the party organization. See the comments by Charles Evans Hughes, "The Fate of the Direct Primary," *National Municipal Review*, 10 (1921), pp. 23-31.

papers, and often by individuals consumed by an ambition for office.

Scattered signs suggest that, after forty years of penance, party organization may work its way back into some modification of its ancient role. A realization seems to be arising that the business of developing and pushing candidates for office cannot be left to be settled more or less exclusively by the process of virtual self-selection by those persons who chance to be aspirants for office.[26] In short, the management of the affairs of party demands both continuous effort and a consolidation of the forces of leadership, if party is to perform effectively its role as an instrument of popular government.

The scattered incidents—which do not necessarily make a trend—toward the reconstruction of party organization involve attempts to superimpose over the direct primary modes of selection of party candidates in a more deliberate manner than often prevails in the more or less random processes of the primary system. These incidents, furthermore, can be interpreted in the light of the general theme that the role and nature of intraparty politics depend generally upon the balance of power between the parties.

In the states in which the balance of electoral strength between the parties tends to be nearly even are to be found the most notable instances of attempts by party organizations to play a positive and controlling role in the nominating process. In some of the close states the old convention process, of course, remains more or less in its pure form and serves as a means for agreement upon party candidates. In several primary states with fairly closely balanced party divisions within the electorate the consolidation of party leadership has been attempted by means of pre-primary conventions or informal party assemblies to settle intraparty differences prior to the direct primary. To

[26] See the report by a committee of the National Municipal League under the chairmanship of Joseph P. Harris, *A Model Direct Primary Election System* (1951).

the extent that these endeavors succeed, an official party slate is entered in the direct primary and wins the nominations more or less as a matter of course. While many exceptions undoubtedly occur, the rational presumption would be that the echelons of leadership would tend most to seek internal unity when the outcome of the campaign against the opposition is expected to be quite close or in doubt. When a party is assured of election victory, no restraints need mark its internal struggles for nomination and for position.

Illustrative of the general argument is the recent experience with the pre-primary convention in Massachusetts. Since 1928 the balance of party strength has been such that either party could hope to win—or expect to lose—the governorship and other statewide offices. In both 1948 and 1950 the Republicans had slates for statewide offices composed entirely of Yankee Republicans. Their bad luck in these years led some Republican leaders to surmise that their failure to take into account in their slates the ethnic realities of Massachusetts may have had something to do with their misfortunes. Yet to nominate in a free and untrammeled primary anybody other than a Yankee was difficult, given the class of people voting in the Republican primaries.

Under Republican leadership, with some aid from Italo-American Democrats restive under Irish domination of their party, the 1951 legislature voted to authorize pre-primary conventions. Governor Paul Dever vetoed the bill, but the Republicans proceeded in 1952 to hold informally a "grass roots" assembly of 1200 delegates to endorse a primary ticket. A nicely rounded slate emerged from the deliberations of the assembly: three Yankees, two Jewish-Americans, an Italo-American, and an Irish-American woman. The convention slate won handily in the primary; in fact, only one of the convention endorsees had primary opposition.

With the election of a Republican governor and legislature in 1952 the way was cleared for adoption of legislation on pre-primary conventions. The bill, enacted in 1953, provided for the appointment of delegates to the convention by ward and town committees, if a party exercised the option to hold a pre-primary convention. The endorsees of the convention are placed first on the primary ballot. Acting under the new law, the 1954 Republican pre-primary convention ground out another slate that took into account the ethnic facts of Massachusetts political life. The convention slate encountered no opposition in the primary.

Republican experience with the pre-primary convention points to an important factor in determining how this marriage of the convention and primary system works. The Republican state committee in these two situations was well enough unified and well enough provisioned with the materiel of political warfare to compel acceptance in the leadership ranks of the convention decisions. Some individuals who got no endorsement from the convention or received support only for a lesser nomination than that to which they aspired sputtered but yielded before a force that would have overwhelmed them had they made a primary fight against the convention designees. The absence of similar inner cohesion within the Democratic party has made the success of its pre-primary conventions something less than spectacular. Under an earlier pre-primary law the Democratic pre-primary convention of 1934, dominated by the forces of Governor Joseph Ely, recommended a slate that did not include James Curley, a great favorite of the Boston Irish. Curley carried the fight into the primary and overwhelmingly defeated the convention designee for the gubernatorial nomination. In 1936 the Democratic convention again failed to consolidate the party leadership behind its slate which had rough going in the primary. The existence of the direct primary, of course, creates opportunity for the exploitation of conflicting group sentiments in the rank and file of the party. The pre-primary convention only provides an arena for endeavors to reconcile competing ambitions within the party leadership. For the pre-primary convention to amount to much of anything those endeavors must either result in strong consensus within the leadership or the controlling leadership core must possess the means to make challenge of the convention decision in the primary unrewarding.

The Massachusetts legislature abolished the state's first pre-primary convention in 1937. After its re-introduction in 1953, the Democrats again demonstrated considerably less capacity to settle their internal differences in the confines of the convention than did the Republicans. Like the Republicans, they were plagued with the problem of what ex-Mayor James Curley was wont to call "the newer races." Under circumstances of quite close party competition the Irish Democratic leadership felt compelled to make at least a gesture toward a balanced slate and in 1954 the ticket was leavened by a senatorial candidate of Italian and Irish descent, Foster Furcolo. And in various districts the top Democratic Irish leaders exerted their powers of threat and persuasion to induce fellow Irishmen to leave the primary field clear for Jews and others not of the Green.

The point of the discussion is not to emphasize the uses of the pre-primary convention in the unedifying process of preparing balanced tickets—although a balanced ticket may be no more unedifying than a solid Yankee ticket or a straight Irish slate. The moral of the tale, rather, is that under conditions of fairly even party competition the impulse to develop ways and means to consolidate the leadership of the party finds encouragement from the necessities of the party battle. Under other circumstances of close competition the impulse to close ranks against the enemy might be directed toward the reconciliation of geographical differences, the healing of factional wounds, the balancing of divergent policy drives, the drafting of candidates, or the minimization of the divisive effects of personal ambitions more numerous than places on the ticket.

A number of other instances in which states have superimposed the pre-primary convention over the primary or have developed other instruments for consolidation of party forces conform to the general argument that the urge toward party unification should find special encouragement under conditions of relatively even party competition. Thus, Utah in 1947 enacted legislation to provide for pre-primary conventions. This state, whose gubernatorial politics has been fairly evenly balanced between the parties,[27] abandoned the convention system for the direct primary in 1937, quite late in the primary movement. Under the 1947 Utah law the names of the two candidates receiving the most convention votes are placed on the direct primary ballot. Thus the number of primary contestants is kept down to no more than two; aspirants for nomination can gain a place on the primary ballot only by convention endorsement.[28]

Similarly, in New Mexico, another state fairly closely competitive at least over the long run,[29] the direct primary came into use late and has recently been supplemented by a pre-primary convention. This state continued to use the convention system of nomination until 1940, and soon thereafter many political leaders of the state began, either covertly or openly, to urge repeal of the primary law. Quite apart from the usual assertions that the primary caused a disintegration of party leadership, circumstances peculiar to New Mexico created special problems. The free and open primary—in 1946 for 14 Democratic nominations 57 candidates competed—made difficult the balancing of either party ticket to take into account the Anglos and Spanish and the divergent territorial interests within the state. After considerable controversy, in 1951 a pre-primary convention law went on the books. It applied to statewide offices only and provided that aspirants for nomination would be placed on the primary ballot only by convention certification. Those aspirants who receive at least 20 per cent of the con-

[27] The mean Democratic percentage of the Utah gubernatorial vote, 1912-1952, was 50.9, which would place Utah in the category labelled competitive in Table 9.

[28] For a summary of the Utah legislation, see R. N. Ballard, *The Primary Convention System in Utah* (Salt Lake City: Institute of Government, University of Utah, 1947); on the general nature of Utah politics, see Frank H. Jonas, "Utah: Sagebrush Democracy," in *Rocky Mountain Politics,* (Albuquerque: University of New Mexico Press, 1940).

[29] The mean Democratic percentage of the gubernatorial vote, 1916-1952, was 51.5, which would place the state in the leaning Democratic category in Table 9.

vention vote win a place on the ballot; they are ranked on the primary ballot in the order of the size of the convention vote.[30]

The dispute over nominating methods continued after the adoption of the pre-primary convention, and the 1955 legislature voted to return to the unadulterated direct primary after defeating a proposal to restore the pure convention system. The most spirited advocacy of the liquidation of the pre-primary convention came from the press and from the wing of the Democratic party led by Senator Dennis Chavez. Whatever the motivation of the New Mexico press, its action was in accord with a common pattern. Publishers can probably exert a greater influence over nominations by primary. The Chavez group, a minority faction, has been unable to control the Democratic organization of the state, although the Senator himself seems to be unbeatable. His group perhaps felt that its chances were better under the primary than the convention. In any case, rivalry between party factions led by governors and by United States Senators recurs in many states and points to a serious problem in the maintenance of working unity within state parties.

Massachusetts, Utah, and New Mexico make an odd kettle of fish, but they have in common the fact that in each of them both parties can look forward sooner or later to victories in state elections. Perhaps the necessity to consolidate party strength to maximize the chances for victory under competitive conditions provides the fundamental explanation for their experimentation with the pre-primary convention.[31] In sev-

[30] See Paul Beckett and Walter L. McNutt, *The Direct Primary in New Mexico* (Albuquerque, 1947); C. B. Judah and O. E. Payne, *New Mexico's Proposed Pre-Primary Designating Convention* (Albuquerque, 1950); Dorothy I. Cline, "New Mexico Retains Primary," *National Municipal Review*, 39 (1950), pp. 233-236; Jack E. Holmes, *Problems Relating to Various Nominating Procedures in New Mexico* (New Mexico Legislative Council Service, 1955); New Mexico *Laws*, 1951, ch. 180.

[31] The same hypothesis, in reverse, may at least partially account for the abandonment of the pre-primary convention in Nebraska and in South Dakota. In such one-party states the factors conducive to party unity and the role of the primary itself are markedly different from the competitive states. On the Nebraska repeal, see A. C. Breckenridge, "Pre-primary Trial Dropped," *National Municipal Review*, 43 (1954), pp. 186-

eral other states, somewhat similarly situated, the tendency toward activation and consolidation of party leadership on the question of nominations has taken the form of extralegal conferences and assemblies to recruit and endorse slates of candidates. California's development of informal pre-primary assemblies is one of the more striking instances. The convention of the Republican Assembly endorses primary candidates and, on occasion, when no suitable aspirant turns up on his own motion the Assembly searches out a prospect and persuades him to seek the nomination with its endorsement. The California Democratic party can claim a large popular following, as the results of presidential voting show, but its leadership on the local scene has been so inept that its place in state politics has been inconsequential. With the Republican precedent and the hope that better organization might lead to victory, the California Democratic Council was formed in 1953 to make pre-primary endorsements. After the 1954 primaries, it could be said that "although the direct primary election remained the formal method of nomination in both parties, the actual decision was made by extralegal groups, with few other aspirants entering the primary." [32]

All these instances of experimentation with nominating procedures are indicative of a realization that if the political party is to play a positive role in leadership it must be equipped

---

191. On South Dakota, see C. A. Berdahl, "The Operation of the Richards Primary," 106 (1923), pp. 158-171; "New South Dakota Primary Law Applies Short Ballot Doctrine," *National Municipal Review*, 19 (1930), pp. 235-238.

[32] Thomas S. Barclay, "The 1954 Election in California," *Western Political Quarterly*, 7 (1954), p. 597. See also Hugh A. Bone, "New Party Associations in the West," *American Political Science Review*, 45 (1951), pp. 1115-1125; Currin V. Shields, "A Note on Party Organization: The Democrats in California," *Western Political Quarterly*, 7 (1954), pp. 673-683; Dean R. Cresap, *Party Politics in the Golden State* (Los Angeles: The Haynes Foundation, 1954), chap. 7. In the 1920's in Minnesota the Farmer-Labor conventions began to endorse slates prior to the primaries. Later the Republicans, to develop solidarity in the face of the Farmer-Labor threat, also began to hold endorsement conventions. See G. H. Mayer, *The Political Career of Floyd B. Olson* (Minneapolis: University of Minnesota Press, 1951), pp. 38-39, 93.

with means of exercising that leadership. By the same token, these instances also reflect a belief that leadership is apt to be splintered and disorganized by sole reliance on the processes of the unmodified direct primary to provide party standard bearers in election campaigns. Yet it is significant that these endeavors to close the party leadership ranks have occurred principally in states with either the reality or the prospect of relatively close competition between the major parties. Among those states whose party systems rank toward the one-party extremes of the party spectrum, the major political disputes occur within the primary and the stimulus to consolidation provided by a threatening opposition does not prevail. In such states, of course, primary contests are the politics of the state and the unification of party leadership—through pre-primary conventions or through informal means—would be a negation of popular government.[33]

Two convention states—Connecticut and Indiana—have recently modified their convention practices in part to offset agitation for the adoption of the direct primary. Connecticut legislation of 1955 provides for an optional post-convention primary. In its application to statewide nominations the act, in essence, permits unsuccessful aspirants for nomination who receive at least 20 per cent of the state convention vote to appeal

[33] In overwhelmingly one-party states, two pre-primary conventions would make more sense than one. In fact, in a few such states informal procedures prevail by which the competing factions within the dominant party center their strength on slates of candidates. In Louisiana, by negotiation among the leaders of the Long and anti-Long factions, slates of primary candidates are usually agreed upon. In North Dakota, the Non-Partisan League and the Republican Organizing Committee have presented slates in the Republican primaries. In Wisconsin, the Republican party of Wisconsin, an extralegal voluntary committee formed outside the official party system, developed to challenge the La Follette wing, which was a rather well-disciplined faction itself. It survived to carry the party battle against a similar group formed within the official structure of the Democratic party. See Frank J. Sorauf, "Extra-Legal Political Parties in Wisconsin," *American Political Science Review*, 48 (1954), pp. 692-704. The Richards law of South Dakota set up detailed pre-primary procedures through which party factions in a one-party state could present alternatives at the primary. See references cited in note 31, this chapter.

from the convention decision to the party voters in a direct primary. The primary procedure may be set in motion by a petition signed by 5,000 members of the party and a deposit equal to 5 per cent of the annual salary of the office in question. In the absence of such an appeal the convention nomination is final.

The 1947 Indiana legislature acted to meet complaints about the state's convention system. A handful of party bosses was said to dominate the delegates. The nominees for major office, who had been customarily chosen early in the convention proceedings, were said to be able to dictate the rest of the ticket. Furthermore, after the settlement of the major nominations, at times after a warm contest, most of the delegates would leave the hall after giving their proxies to their county chairmen who voted for the nomination of the pre-arranged slate of minor nominees. To separate major and minor nominations, the 1947 action reversed the order of nominations. So long as major nominations were in doubt, less likelihood of dictation of minor nominations existed. This reform has since been modified to give party conventions the option of voting simultaneously on all candidates, an option exercised by the Republicans.

The more novel reform was the introduction of a secret convention vote through voting machines. Under this change the 2,000 or more delegates are assigned, by counties or groups of counties, to 30 or 40 voting machines scattered about the convention hall. Instead of voting by roll call, the delegates file to the assigned machine and vote in secret. No person may hold more than one proxy, a limitation that removes the possibility that party leaders, with wads of proxies, might vote the machines like cash registers. Since the changes a sharp increase has occurred in the number of aspirants for nomination, especially for the lesser offices. Party leaders still exert considerable influence over the selection of candidates. Both before and after the reform, convention decision was reached in a balance of influence between a small clique of party leaders and the mass of delegates. Perhaps the reform added some weight to the delegates' side of the balance.

5. The Primary and the Party System

While it is clear enough that the direct primary handicaps the operations of party leadership, it seems also equally clear that the shortcomings of the party systems of the American states stimulated the development of the primary. The direct primary made possible a popular government of sorts, although it seems fairly apparent that there has not come along with the primary any innovation in the organization of political leadership superior to a well-ordered party system as an instrument of popular government. Yet if there is to be a reconstruction of party in the government of the American states, it will need to be accompanied by a reorientation in popular thought about party politicians. That popular theory of belittlement and condemnation which reached its full flowering in the Progressive era aided in the disintegration of political organization and forced the retreat of most of the remnants of organized politics into the backroom. True, only an abject people holds its politicians in awe, and even if a people merely respects its politicians, the republic may be ailing. Yet the functions of party politicians have to be performed. It may be just as well to create institutional conditions that both permit them to do their work and allow the people to watch them like a hawk.

If the strivings to construct party systems more nearly commensurate with the needs of the states are to bear fruit, a sober reconsideration of the direct primary procedure of nomination will have to be made. Yet the simple formula of the old-style politician, back to the convention system, makes little sense as a practical slogan. The direct primary enjoys great strength as a symbol, a strength derived from its enemies. The principal campaigns against the primary have been transparently anti-democratic; they have been led on the whole by pious frauds, self-styled exponents of republican government. Whether the direct primary really functions as an instrument of popular government—and sometimes it undoubtedly does—it will probably demonstrate great staying power. Proposals to revert to the pure convention system would encounter an obdurate opposition; the American tradition is to destroy institutions patently oligarchical or to transmute their reality into conformity with democratic forms.[34]

Perhaps the solution will rest in the contrivance of circumstances and practices favorable to the development of leadership cliques adequate to the performance of party functions yet subject to popular control. The combination of the primary with the pre-primary convention may foreshadow the line of evolution that will occur although other arrangements may better serve the purpose. In any case, the nominating procedure is something of an accessory after the fact. The basic problem of party government rests in the party leadership worthy of popular confidence. Only a romantic can say much for party leadership in most of the states, either now or in the good old days, although encouraging signs appear from place to place. And the direct primary does not explain entirely the condition of party leadership although it has a relevance. An equally prominent place among the villains is held by those good people who have discouraged partisanship as civic wickedness and have caused the diversion of vast quantities of social energy from party channels to nonpartisan activity or simply to inaction.

One moral of the analysis that can scarcely be disputed is that any reconstruction of state politics must take into account the peculiar aspects of the situation in each state. American governmental reformers have been fond of procedural and organizational schemes designed for adoption in all sorts of circumstances. For some types of problems uniform prescriptions may be both feasible and desirable, but certainly that is not the case with the organization of political leadership. Given, for example, the circumstances that generate an overwhelming electoral attachment to a single party in well over a third of the

[34] Consider the fates of the congressional caucus and of the legislative election of Senators. See W. G. Carleton, "The Collapse of the Caucus," *Current History,* 25 (1953), pp. 144-150; W. H. Riker, "The Senate and American Federalism," *American Political Science Review,* 49 (1955), pp. 452-469.

states, it is most improbable that any substitution of party politics for the intraparty politics of the direct primary will soon occur in these states. Neither can it be said that anybody has contrived a plausible substitute for the rather chaotic politics of the primary in one-party cities, counties, and districts. On the other hand, in states with a normal electoral division hovering around or moving toward the 50-50 point the prospects for a reconstruction of party organization and a vitalization of party competition are better.

Chapter 5

Participation in Primaries: The Illusion of Popular Rule

The American political tradition caps decisions made by popular vote with a resplendent halo of legitimacy. Therein lies a source of the strength of the direct primary as an institution. In its form and spirit the primary appears to be a means for mass decision. In practice, not many people go to the trouble of using this great mechanism for the registration of the popular will. While it is well enough known that few voters turn up at the polls on primary day, relatively little effort has been devoted to the determination of precisely how many do so. Random thoughts about the significance, if any, of wholesale boycotting of the primaries by the voters have run to the effect that a small turn-out assures a victory for the party organization's slate or that the whole problem has no importance one way or another. Yet reflection on the actual facts of primary participation suggests important questions about the nature of the politics of the states. Here some preliminary explorations of the numbers and sorts of people who vote in direct primaries may at least get some of the facts out on the table and indicate tentative conclusions about the consequences of variations in levels of participation.

1. Levels of Participation in Gubernatorial Primaries

A few simple facts about the numbers of persons who vote in the direct primaries will aid in the estimation of the extent to which the primary is an instrument of popular government. To lend significance to such figures, it need not be assumed that the larger the number of voters the more "democratic" the process or the better the results. If 90 per cent of the potential electorate shares in the nomination of candidates, obviously a different sort of political order exists than if only 10 per cent of the maximum possible number of participants feels sufficiently concerned to go to the polls on primary day.

How many people do vote in primaries to nominate candidates for governor? The answer to so simple a question becomes a bit involved. It all depends on the time, place, and circumstances. The level of participation must be described in terms of distributions, frequencies, ranges, and averages rather than by a set figure.

In a sample of 15 nonsouthern states over the period 1926-1952, in three out of four primaries not more than 35 per cent of the potential electorate voted in the primaries of one or the other of the major parties. That is, the total Democratic primary vote plus the total Republican primary vote did not exceed 35 per cent of the number of citizens 21 years of age or over. In about one of six primaries the voters in Democratic and Republican gubernatorial primaries did not exceed 20 per cent of the number of citizens 21 and over. At the extreme of high participation in only one out of twelve primaries did more than 50 per cent of the potential vote turn up at the polls. Most often between 25 and 35 per cent of the potential electorate voted in the primaries. About four out of ten of the primaries in the sample states fell within this range of participation, as may be seen in Table 15.

The levels of interest shown to prevail in gubernatorial primaries are far exceeded, of course, by the participation in gubernatorial general elections. Characteristically, well over one-half the potential electorate votes in the general elections while the great bulk of primaries draw less than one-third of the voters. The third column of Table 15 shows the distribution of

TABLE 15

Gubernatorial Primaries in Selected States According to Percentage of Potential Electorate Voting in Republican or Democratic Primary, 1926-1952[a]

PARTICIPATION PERCENTAGE	NUMBER OF PRIMARIES[b]	PERCENTAGE OF PRIMARIES	PERCENTAGE OF GENERAL ELECTIONS
10-14	9	5.1	0.0
15-19	22	12.5	0.0
20-24	23	13.1	0.0
25-29	37	21.0	1.1
30-34	39	22.2	2.8
35-39	15	8.5	5.7
40-44	5	2.8	4.5
45-49	10	5.7	9.7
50-54	9	5.1	13.1
55-59	4	2.3	8.0
60-64	2	1.1	13.6
65-69	1	0.6	14.2
70 and over	0	0.0	27.3
	176	100.0	100.0

[a] *The states included in this tabulation are Vermont, North Dakota, Maine, Wisconsin, Michigan, New Hampshire, Pennsylvania, Kansas, Massachusetts, Illinois, Wyoming, Ohio, Colorado, West Virginia, and Missouri. The selection of states for inclusion in this table was dictated chiefly by the availability for the period covered of the types of data needed for the analyses made in Table 16 and Figure 14.*

[b] *In the enumerations of this column one primary equals a pair of simultaneous primaries, Republican and Democratic. Thus in nine primaries, so defined, between 10 and 15 per cent of the potential electorate voted for either Democratic or Republican aspirants for the gubernatorial nomination.*

general elections in the sample of 15 states according to the proportion of the potential electorate turning out to vote.[1]

What factors account for the variations in the rates of participation in gubernatorial primaries? Perhaps some meaning may be squeezed from the figures on participation rates by a search for the explanation of why one primary day sees 10 per cent of the voters at the polls and another 50 per cent. One broad category of explanations for these differences consists of factors peculiar either to a particular state or even to a particular primary. In any state when neither primary is contested the turnout is apt to be low. In Illinois, for example, when the state organization happens to be split and a factional fight occurs in the primary the turnout tends to the high side. When the party organization unites on a candidate for the nomination the vote is small. An especially warmly fought primary may pull the turnout for a particular primary far above the usual level for a state. Thus the 1938 Pennsylvania Democratic primary, in which the Mine Workers and the regular Democrats fought out their differences, brought the turnout much above the usual level for the state.

In a few states the entire primary voting record is considerably higher than participation rates for the bulk of the primaries analyzed in Table 15. The average participation rate for all the primaries shown in Table 15 is 31 per cent. On the other hand, the mean rate for the North Dakota primaries included in the table is 53 per cent; for West Virginia, 49; for Wyoming, 40. These deviant rates are undoubtedly clues to peculiar characteristics of the political systems of these states. In all three of these states a habit of high political participation prevails; they rank, for example, quite high among the states in the percentage turnout at general elections. Perhaps that habit spills over into the primaries and brings a high primary turnout. The high rate for North Dakota doubtless flows also in part

[1] A subdivision of these general elections to contrast participation rates in years of presidential elections and in nonpresidential years appears in Table 1 on p. 16.

TABLE 16

Mean Proportions of Potential Electorate Voting in Major-Party Gubernatorial Primaries in Sure Republican States and in More Competitive States, by Years, 1926-1952

YEAR	SURE REPUBLICAN STATES [a]	MORE COMPETITIVE STATES [b]
1926	30.8	25.9
1928	24.4	33.1
1930	34.1	26.4
1932	41.3	41.1
1934	34.9	36.3
1936	34.7	39.3
1938	35.8	35.7
1940	31.9	37.9
1942	20.0	20.0
1944	20.0	20.6
1946	23.6	16.9
1948	29.1	28.0
1950	29.1	24.0
1952	35.2	31.8

[a] *Vermont, North Dakota, Maine, Wisconsin, Michigan, New Hampshire, Pennsylvania, Kansas.*

[b] *Massachusetts, Illinois, Wyoming, Ohio, Colorado, West Virginia, Missouri. The two groups of states are not identical with the groups with similar labels in Table 9. The grouping in this table was governed by the availability of suitable data to compare primary participation in two groups of states with contrasting degrees of party competition. Even so, the series on the more competitive states is influenced by the fact that the calendars of elections of states included cause the composition of the group to differ slightly in off years and presidential years.*

from the lively duels within the Republican party between the Non-Partisan League and the Republican Organizing Committee.

Some of the variation in primary turnout in Table 15 undoubtedly comes from factors common to all states. Studies of public concern about presidential politics have shown that great waves of interest and disinterest affect the voters of most of the states in much the same manner. At times the gravity of public issues brings a larger proportion of the potential electorate into the circle of the politically involved. At other stages tranquillity prevails, or perhaps hope dies, and the circle of the involved shrinks. It is evident that to some extent these variations in the public's political temperature affect interest in direct primaries as well as participation in presidential elections. These variations in primary turnout from time to time appear in Table 16, which transform the data of Table 15 into a pair of time series showing the average rates of primary turnout by years for a group of sure Republican states and for a group of more competitive states. In both sets of states the primary turnout responded to the great waves of political concern or unconcern that swept the country during the period 1926-1952. In 1932 the numbers of primary voters jumped quite sharply over that of 1928, and a high level of interest was maintained in 1934, 1936, and 1938 in keeping with the intensity of the political debates of the time. In 1942, 1944, and 1946, primary turnout dropped sharply as did interest in other types of elections, while in 1952 there was a marked upturn in primary voting as well as in turnout at the presidential election.

An interesting, and perhaps significant, feature of the data of Table 16, is that total primary turnout in the group of sure Republican states runs at about the same level from year to year as in the group of states called more competitive. That is, no matter how those persons sufficiently concerned to vote in primaries divided between the parties, roughly similar proportions voted in one or the other major party primaries.[2] To show in more detail what underlies the figures of Table 16, the data of the table are broken down by the primaries of the major parties in the graphs in Figure 14. The curves in that figure show the average percentages of the potential vote participating

[2] Even within the one-party states of the South the range of participation in gubernatorial primaries is not radically different from that for states outside the South, as indicated by the sample in Table 15. See Key, *Southern Politics*, pp. 504-505.

in the primary of each party over the period 1926-1952. In the sure Republican states, shown in the upper panel of the drawing, the mean participation rate in the Republican pri-

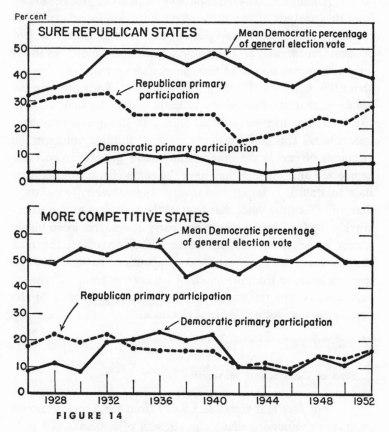

FIGURE 14

Mean Proportions of Potential Electorate Voting in Republican and Democratic Gubernatorial Primaries in Sure Republican States and in More Competitive States, 1926-1952

maries consistently exceeded by a wide margin that in the Democratic primaries over the entire period. In the more competitive states the participation rates ran more closely together over the period, although, insofar as primary participation measures competitiveness, the Democrats occupied a weak position in these states in the early period covered by the graphs.

About the only indisputable conclusion to be drawn from this analysis of the levels of participation in gubernatorial primaries is that not many people take a hand in this sort of political business. Yet the tendency toward similar levels of turnout under similar conditions suggests a speculative inference about the workings of state political systems. Perhaps there exists a sector of the population, of more or less the same relative size from state to state, with an especially strong concern about state affairs. This concern expresses itself through voting in the primaries of one or the other of the major parties.[3] Who these people are and whether they have the same characteristics from state to state it is impossible to say. Nevertheless, few though they are, it is their votes that control the gateways to the governorship. In fact, in the strong one-party states, this more highly concerned sector of the electorate makes, in effect, the final choices. As states approach dual competition the final decision tends to be taken from the hands of the narrow group of primary participators and transferred to the much larger sector of the population that votes in general elections.

2. Size of Controlling Minorities

The fact that voters stay away from the direct primaries in droves profoundly affects the strategy of gubernatorial politics in the American states. So few votes determine the party nomination that aspirants for office need only command the

[3] Of a 1952 national sample, 27 per cent had a "high" degree of political participation in that year, i.e., they voted in the general election and also engaged in other sorts of political activities. It may not be entirely coincidental that this group of highly concerned individuals was so nearly the same size as the average rates of primary participation appearing in Table 15. See Angus Campbell and others, *The Voter Decides* (Evanston: Row, Peterson, 1954), p. 31.

loyalties of a relatively small following to win a place on the party ticket. Once on the ticket, the candidate's fortunes may be governed by the traditional voting pattern of the state, the great accidents of general election politics, or even by the sound preferences of a majority of those who vote in the general election.

From earlier analyses it has doubtless been deduced that the primary vote polled by the winner of a nomination must be a quite small proportion of the electorate, although no calculations have been presented on the point. That omission is corrected in Table 17 which presents the data on the proportions of the potential electorate supporting Republican nominees in the primaries in 21 states grouped, as in Chapter IV, according to their political complexion. As would be expected from the earlier tabulations, Republican nominees in strong Republican states on the average attract the support of a larger proportion of all voters than do Republican nominees in more closely fought states.

Yet no matter what the balance of partisan power may be in a state the primary vote of the Republican nominee amounts to an extremely small proportion of the total potential electorate. Even in the group of states classified as strong Republican, in which the Republican nominee was almost certain to win, 63 per cent of the Republican candidates for governor polled a primary vote of less than 15 per cent of the potential electorate. In the same group of states a primary victor most infrequently drew as much as 25 per cent of the potential electorate—about one out of ten times. In the states categorized as competitive and as leaning Democratic about nine out of ten Republican nominations were made by less than 15 per cent of the potential vote.

It is unnecessary to encumber the discussion with the complete companion table for the Democratic primaries. The Democratic primaries, in general, present a set of relationships just the reverse of that shown for the Republican primaries in Table 17. In the strong Republican states, the votes polled by winners of Democratic gubernatorial primaries are minute proportions of the potential electorate. Of the Democratic nominations in these states, 64 per cent were made by less than 5 per

TABLE 17

Distribution of Votes of Nominees of Republican Gubernatorial Primaries as Percentages of Total Potential Electorate, According to Political Complexion of State[a]

STATE GROUP	VOTE AS PERCENTAGE OF POTENTIAL ELECTORATE						
	0-4	5-9	10-14	15-19	20-24	25 PLUS	
	PERCENTAGE OF NOMINEES						100%=
Strong Republican	2	22	39	19	9	9	165
Less Strong	2	23	46	19	8	2	52
Competitive	5	45	40	8	2	0	78
Leaning Democratic	7	59	23	11	0	0	56

[a] *The states and periods covered by this analysis, as well as the groupings of states, are identical with Table 9.*

cent of the electorate. On the other hand, in states with relatively stronger Democratic parties the winners of Democratic nominations attract a higher proportion of the potential electorate. The proportions of Democratic nominations made by less than 10 per cent of the potential electorate for the various groups of states were as follows:

Strong Republican	96%
Less-strong Republican	93
Competitive	77
Leaning Democratic	55

Generally, Democratic nominations are made by smaller proportions of the total electorate—at least in the states analyzed—than are Republican nominations. And turnout at Democratic primaries tends to be smaller in relation to the party's general election vote than at the Republican primaries. In part this difference reflects the fact that in most of the states examined the Republican nomination is worth more—and is probably sought more diligently—but the difference may also reflect the fact that the Democratic following consists in the main of persons less disposed to vote than are Republicans.

The relatively small numbers of voters that an aspirant must rally to his support to win the nomination is related to the fact that commonly outside the South a plurality, rather than a majority, of those voting at the primary is necessary to carry the day. In Tables 12 and 14 in Chapter IV the facts were arrayed to indicate the proportions of gubernatorial nominations made by less than 50 per cent of the primary vote. These proportions, according to party and to political complexion of state groups, were:

STATE GROUP	REPUBLICAN	DEMOCRATIC
Strong Republican	38%	6%
Less-strong Republican	41	32
Competitive	32	17
Leaning Democratic	28	44

Nominees who win with less than 50 per cent of the primary vote attract, of course, the support of an exceptionally small proportion of the total electorate. Nor in general did capture of the nomination by less than half the primary vote reduce the chances for ultimate victory.[4]

----

[4] It might be supposed that the plurality nominations could be analyzed to test the supposition that a warm primary fight splits the party and reduces the chance for victory in the general election. While such may undoubtedly be the consequence in particular situations, test runs of the data reveal no sharp differences in general election fortunes of plurality and majority nominees as groups. In fact, the Democratic nominees by a plurality in the strong Republican states, few though they were, won far more frequently than did majority nominees. Thus, the Democratic nominees in Maine in 1914 and 1932 polled less than a majority of the primary vote but went on to win the general election. This suggests that at times a three-way primary fight may be a function of

Whether men who squeeze through the primaries with the support of a small proportion of the electorate are any better or worse than those with slightly larger followings it is impossible to know. More or less horrible examples may be found to be sure. In Ohio in 1934 Martin L. Davey won the nomination with votes equal to 5.3 per cent of the potential electorate and carried the state in that year of great Democratic strength over the nation as a whole. In 1920 Len Small received a primary vote of 10.9 per cent of the potential Illinois electorate and rode into office on the great Republican landslide of that year. On the other hand, many governors with eminently respectable records have gained office in the same manner. The records suggest something of the fortuitous and capricious nature of elective process. A man who chances in the primary to win the votes of 5 to 10 per cent of the potential voters, with the aid of luck and landslides, can be elevated to the governorship of an American commonwealth. The seemingly rational processes of democratic politics contain an element of the lottery.

Yet the small size of the blocs of voters necessary to win nominations has a most significant consequence for the nature of the party within the states. The direct communion of potential candidates with small groups of voters places enormous difficulties in the way of those party leaders disposed to look beyond the primaries to the general election and to put forward the most appealing slate. Individual politicians with a grasp on a small bloc of voters which can be turned into a primary victory are difficult to discipline or to bargain with. The support of even a weak personal organization, the loyalties and admiration of an ethnic group, a wide acquaintance within a religious group, simple notoriety achieved in a variety of ways, an alliance with an influential newspaper—these and a variety of other elements may create power within the narrow circle of

---

the belief that the general election prospects are unusually good. When Maine Democrats begin fighting among themselves for the gubernatorial nomination, the chances are that the outlook for the Republicans is gloomy.

people who share control in the politics of the direct primary.

3. Biases in Primary Constituencies

The smallness of the primary vote would not affect the results if those who voted constituted a representative sample of the adherents of a party. A minute group of voters—as small even as one of Mr. Gallup's samples—would make about the same nominations as would a turnout of 100 per cent, if the principal elements of the party were proportionately represented in the group. The fact seems to be, however, that those who vote in the primaries do not make up miniatures of the party membership. Perhaps in those one-party states with extremely high primary participation and in which the primary is indubitably the election the primary voters approximate a more or less representative sample of those who would vote in the general election if the general election were of any importance. Yet in states with a modicum of interparty competition primary participants are often by no means representative of the party.

Although a sample survey could be used to determine with some exactness the characteristics of those few persons who bestir themselves to express preferences for party nominations, an exercise in the arithmetic of election returns can reveal some gross dimensions of the active primary constituency. A plausible hypothesis with which to begin an inquiry is the supposition that in statewide direct primaries—to make nominations for governor, United States Senator, and other offices filled by elections at large—a disproportionate part of the vote would be cast by residents of areas strongly attached to a party. Virtual one-party Republican counties, for example, would be agitated over Republican nominations for local office and the Republican primary turnout would be exceptionally heavy in such counties. Their contribution to the total vote in statewide nominations would incidentally also be large. In the same counties Democrats, faced by hopeless prospects in local races, would vote in small numbers in the primaries and incidentally contribute a relatively small proportion of the state vote in the gubernatorial primaries. In counties controlled locally by Democrats the reverse of this pattern of participation would be expected to prevail.

The hunch is, then, that strong Democratic localities would vote especially heavily in statewide primaries, while strong Republican areas would contribute a similarly large part of the total vote in statewide Republican primaries. Whether this state of affairs actually prevails can be determined quite easily. An illustrative calculation on a New Hampshire gubernatorial primary will explain a technique to be applied to a few other situations. In the 1950 gubernatorial primaries in New Hampshire the Democrats nominated Robert P. Bingham, while the Republican nomination was won by Sherman Adams, a man later to gain some notoriety on the national political scene. In Hillsborough County, the strongest Democratic county in the state, the total Democratic primary vote was 89.6 per cent of the total Republican vote. This ratio, which we may call the index of primary balance was used, it may be recalled, in Chapter IV as a convenient measure of the relative strength of partisan groups within the electorate. In Hillsborough County the Democratic primary vote was 43.2 per cent of the Democratic general election vote and the Republican primary turnout was 64.8 per cent of the Republican general election vote. At the opposite extreme from Hillsborough County was Carroll County, an area of dedicated Republicanism in which the Democratic primary turnout amounted to only 3.8 per cent of the total Republican primary vote. In Carroll County the Democratic primary vote was only 13.2 per cent of the Democratic general election vote and the corresponding Republican figure was 81.4 per cent. The association between party strength and primary turnout may be clearer from the array of these figures on page 147.

At the right-hand column is a puzzling "index of primary participation distortion," which is simply the Democratic primary vote (as a percentage of the Democratic general election vote) minus the Republican primary vote (as a percentage of the Republican general election vote). This measure of the spread between the two parties in primary participation may serve as a rough measure of the tendency for participation in the

COUNTY	INDEX OF PRIMARY BALANCE	DEMO- CRATIC PRIMARY VOTE AS % OF GENERAL ELECTION VOTE (A)	REPUB- LICAN PRI- MARY VOTE AS % OF GENERAL ELECTION VOTE (B)	INDEX OF PRIMARY PARTICIPA- TION DISTORTION (A)-(B)
Hillsborough	89.6	43.2	64.8	−21.6
Carroll	3.8	13.2	81.4	−68.2

two party primaries to vary with the relative strength of the parties. If the index declines in value as Democratic strength decreases from county to county (in this case becomes a larger negative number), the tendency prevails. In this instance in Republican Carroll County the index is much lower in value than it is for Hillsborough County which reported a Democratic majority.

With this explanation of the method of testing the matter out of the way, a few quick checks may be made to determine whether the supposed differentials in participation in different types of counties really occur. Table 18 summarizes an analysis of the Ohio gubernatorial primaries of 1944, when the Democrats nominated Frank Lausche and the Republicans, James G. Stewart. The differentials in primary voting among the 88 counties of Ohio conform roughly to the expectation that the strong Republican counties would contribute relatively more to the Republican primary vote than to the Republican general election vote and that strong Democratic counties would play the same role in Democratic statewide primaries.

In Table 18, however, the averages for the groups of counties do not stair-step down regularly in every instance as one reads down the table from the strong Democratic counties to the strong Republican counties. This fact plus the rather wide

TABLE 18

Differentials Among Counties in Participation in Ohio Gubernatorial Primaries of 1944, Related to Variations in Balance of County Party Strength

INDEX OF PRIMARY BALANCE: RANGE[a]	NUM-BER OF COUN-TIES WITHIN RANGE	PARTY PRIMARY VOTE AS PER-CENTAGE OF ITS GENERAL ELEC-TION VOTE, MEAN		MEAN INDEX OF PRIMARY PARTICI-PATION DISTOR-TION[b]	MEAN NUMBER OF DEMO-CRATIC COUNTY OFFICERS PER COUNTY
		DEMO-CRATIC	REPUB-LICAN		
110-431	13	37.7	22.0	+15.7	6.92
70-109	13	22.2	24.3	− 2.1	5.77
50-69	13	20.0	31.4	−11.4	4.08
39-49	12	17.7	28.4	−10.7	1.00
27-35	12	16.0	34.0	−18.0	0.58
21-26	13	13.2	39.5	−26.3	0.46
11-19	12	14.6	46.2	−31.6	0.08

[a] *This index is the total Democratic gubernatorial primary vote as a percentage of the total Republican gubernatorial primary vote within a county.*
[b] *This index is simply the difference between the two columns to its left. When the value of the index is positive the Democrats polled in the primary a vote larger in relation to their general election vote than did the Republicans. When the value is negative the reverse is true. The larger the number, either positive or negative, the wider is the difference in primary participation between the two parties.*

dispersions of the figures making up the averages for the county groups suggested that some factor in addition to the balance of party strength contributed to variations in primary participation. Table 19 records a second analysis in which the counties of the state were divided into two groups: one group including the counties with populations of over 70,000 and the other, the less populous counties. This breakdown nicely irons out the irregularities of Table 18. Among the more populous counties primary participation tends to increase from county to county with local party strength. The same relationship prevails among the less populous counties. The differences among each of the two sets of counties exist at different levels of participation. The fact

TABLE 19

County Differentials in Participation in Ohio Gubernatorial Primaries, 1944, Related to Variations in Balance in County Party Strength, According to Population of County

INDEX OF PRIMARY BALANCE: RANGE	MEAN INDEX OF PRIMARY PARTICIPATION DISTORTION			
	COUNTIES UNDER 70,000		COUNTIES OVER 70,000	
	N	INDEX	N	INDEX
110-431	10	+22.8	3	− 7.8
70-109	7	+ 4.0	6	− 9.2
50-69	5	− 6.4	8	−14.7
39-49	11	− 9.8	1	−19.9
27-35	11	−17.5	1	−24.3
21-26	9	−25.1	4	−28.9
11-19	12	−31.6	0	

seems to be that urban Republicans, impelled both by their compulsions to do their civic duty and by the newspapers, vote in rather high degree in the primaries considering that their local cause is more or less hopeless. Urban Democrats are not especially moved by such drives although they go to the primary in greater numbers in cities in which their party is extremely strong than in the populous counties where their party is weak.

In Ohio the broad expectation about differentials in primary participation holds, though account needs to be taken of the fact that another type of difference in primary participation prevails between counties of large population and those of smaller population. The same type of analysis applied to the 1950 Colorado primaries for the nomination of candidates for lieutenant-governor yields another confirmation of the supposition that primary participation is warped by variations in the balance of power between the parties. Special heed ought to be given

TABLE 20

County Differentials in Participation in Primaries to Nominate Candidates for Lieutenant-Governor, Colorado, 1950, Related to Variations in County Party Strength

INDEX OF PRIMARY BALANCE: RANGE [a]	NUMBER OF COUNTIES WITHIN RANGE	MEAN INDEX OF PRIMARY PARTICIPATION DISTORTION [b]	MEAN NUMBER OF DEMOCRATIC COUNTY OFFICERS PER COUNTY
139-448	11	+21.5	9.5
101-135	13	+ 5.4	6.0
73-100	13	+ 4.8 [c]	4.2
50-72	13	− 6.3	3.4
23-49	13	−19.6	3.1

[a] *Democratic primary vote as percentage of Republican primary vote for lieutenant-governor.*
[b] *For definition of this index see note to Table 18.*
[c] *A single deviate county makes the mean for this group of counties somewhat higher than might be expected. Without the index of 32.8 scored in Hinsdale County (where the Democrats got 64 of their 73 general election voters out to the primary yet polled only 37.4 per cent of the general election vote) the mean index for the group of counties is 2.5.*

to the column of Table 20 showing the average numbers of Democratic county officers for the counties of each group. The counties ranked high in numbers of Democratic county officers also ranked high in Democratic primary participation and low in Republican primary participation (in relation to general election vote). If our general suppositions are correct, the primary contests for Democratic county nominations in strong Democratic counties attract voters to the primaries and help swell the vote in these counties on Democratic statewide nominations. Meanwhile, local Republicans, unmoved by the prospects for local victory and relatively untouched by the urgings of local candidates for their vote, stay away from the primaries. A reverse set of relationships apparently prevails in the strong Republican counties.

An extensive analysis would be necessary to ascertain whether these broad differentials in primary participation prevail in all states and at all primaries. Doubtless in some sets of circumstances the relationships do not exist,[5] yet the tendency for areas strongly attached to a party to gain a disproportionate weight in statewide primary nominations is doubtless sufficiently widespread to be of importance.[6]

The method used here does not identify all the significant characteristics either of those who vote in primaries in high degree or of those who refrain from voting in high degree. The technique yields a finding that primary participation in some areas far exceeds that in others. Within the areas of high partici-

[5] An analysis of the 1950 Pennsylvania gubernatorial primaries by the same method reflects the existence in that state of the tendency for primary participation to vary more or less directly with the balance of party power from county to county. Analyses were made of the 1940 Washington gubernatorial primaries, the 1948 Montana and the 1944 Idaho primaries to nominate candidates for attorney-general. While the relation between index of primary balance and index of primary distortion were broadly associated, many counties deviated widely from the general relationship. Idaho and Montana had open primaries while Washington employed the so-called blanket primary. It may be that under open primary conditions—in which voters are free to vote in the primary of either party—the pulling and hauling of county nomination contests are especially effective in moving voters to and fro across party lines. These migrations from party to party in local contests may produce the erratic voting behavior in some counties in the nominations of statewide candidates.

[6] One other test of the relation between primary participation and party balance may be noted for the record. In the 1938 Massachusetts gubernatorial primary the index of primary distortion ranged from plus 52.9 for Suffolk County to minus 26.6 for Nantucket County. The rank-order coefficient of correlation between the index of primary balance and the index of primary participation distortion for the counties of the state was plus 0.92.

pation voters of some income classes may vote in higher degree than do others, members of some ethnic groups may be more highly involved than others, and many other types of variation may exist that our technique of analysis cannot reach.[7]

4. Consequences of Unrepresentative Primary Turnout

Our analyses make it clear enough that the effective primary constituency may often be a caricature of the entire party following. The question immediately arises, what of it? The answer must be to a considerable degree conjectural. A suggestive line of speculation may be to consider the problem as a special case of the more general question of the interaction between public officials and their constituencies. A time-worn axiom of American politics proclaims the proposition that politicians keep their ears to the ground. Different politicians keep their ears to different sorts of soil, a fact that makes it possible to ascertain whether they pay any heed to what they hear. It is quite plain, from several systematic analyses, that not only does the character of the constituency affect the type of person elected but that after representatives are elected their voting records have, on the average at least, a demonstrable relationship with the characteristics of the people of their constituency.[8] The same general idea has served to explain some of the differences in the behavior of a variety of public functionaries. Thus, it is often

    [7] Another primary phenomenon associated with variations in party strength from county to county is of some interest. In Tennessee, Kentucky, and West Virginia statewide primary candidates supported by the state administration usually draw quite high proportions of the Democratic primary vote in the Republican counties, which are chiefly mountain counties. Local Democrats with no access to county office are especially amenable to management by patronage or at least those amenable to such management constitute in such counties a very high proportion of the Democratic primary vote.
    [8] See Julius Turner, *Party and Constituency: Pressures on Congress* (Baltimore: Johns Hopkins Press, 1951); Duncan MacRae, Jr., "The Relation between Roll Call Votes and Constituencies in the Massachusetts House of Representatives," *American Political Science Review,* 46 (1952), pp. 1046-1055.

said that United States Senators, with their large constituencies including many interests and types of people, are apt to take a different viewpoint than Representatives who often speak for relatively homogeneous—farmer, worker, suburban—districts. Or that the President must concern himself with all the people and, hence, may be moved to take a position diverging from that of a Senator or a Representative who responds to the tugs of a narrower constituency.

This broad tendency for the elective official to reflect the characteristics of his constituency may have a special significance if it also applies to the highly unrepresentative "constituencies" of actual participators in statewide direct primaries. Over the long run, the effect may be to mold the party leadership, or at least the bulk of the party candidates, more and more toward the image of that sector of the party stimulated by circumstances to participate in the primaries in high degree. By the same token, the composition and orientation of the party leadership would come less and less to take into account those elements of the party indisposed by circumstances to play a role in the primary.

The exact form of these consequences would, of course, be expected to be a product of the facts of the situation as they existed in a particular state at a particular time. Depending on the precise nature of those facts, the effective primary constituency of the state as a whole may come to consist predominantly of the people of certain sections of a state, of persons chiefly of specified national origin or religious affiliation, of people especially responsive to certain styles of political leadership or shades of ideology, or of other groups markedly unrepresentative in one way or another of the party following. The consequences would, thus, probably be most notable when the party following contained large and diverse groups of voters. Under some circumstances the minuscule and unrepresentative primary constituency may project its features upon the party leadership and handicap the party in polling the maximum party strength in the general election. On occasion, when extraneous influences such as presidential landslides control state elections, nominations dominated by warped primary constituencies may lead to general election victories mightily embarrassing to the responsible elements of the party as well as impairing the usefulness of the party in the larger cause of the government of the state.

The testing of these general notions and precise identification of the types of circumstances under which they would tend to prevail would require the most extensive investigations. An examination of the workings of the primary system in Massachusetts, however, will serve as an illustrative instance, although it should by no means be supposed that the effects of the primary system take exactly the same form in other states. As a first step in the examination of the transformation of Massachusetts parties under the direct primary system Tables 21 and 22 deserve careful inspection, for they identify some long-run tendencies that suggest lines of speculation in relation to our general proposition about the effects of the primary.

Since the introduction of the primary system of nomination for statewide office in 1912 the geographical distribution of Democratic nominees for statewide offices has been gradually but radically altered. In the first decade of the century only one out of four Democratic nominees for such posts resided in Boston and vicinity, as defined in Table 21. By a slow but steady movement Boston Democrats after the introduction of the primary increased their proportion of the nominations to 82.9 per cent for the decade 1942-1952.

Over the same period the geographical distribution of the membership of Republican slates also underwent drastic changes, which are pictured in Table 22. The shifts in the sources of Republican candidates differed from those for the Democrats although probably the same types of underlying influences brought them about. Under the convention system the strong Republican territory of western Massachusetts contributed about one out of three Republican candidates for statewide office. Under the direct primary the leaders of the loyal Republicans dispersed over the western counties gained smaller and smaller shares of the posts on the slate and eventually they came to win no places on the ticket.[9] Fewer and fewer Republican nominees claimed Boston as their residence. In 1900-1911 about 40 per cent of the Republican statewide nominees were Bostonians; in 1942-52, only 12 per cent. It may be sus-

TABLE 21

Trend in Residence of Democratic Nominees for Statewide Office in Massachusetts, 1900-1952

		FROM BOSTON AND VICINITY[b]		ELECTED	
PERIOD	NUMBER OF NOMINEES[a]	#	%	#	%[c]
1900-1911	72	18	25.0	3	4.2
1912-1920	56	26	46.4	11	19.6
1922-1930	34	15	44.1	6	17.6
1932-1940	32	21	65.6	17	53.1
1942-1952	41	34	82.9	22	53.7

[a] *Includes nominees for all statewide elective offices and for the United States Senate since 1916.*

[b] *Includes Suffolk County, Cambridge, Medford, and Somerville.*

[c] *That is, percentage of all Democratic nominees elected, not of those from Boston and vicinity only.*

pected that this shift parallels the movement of Yankees from Beacon Hill to the suburbs, but it also probably reflects a gain in capacity to win nominations by persons with a claim on considerable local concentrations of Republican voters.

The analysis of changes in geographical distribution of candidates rests on no assumption that geographically balanced tickets are a "good thing." Rather the changing pattern of the

[9] From 1913-1920, 18.3 per cent of the aspirants for Republican nominations were from the western counties. From 1942-1952 only 6.1 per cent of the aspirants for nomination were from these counties. Evidently the westerners gradually learned that their cause was hopeless against those leaders who could draw more readily on the concentrations of Republican voters in the eastern counties.

nominees suggests that under the direct primary a marked alteration in the location of the controlling power points in the nominating process has occurred. That alteration is mirrored in the changing geographical distribution of the party nominees.

In the Democratic party the changes in sources of statewide nominees apparently paralleled a gradual disintegration of the statewide Democratic organization. In the convention epoch that organization allocated nominations over the state.

TABLE 22

Trends in Residence of Republican Nominees for Statewide Elective Office in Massachusetts, 1900-1952

PERIOD	TOTAL NOMI- NEES	FROM BOSTON		FROM EASTERN COUNTIES[a]		FROM WESTERN COUNTIES[b]	
		#	%	#	%	#	%
1900-11	72	29	40.3	14	19.4	25	34.7
1912-20	56	17	30.3	22	39.3	14	25.0
1922-30	34	9	26.5	23	67.6	2	5.9
1932-40	32	9	28.1	20	62.5	3	9.4
1942-52	41	5	12.2	36	87.8	0	0.0

[a] *Included in this category are nominees from Essex, Middlesex, Norfolk, Bristol, and Plymouth counties.*
[b] *This group of counties consists of Berkshire, Franklin, Hampshire, Hampden, and Worcester.*

Even after the adoption of the primary the state organization continued to sponsor more or less balanced slates in the primaries. Its capacity to carry its slate in the primary became less and less with the passage of time as the organization became weaker and weaker. Ultimately in large measure the determination of nominations came to rest largely in the hands of those leaders with a hold on large concentrations of primary voters in strong Democratic territory. And these leaders tended to be individualists who got themselves nominated.

It might well be supposed that the primary system of

nomination had nothing to do with these tendencies. Undoubtedly other factors were at work. One possibility, however, can be ruled out. Did the changing origins of candidates simply parallel a change in the location of the Democratic vote? In fact, the division of the Democratic vote between Boston and vicinity and the rest of the state remained fairly constant. The primary, in combination with the distortions in primary participation, gave the Boston Democratic vote a mighty leverage in nominations. Some averages for the periods 1913-1920 and 1942-1952 will make clear what happened:

	1913-20	1942-52
Average percentage of total Democratic primary vote on statewide nominations from Boston and vicinity	56.0	52.4
Average percentage of Democratic candidates' general election vote from Boston and vicinity	33.1	29.6
Average percentage of total general election vote from Boston and vicinity	26.0	23.9
Total Democratic primary vote in Boston and vicinity as percentage of nominee's statewide general election vote, mean	18.8	15.4

These figures give the characteristics of the situation which facilitated the pyramiding of a small following of voters into a nomination for statewide office. Boston and vicinity, as defined in Table 21, accounted for about one-half the statewide Democratic primary votes against around one-third of the statewide general election vote for Democratic candidates. The total Democratic primary vote in Boston and vicinity averaged in the two periods 18.8 and 15.4 per cent of the Democratic nominees' statewide general election vote. Men with the capacity to win the support of voters in Boston equal to 10 per cent or so of the statewide Democratic general election vote obviously would have enormous advantage in capturing statewide nominations.

A factor that doubtless contributed to the disintegration

of statewide Democratic organization, as reflected in the distribution of nominees, arose from the increasing prospects over the period for Democratic statewide victory. So long as Democratic candidates had little chance for victory the state organization could designate and nominate through the primary more or less balanced slates. In truth, when the nominations were worthless, it took precious little statewide organization to produce a balanced slate. As the probability of victory grew, however, the latent cleavages within the party became manifest through sharp competition for primary nomination. In other words, when the Democratic nominations for state office became worth something, Boston Democratic politicians had a stronger incentive to exert the great leverage of their local followings in the statewide primaries. The right-hand column of Table 21 indicates the changes over a half century in the probability of victory for Democratic nominees.[10]

For many years after the introduction of the direct primary the Democratic state organization, through the state committee, the state convention, or less formal means, prepared slates of organization candidates for the primary nomination. Gradually whatever cohesiveness the organization ever possessed became inadequate to curb the tempting opportunity to fight out differences in the primary. In fact, in due course even the factional elements of the party became so ineffectively linked with the voters that the outcome of primary contests, at least for the lesser offices, became almost a matter of chance.

For well over thirty years important actors in the internal wars of the party were David Ignatius Walsh, of Fitchburg, and James Michael Curley, of Boston. Although they never met as opposing candidates, their allies and associates often sparred

[10] The change in competition for Democratic nominations for statewide office associated with increasing prospects of general election victory is suggested by the fact that from 1913-1920, 85 per cent of the Democratic primary nominations were made without contest; from 1942-1952, the percentage made without contest was only 31. From 1913-1920 only 4 per cent of the Democratic primaries involved three or more aspirants for the nomination; from 1942-1952, 45 per cent of the primary races involved 3 or more contestants.

in the primaries. Walsh, with the benefit of the Republican rifts of the Progressive era, won the gubernatorial election of 1913 and as governor established a record as a progressive himself. In 1918, a year of Democratic disaster over the nation, he won a United States Senate seat and remained in the Senate most of the rest of his life. Over the years he built up and maintained a following adequate to keep him in the Senate yet not sufficient to control the Democratic party of the state. The first Catholic governor of the state, Walsh's style of politics was adapted to political longevity in his environment. Irish by origin and for his day liberal, he had an appeal to the Massachusetts Irish, an appeal re-enforced by his isolationism. Yet he proclaimed, "Let every man of Irish blood face his duty as an American citizen in passing judgment on national and international questions. Let us remember to be Americans first." [11] So mellow a view coupled with a moderate economic outlook earned for him independent and, on occasion, Yankee Republican support that contributed to his capacity to survive despite the misfortunes of his party.

Curley's style of politics, radically different from that of the upstater Walsh, served his purposes and needs also. Curley, his biographer Joseph F. Dinneen observes, was a "creation of a curious society known everywhere as 'The Boston Irish,' as distinguished from all other Irish." [12] Curley built a political career on his uncompromising championship of the Boston Irish. A man of exceptional histrionic skill, he had great capacity to play upon the sentiments of the more exuberant strains within the Boston Irish community.

Scarcely had the direct primary been put into operation when Curley, from his base as mayor of Boston, challenged a primary recommendation of the Democratic state committee. In 1913 the committee backed Walsh for the gubernatorial nomination and Richard H. Long, of Framingham, for the nom-

[11] Dorothy G. Wayman, *David I. Walsh, Citizen-Patriot* (Milwaukee: Bruce, 1952), p. 108.
[12] *The Purple Shamrock* (New York: Norton, 1949), p. 9.

ination for lieutenant-governor. Curley's man, one Edward P. Barry, of Boston, won the latter nomination. At intervals over the years Curley men and Walsh men crossed swords. In 1930 Joseph B. Ely, a western Massachusetts Democrat, a Protestant, and early in his career a protégé of Walsh, easily won the gubernatorial nomination over a stalking horse backed by Curley.[13] The state convention of 1934 endorsed Walsh for the United States Senate and Charles H. Cole, an Ely-Walsh man, for governor. Curley carried the fight to the primaries and won the gubernatorial nomination for himself but his man Edward P. Barry made a poor showing in the primary against Senator Walsh. Curley won the senatorial nomination in 1936 but, in a year when any Democrat should have won, lost to young Henry Cabot Lodge. Again in 1938 he won the primary nomination for governor but lost to Leverett Saltonstall in the general election. Curley's strong hold on a substantial block of Boston voters made him a formidable candidate in statewide Democratic primaries. No matter how faithfully he mirrored his own immediate constituency, he made a poor candidate in the larger arena of the state. He managed to win only one statewide race, that for governor in 1934, a year when probably Democratic popular strength in the nation generally reached its peak.

The gradual increase in the proportions of Democratic nominations captured by Bostonians did not reflect by any means solely the fortunes and exertions of prominent factional leaders. It came more and more to result from the unguided and unbossed actions of primary voters in supporting names familiar to them, usually those of local notables. Primary maneuvers to divide the vote, by a multiplicity of candidacies, became more common and increased the probability that this or that extremely small minority would control the nomination. The case of Francis E. (or Frankie) Kelly is illustrative. A Bostonian and a professional Irishman with a picturesque manner, an uninhibited tongue, and a great capacity to make political capital

---

[13] In Curley's old Boston ward the primary vote was 180 for Ely against 2370 for Fitzgerald, the candidate backed by Curley.

of the oppressions of the Irish in both the Old World and the New, Frankie won several statewide nominations by attracting less than half the Democratic primary vote. In 1936, with 45 per cent of the vote in a three-way primary race, he defeated the Democratic convention's choice for lieutenant-governor, Philip Philbin of Clinton in Worcester County. He eked out a general election victory with a lead of 7,347 votes over Leverett Saltonstall, in a year when Roosevelt's coattails had tremendous supportive power. During Frankie's tenure the unhappy governor, a fellow Democrat, was most reluctant to leave the state and thus place the affairs of the Commonwealth in the hands of the irrepressible lieutenant-governor.[14] In 1944, 1946, 1948, and 1952, Frankie won the nominations for attorney-general by pluralities. Organization leaders with a statewide view regarded him as no asset to the ticket; yet they did not have the means to block him in the primary. His defeats and victories in the general elections seemed to be the more or less fortuituous consequence of the general drift of partisan sentiment; once over the primary hurdle the fortunes of a candidate for a minor office in a close state are in the laps of the political gods.

These cases suggest that the direct primary in Massachusetts, along with its distorted effective constituency, had consequences for party leadership that are not so easily measured as are changes in residence of candidates. In any case the problem of geographical balance is generated by the practice of electing officials who might in the main better be chosen otherwise. Geographical balance may not be a matter of as great importance in party victory[15] as is balance in the sense of selecting

[14] See Robert S. Allen, *Our Sovereign State* (New York: Vanguard, 1949), p. 31.

[15] There may be skepticism whether a balanced ticket, in the sense of a ticket geographically balanced or representative of religious sects and national-origin groups, is in fact advantageous in the practical business of getting votes for the entire ticket. The question has, in actual politics, no uniform answer. Sometimes balance helps; sometimes it has no discernible effect. It seems fairly clear, however, that elements of residence, national origin, religion, and the like have far greater bearing on votes in the primary than in the general election when party considerations come into play.

candidates whose style of politics and whose policy orientations strike somewhere near the common denominator of the party membership. In this sense a ticket with only one candidate may be "balanced" or "unbalanced." In the internal politics of American parties a recurring problem of party leadership is to keep in check the extremists in the party—ideological extremists, regional special pleaders, deviant groups of whatever sort—and to nominate candidates and advocate causes that hold the support not only of most elements of the party but reach out and attract the uncommitted voter and the milder adherents of the opposition. The accomplishment of that task is inevitably difficult, but under some circumstances the primary procedure creates especially formidable obstacles.

Massachusetts Republicans have also had their troubles in maintaining a leadership adequate to obtain nomination through the primary of suitable statewide candidates. The problem is illustrated by the confusion among Republican primary voters over the names of Charles L. Burrill and Fred J. Burrell. Charles L. Burrill won the Republican nomination for state treasurer in 1913 and won both nomination and election in 1914, 1915, 1916, 1917, and 1918. In 1919 he did not seek renomination, but one Fred J. Burrell, age 31, was nominated and elected. After a few months in office, he got into difficulties. The legislature initiated an inquiry looking toward impeachment proceedings. Banks had complained that to obtain deposits of state funds they needed to place their advertising through an agency designated by Mr. Burrell. The young treasurer resigned under pressure. He denied any wrong-doing and explained his resignation as an act of filial piety to save his aged mother from the pain of critical publicity. Governor Calvin Coolidge named James Jackson to the vacancy. Mr. Jackson won re-election in 1920 and 1922 but not without first having to defeat Mr. Fred J. Burrell in the Republican primaries, a task that also fell to the lot of Wm. S. Youngman, the Republican nominee for treasurer in 1924.

Fred J. unsuccessfully sought the Republican nomination for treasurer in 1928 but he was back in the running for the 1930 nomination against Charles L. Burrill and six other candidates. Both Mr. Burrill and Mr. Burrell were identified on the ballot as "ex-Treasurer" and Fred J. Burrell came out ahead with 20.8 per cent of the Republican primary against Mr. Burrill's 19.9 per cent. The electorate proceeded to protect the state from the folly of the Republican primary voters. Fred J. Burrell was hard to discourage. He tried for the nomination for treasurer again in 1936. In 1942 he actually won it, and again he was defeated in the general election. Undaunted he tried, without luck, for the nomination in 1946. In 1950 he returned to the wars and defeated in the primaries Roy C. Papalia, a young Italo-American Republican, only to lose the election. In 1952 Papalia, with the endorsement of the pre-primary convention, carried the primary against Burrell.

Obviously when candidates of questionable capacity whose names are household words—or who have the same name as somebody whose name is a household word—can become formidable contestants in primaries, party organization no longer has much capacity to lead the voters, a condition that may be more ominous than that which prevails when the primary rubber-stamps the organization slate.[16]

[16] The saga of the Hurleys in Massachusetts politics further illustrates the matter. In 1930 Francis X. Hurley won the Democratic nomination for auditor and Charles F. Hurley won the Democratic nomination for treasurer. Both went on to victory and in 1932 were renominated and re-elected. Four years of publicity for the Hurley name gave it a political potency. In 1934, as Charles F. Hurley, unsuccessful in his bid for convention endorsement for governor, had to be content with a renomination for treasurer, one Joseph L. Hurley turned up on the scene and won the nomination for lieutenant-governor. Elected as lieutenant-governor, he shared the stage with Treasurer Hurley for a couple of years and the name of Hurley became more and more of a household word. The two Hurleys, Charles F. and Joseph L., vied in 1936 for the convention endorsement for governor. Charles F. won the nod and Joseph L. disappeared from the limelight. The magic of the name Hurley seeped over into the Republican ranks and, also in 1936, the Republicans endorsed and nominated a William E. Hurley for treasurer, the post held by the Democrat, Charles F. Hurley, now running for governor. Simultaneously, the Democratic convention proposed J. C. Scanlon for the treasury post, but one James M. Hurley won the primary nomination for the place that

The impact of different groups within the highly restricted primary constituency upon party nominations differs from state to state with the structure of the groups within the party, with the sorts of people who make up the high participating element of the party, and doubtless with many other variables. Yet it is probably correct that the fact that primary constituency bias tends to determine the nature of party leadership may become of special significance for the minority party which is especially weak, i.e., not too weak to hope for victory but not strong enough to win except on infrequent occasions. Leaders of such a party who are ambitious for statewide victory confront a real difficulty in overcoming the preferences of a primary constituency for its own peculiar kind. Yet to win now and then such a minority must put forward nominees with an appeal to the independents and to the inconstant fringe of the majority party. In the states of the North the minority's problem in fielding an attractive ticket is principally a Democratic problem. Where the Republicans normally occupy the minority position, they have their difficulties.

In New Mexico, Jack E. Holmes has pointed out in an able analysis,[17] to win state elections the Republicans of the small number of Republican counties must desert their own and put up candidates from elsewhere in the state. Nevertheless, during the period 1940-1950 most of the voters in the Republican primaries and a majority of the Republican nominees came from five counties of the Rio Grande Valley. Republican personalities of these counties can readily obtain primary nominations for statewide office. Yet, Mr. Holmes observes, "individuals nominated from such a narrow base of old friends and neighbor's support will hardly appeal to the dissident Democrat

---

had been so adequately filled by Charles F. Hurley. Mr. Charles F. Hurley went on to win the governorship but his colleague Mr. James M. Hurley, of Marlborough, fell before the campaign of Mr. William E. Hurley, the Boston Republican.

[17] Jack E. Holmes, *Problems Relating to Various Nominating Procedures in New Mexico* (Santa Fe: New Mexico Legislative Council Service, 1954).

from the East side who is looking for a respectable chance to vote his convictions on policy on those occasions when he might feel that his own party has not given him and his neighbors a fair shake." [18]

5. Queries about Mass Control of Party Hierarchies

A favorite argument of some of the more sophisticated advocates of direct primary used to be that the primary afforded a means for popular correction of the errors and misjudgments of the party organization in the nominating process. They recognized the uses of party organization and thought that the party leadership would and should propose slates of candidates to the judgment of the party membership in the primaries. The party voters could then approve or reject or selectively substitute in the primary the virtuous challengers of the wicked men proposed by the organization. The facts of experience about mass interest and participation in the direct primaries make it evident that the expectation that the primary would function as a mechanism for control of the party hierarchy requires revision. The data on participation over a long period and under widely varied conditions make it plain that only under the most exceptional circumstances will more than a handful of the voters turn out at the primary. The thinness of participation is perhaps not so significant a factor in the re-estimation of the possibilities of membership control of the party hierarchy as is the unrepresentative character of the segment of the party that does participate.[19]

If any moral at all obtrudes from the various compara-

[18] *Ibid.*, p. 34.

[19] The observation has often been made that primary participation may be low but it is far greater than ever occurred in the caucuses and "primaries" that operated at the first step in the choice of convention delegates. From this it is said to follow that the primary is "better." Whether one level of participation is better than another can be argued endlessly and fruitlessly. The point here is that under the primary a new type of situation, a new structure of influence, is created that over the long run may alter the results of the process.

tive analyses, it is that the practical realities of particular institutional arrangements vary with the nature of the situation into which they are introduced. So it is with the estimation of the significance of the biases in the effective primary constituency. The form of the bias is fixed by the peculiar situation in each state as are its consequences and significant elements of that situation may change from time to time within an individual state. It is therefore most perilous to attempt any general observations on the basis of the sample inquiries reported in this chapter; far more extensive study would be required to estimate the frequency of occurrence of particular types of actions associated with the primary system of nomination and to define the circumstances under which particular types of actions might be expected to take place. About all that can be said is that under some circumstances the unrepresentative block of participators in the primary, by nominating candidates in their own image, seriously handicap the party in carrying the battle to the opposition in the general election. The elevation of such minorities to power within the nominating process—through the smallness of total participation and its bias along with the accidents of plurality nomination—may affect more than the capacity of the party to wage political war. At times the swings of partisan sentiment are enough to throw into office the most improbable sorts of characters who have won nominations through the vagaries of the primary.

It may well be that these sorts of consequences of the bias in participation are most apt to occur in states fairly competitive between the major parties and in states in which one or the other of the parties contains within itself a congeries of groups of voters susceptible to management and manipulation by would-be candidates. Another range of consequences may develop as one moves into states that are dominated by a single party although the difference may be one of degree.[20]

[20] In the workings of the direct primary another factor that may be of considerable importance in the differing situations from state to state is the absolute size of the electorate. At least a priori, it would seem

A focus of attention on these aspects of primary participation points to special difficulties in maintaining a cohesive party hierarchy extending over an entire state under the statewide direct primary. A party organization, representative of all segments of the party and with an eye on statewide victory, would almost of necessity propose slates in one way or another unappealing to the unrepresentative sector of the party voting in the primary. Statewide party hierarchies seem to disintegrate under the impact of the influences given free play by the primary. They cannot thrive under repeatedly successful assaults upon their proposals by those who, on the basis of some special or parochial appeal, can manage to win nominations through the primary. Only under rather exceptional sets of circumstances—of party homogeneity, of monopolization of sources of campaign funds, of common desire for victory—can formal party leadership maintain much control over the nominating process. The more common tendency seems to be that competing centers of power—competing informal hierarchies based on localities, regions, groups, personal followings—develop their electoral support in the direct primary. These little hierarchies—under one-party conditions approach, of course, the reality of political parties themselves.[21]

---

that the informal channels for the dissemination of information about politics and politicians in Wyoming would probably make for a much better informed primary electorate than would the same channels in Ohio, Illinois, or Massachusetts. Metropolitan populations live, to be sure, under the beneficent influence of the great modern instruments of communication. Yet not much by way of helpful political intelligence flows through these great mechanisms of communication that do not have much to communicate.

[21] Variations in primary participation may take on a special statewide significance when a large concentration of primary voters is deliverable by a local machine. Thus in Kansas City, Missouri, in 1932 the Democratic gubernatorial primary participation was 72 per cent of the Democratic general election vote. The corresponding Republican figure was 36 per cent. Of the Democratic primary vote 91 per cent went to the candidate supported by the Pendergast organization. In 1936, similar ratios between primary vote and general election vote prevailed for Republicans and Democrats, but on this occasion 98 per cent of the Democratic primary turnout was marked up for the candidate favored by Pendergast for the nomination.

The dilemma with which the analysis confronts us is essentially that the introduction of means for popular control of party hierarchies also plants the seeds for the fission, if not the destruction, of statewide party organization. The primary mode of nomination gives free play to forces that make it difficult for the party hierarchies to do much by way either of good or evil. The observation that such consequences tend to prevail should not be interpreted as an argument for the return of the old-style convention system, which had its erraticisms as well. The point is rather that under the processes of the primary we have a wide range of consequences, by no means all to the good, more or less totally unforeseen by the architects of this system of nomination.

Chapter 6

Atrophy of Party Organization: A Study of Legislative Nominations

By the addition of analysis after analysis, an impression begins to build up of the complexity and variety of the political systems of the American states. The great sectional impact of the Civil War on American national politics left a lasting imprint on the form of the politics of the older states; it warped them, in varying degrees, toward a one-partyism of either Democratic or Republican persuasion. The direct primary facilitated the supplementation of partisan divisions with an intraparty factional politics, itself most diverse in form. The classic pattern of competition between parties remained in some of the states, but the reality of politics in many states became the politics of intraparty factions. As the analysis of these matters proceeded, clues began to appear which suggested that perhaps the new rules of the game—the direct primary—created circumstances that made difficult the maintenance and operation of statewide party organization. The new channels to power placed a premium on individualistic politics rather than on the collaborative politics of party.

The question presents itself whether the direct primary mode of nomination may not set in motion forces that tend to lead to the atrophy of party organization. The primary may stimulate the substitution of an intraparty politics for an inter-party politics. Party candidates continue, to be sure, to appear on the general election ballot but often the final decision has in reality already been made at the stage of nominations. Does the continued focus of attention and political effort on the primary of the majority party lead to a gradual dissolution of the leader-ship clique of the minority, disillusioned by the patent fruitless-ness of its efforts? What of the effects of the process on the majority? Does the continued concentration of popular conflict within its primaries tend to break it into factions and leave it a party only in name? [1]

The answers to such questions, if indeed there are an-swers, can be found only by the most careful analysis. A re-spectable body of opinion holds to the view that the formally prescribed rules of procedure and practice of politics have no effect on the way people behave in their political activities. When pushed to the extreme, the argument would be that the results of the struggles of politics will be the same, whatever the formal rules or procedures of the game may be. The view here is that the more probable truth is that the formal rules sometimes affect or influence the informal organization of politics and that the analytical problem is to ascertain the types of circumstances under which the supposed effects do and do not prevail.

A narrow sector of the general question whether the direct primary brings with it party atrophy may be attacked by an analysis of the nomination and election of members of the lower house of the state legislatures in representative two-party states. [2] Since there are many state legislators, the facts of their nomination and election may be checked under a variety of circumstances and in sufficient numbers to give some confi-

---

[1] An earlier version of this chapter, "The Direct Primary and Party Structure: A Study of State Legislative Nominations" *American Political Science Review,* 48 (1954), pp. 1-26, presents the argument in more detail.

[2] For reasons that will become apparent, it is unlikely that the method applied here would yield much when applied to states with a marked imbalance between the parties.

dence in the findings that develop. An examination of the data about legislators can, of course, throw light on only part of the larger question of the relation between party organization and the mode of nomination. The findings may or may not be applicable in other sorts of situations.

1. Patterns of Primary Competition

A first step toward the solution of our problem will be to set out some facts about the workings of the primary in the nomination of candidates for state legislatures. For the immediate purposes the most relevant aspect of the operation of the primary system of nomination consists in the wide variation in the extent to which political hopefuls vie for primary nominations. It might be expected that within each legislative district two or more Democrats would fight it out in the primary for the nomination and two or more Republicans would flex their political muscles in the primary of their party. The victors in each primary would then proceed to campaign against each other for the support of the voters at the general election. If this pattern prevailed, each legislative district of a state would be characterized not only by competition at the general election but also by rivalry in each of the party primaries.

In actual practice the process of primary nomination diverges rather markedly from these suppositions of universal competition. The departures from the expectation of the uniform existence of competition are associated with variations in the more or less normal division of general election strength between the parties. In states with a two-party system the legislative districts usually range from those committed to the Republicans by overwhelming majorities to those that are customarily Democratic by equally wide margins. Between the sure Republican districts and the sure Democratic districts are districts that normally divide nearer to the 50-50 line. The gains or losses by the parties at particular elections are in the main among those districts that have a history of rather close division of the popular vote.

Legislative districts thus range from sure Republican districts, through those that are doubtful, to sure Democratic districts. Competition for party nominations varies with these differences among districts. Instead of there being invariably a couple of Republicans who vie for their party's nomination and a pair of Democrats who contend for the right to oppose the Republican nominee, a great many nominations go by default. The extent to which a party's nominations are contested in the primary by two or more aspirants depends in large measure on the prospects for victory for the nominee in the general election. Uncontested nominations for legislative posts are almost the rule in those districts in which a party's cause seems hopeless, while a large proportion of nominations are contested in relatively sure districts. A type situation is described in the graphs in Figure 15 which relate the proportions of nominations contested by two or more candidates in primaries for the Missouri House of Representatives to the division of the vote in the subsequent general election. The division of the district vote at the general election may be regarded as a rough measure of expectations about the outcome of elections.[3]

Although the increase in the incidence of primary competition as the prospects for party victory improve, demonstrated by Figure 15, probably recurs from state to state, the proportion of all nominations contested varies from state to state with a variety of factors. Table 23, with its data on Indiana's 1948 primary, indicates that in Indiana, as in Missouri, the greatest propensity to compete for a party's nominations occurs in those districts in which the nominees have the greatest

[3] The combination of five primaries in Figure 15 smoothes the curve but the fundamental relation shown appears at each election. Throughout, the combination of primaries usually smoothes a curve or pictures a more regular set of relations than appears from the data of a single primary. This effect is most marked in the cells of very small numbers. Enlargement of the sample by the cumulation of data on several primaries would probably iron out most of the irregularities that appear in cells of small numbers in some of the tables that follow.

assurance of victory in the general election. The table also reveals a considerably higher incidence of competition—with general election strength held constant—in Indiana than in Mis-

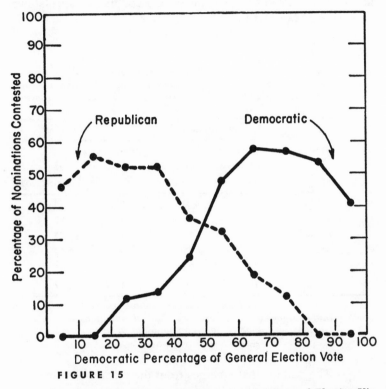

FIGURE 15

Primary Competition and the Prospects for General Election Victory: Relation between Proportion of Nominations Contested and Percentage of General Election Vote Polled by Republican and Democratic Nominees for Missouri House of Representatives, 1942-1950

souri. That difference doubtless points to basic differences in the political structures of the two states, one of which is that relatively more of the Indiana districts are closely contested. Table 23 incidentally suggests some of the limits of the actual

vote as a post facto measure of the expectation of victory; note
that the Republicans competed for nominations to a large proportion of those seats which they lost by a small margin, perhaps
in part a reflection of the rosiness of Republican expectations
before the 1948 upset.[4]

TABLE 23

*Primary Contests in Relation to General Election Vote: Propor-
tions of Democratic and Republican Legislative Nominations
Contested, Indiana, 1948, in Relation to 1948 General Election
Vote in Legislative Districts*

NOMINEES' GENERAL ELECTION PERCENTAGE	DEMOCRATIC		REPUBLICAN	
	NUMBER OF NOMI- NATIONS [a]	PER CENT CONTESTED	NUMBER OF NOMI- NATIONS	PER CENT CONTESTED
Under 40	3	0	9	44
40-44	14	7	21	62
45-49	18	33	30	77
50-54	30	77	18	67
55-59	20	85	13	85
60 and over	11	82	8	87

[a] *Included are those nominations made by party committee rather than by primary. Such nominations are in effect
classified in the percentage computations as uncontested.*

The pattern that emerges from these and other analyses
becomes one in which at one end of the scale primary competition occurs chiefly in the Democratic primary. As the districts become more competitive simultaneous contests for nominations occur a great deal more frequently in the primaries of
both parties. As districts become more firmly committed to the
Republican party, contests for nominations tend to be restricted
to the primaries of that party.

Figure 15 and Table 23 suggest that, on the whole, com-

[4] For relevant comments on Indiana experience, see Charles S.
Hyneman, "Tenure and Turnover of the Indiana General Assembly,"
American Political Science Review, 32 (1938), pp. 51-67, 311-331.

petition for primary nomination tends to become more frequent as the prospects for general election victory improve. Yet the curves in Figure 15 reveal some exceptions to this general proposition. The frequency of primary competition actually declines among the legislative districts in the upper reaches of Democratic and Republican strength, those districts in which general election victory is most certain. How are these departures from the general tendency to be explained? It might be guessed that incumbents are often renominated without primary opposition. Perhaps a greater number of incumbents seek renomination in the sure districts. If they are not challenged in the primary, this would account for the fall-off in primary competition in the districts with the most one-sided general election vote. A check on these suppositions appears in Figure 16 which records an analysis of the primaries of both parties in Missouri for the years 1946, 1948, and 1950. A less extensive collection of Ohio data is analyzed in Table 24. The data of Figure 16 and Table 24 indicate that, at least in the safe districts as we have defined them, primaries in which incumbents seek renomination are less likely to involve competition than are those in which no incumbent is running. The association between primary competition and the probability of general election victory appears considerably closer when only those primaries involving no incumbents are analyzed separately, as may be seen from the relevant curve in Figure 16. For the Ohio legislative districts analyzed in Table 24, the tendency prevails for incumbents to face challenge in the primaries less frequently than nonincumbents. Forty per cent of the incumbents had opposition for renomination while contests occurred in 65 per cent of the primaries involving no incumbents.

The disinclination to challenge a legislator who seeks renomination may not exist everywhere but it does account for some of the variations in primary competition in the states analyzed. Other factors may also have a bearing on the frequency of primary contests. Variations in the social characteristics of districts, for example, may be associated with differences in the frequency of primary contest. Rural districts may, for example, be less given to political commotion than highly urbanized ones. In Missouri Democratic primaries involving incumbents in 1948 a

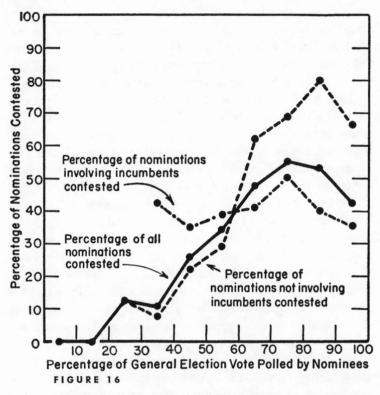

FIGURE 16

Incumbents and Primary Competition: Competition in Primaries Involving Incumbents and in Primaries Involving No Incumbents with Comparable Prospects of General Election Victory, Missouri House of Representatives, 1946-1950

sharp difference existed in the frequency of contests for nomination in those districts over 50 per cent urban and in those under 50 per cent urban. One-half of the nominations in the urban districts were contested; only 10 per cent of the rural districts. A further test of the ruralism-urbanism difference is provided by the more detailed breakdown for the Ohio Republican and Democratic primaries of 1948 which appears in Table 25. That table exhibits some irregularities which would probably disappear by the analysis of a larger number of cases, but generally,

TABLE 24

Incumbency and Competition for Legislative Nominations: Proportion of Ohio House Republican Primaries in Single-Member Districts Contested in 1948, When Incumbents Involved and Not Involved

| REPUBLICAN PERCENTAGE GENERAL ELECTION 1948 | PRIMARY INVOLVING | | | |
| | INCUMBENTS | | NO INCUMBENTS | |
	NOMINA-TIONS	PER CENT CONTESTED	NOMINA-TIONS	PER CENT CONTESTED
30-39	2	100	3	0
40-49	10	20	5	80
50-59	19	47	6	83
60-69	6	50	0	0
70-79	2	0	0	0
100	20	40	3	67
	—	—	—	—
Total	59	41	17	65

within similar ranges of party strength, a higher incidence of primary competition occurs in the more urbanized districts.[5] A lingering doubt remains about the nature of the association between urbanism and competition. It seems clear that the relation between urban population percentage and propensity to compete is not linear.[6] Moreover, metropolitan political systems in which

[5] An element that may influence urban rates in Ohio is the custom of electing many legislators at large from the metropolitan counties. This practice may be conducive to a multiplicity of candidacies for nomination.

[6] The absence of competition seems most noticeable at the extreme of ruralism. Thomas Page, in commenting on the low temperature of competition in rural Kansas districts, observes: "The cold statistics hint that a subtle, informal, and highly personal process of co-optation often goes on in the smallest legislative districts. This leaves no important

no competition occurs in primaries are common enough. Yet the multiplicity of centers of power and of aspiration in highly urbanized areas may require the application of greater effort, ingenuity, and resources to monopolize party position than in otherwise comparable but predominantly rural areas.[7]

TABLE 25

Urbanism and Contests in Primaries: Contests in Ohio Republican and Democratic Primaries to Nominate for State House of Representatives, 1948, in Relation to Nominees' Strength in General Election and to Urbanism of District[a]

NOMINEES' GENERAL ELECTION PERCENTAGE OF DISTRICT VOTE	NOMINATIONS IN DISTRICTS					
	UNDER 50% URBAN		OVER 50% URBAN		TOTAL	
	NUMBER	% CON-TESTED	NUMBER	% CON-TESTED	NUMBER	% CON-TESTED
25-29	2	0	0		2	0
30-39	8	25	8	50	16	37
40-49	26	15	66	67	92	52
50-59	26	58	67	73	93	69
60-69	8	50	7	43	15	47
70-74	2	0	0		2	0
100	21	33	4	75	25	40
Total	93	34	152	68	245	55

[a] *In counties electing two or more members at large, nominations were regarded as uncontested to the extent that the number of aspirants for nomination was less than twice the number of nominations to be made. In the computation of the percentage of the two-party general election vote for candidates in such counties a base was obtained by addition of the vote of a winning candidate to the vote of the highest losing candidate of the opposing party.*

role for the formal election but the registration of the previously implicit consent." See his *Legislative Apportionment in Kansas* (Lawrence, Kansas, 1952), chap. 4.

[7] For related, suggestive comments about rural congressional districts, see Duncan MacRae, Jr., "Occupations and the Congressional Vote, 1940-1950," *American Sociological Review,* 20 (1955), pp. 332-340.

A final question about the incidence of competition for nomination needs to be raised. The preceding analyses have compared different districts at one primary. The fact that electoral decision is actually pushed back in many instances to the uncontested majority primary may lead to the conclusion that many such districts rarely have genuine political competition. Perhaps what happens is that competition tends to occur less frequently in any particular district than the two-year election interval. When an incumbent retires, when an issue divides the community, or when the body politic undergoes disturbance for one reason or another, a contest will develop in the primary. Such events do not occur with the regularity of elections. To test these notions the history of individual districts must be traced through several primaries. Figure 17 records an analysis of Missouri districts through the three Republican primaries of 1946, 1948, and 1950. Those districts were identified in which at least one close contest took place. On the assumption that the incidence of these conditions would vary with party strength, the districts were grouped according to their Republican percentage in the legislative race in the general election of 1948.

When the districts are followed through these three primaries, as may be seen from Figure 17, a much higher proportion of the districts have primary contests in at least one of the primaries than in a single year. Yet the relation between party strength and the incidence of primary competition emerges even more sharply than in the earlier analyses. All this suggests that such factors as urbanism and incumbency may affect the frequency of primary competition through time but that in the long run the incidence of primary competition is a function chiefly of the prospects for victory in the general election.[8]

[8] No entirely satisfactory explanation suggests itself for the sharp fall-off in primary competition in the high ranges of party strength which remains even in the analysis reported in Figure 17, although ruralism seems to be relevant. In the 1948 Missouri general election 34.5 per cent of the completely rural house districts went without contest; 20.3 per cent of the other districts up to 50 per cent urban, and only 6.7 per cent of the districts over 50 per cent urban went without party competition.

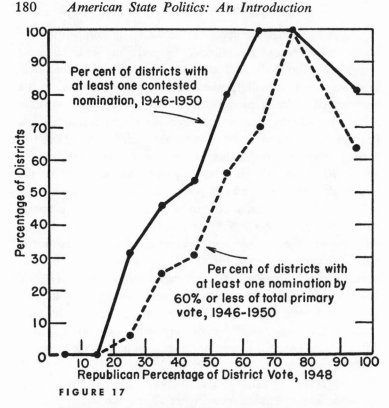

FIGURE 17

Incidence of Competition in Three Successive Primaries: Proportion of Districts with Republican Nomination for Missouri House of Representatives Contested at Least Once in Primaries of 1946, 1948, and 1950, and Proportions Contested Closely at Least Once, Related to Republican Percentage of District General Election Vote, 1948

With a bit of patient puzzling another fact of considerable importance about the workings of party and primary may be pried from Figure 17. The earlier tables and figures showed that in a goodly number of districts no contest occurred in the

Of the seats Republicans won by default, 95.2 per cent were from districts under 50 per cent urban, while the comparable figure for the Democrats was 83.3.

party primary even though the nominee was certain of election. From that fact it might be inferred that among the sure districts for each party there were many in which the organization was so strong that no aspirant dared challenge its man in the primary while in many others the organization was so weak that a primary fight could occur. Figure 17, in which a series of primaries was analyzed, compels a revision of the inference about organization control of the primaries. A primary contest does not occur in the sure districts every two years but in most of these districts a primary contest occurs now and then. This fact suggests that in most of the safe districts the organization either is not strong enough to prevent occasional serious challenge of its man in the primary or perhaps that the organization uses the primary to settle its internal disputes. A look at several primaries in a row, at least in this instance, modifies the inference of organization invincibility that might be drawn from the absence of contest in a considerable number of districts at a single primary.

2. The Primary and the Persistence of Partisanism

The salient fact that emerges from our analyses is that competition for popular primary endorsement tends to concentrate in the districts relatively "sure" for one party. The primary procedure, to a varying extent, transfers popular interest as well as the reality of popular decision from the general election to the primary of the party that has the advantage in voting strength in the district. These findings return us to the broad problem stated at the outset, viz., whether the primary, by changing the rules of the game, has had consequences for the informal organization of party and of power-seeking activity generally. Does the channeling of actual decision into the primary of the stronger party, by its impact election after election over a considerable period, alter the role and structure of the inner party cliques within the legislative districts; attract voter-interest to the primary of the party with the advantage in the general election; tend to bring into the ranks of the stronger party the politically ambitious; and perhaps lead to the atrophy of the informal district leadership once vested with the function of putting forward minority candidates?

While the location of the variations in incidence of primary competition provides material for discussion of such questions, their systematic testing encounters most difficult problems of analysis quite apart from the problem of obtaining relevant data. If consequences for informal practices flow from the primary, the chances are that they accumulate so gradually that they would be beyond capture by field observation unless it were prolonged for a generation. Yet some inferences may be drawn from the elections data.

If the attention of voters and the efforts of aspirants to leadership roles tend to be attracted to the primary of the majority party in legislative districts, the forecast would be that over time a larger proportion of districts would become "sure" districts. In a state in which districts were more or less normally distributed (i. e., a frequency distribution of districts according to party division of the general election popular vote assumed roughly the form of the normal curve), relatively more districts would become sure for both Democrats and Republicans. In a state with a skewed distribution of legislative districts, the proportion of sure districts would increase for whichever party had the advantage in safe districts at the outset. In either case the proportion of districts genuinely competitive between the parties would decline. The effects of these tendencies would be perceptible, of course, only in the absence of countervailing forces.

A test of these propositions appears in Figure 18, which compares the distribution of Missouri House districts according to the percentage division of the two-party vote in 1908, the first year of operation under the direct primary law, and in 1946, 1948, and 1950 combined. Observe that the distribution of districts became more widely dispersed between 1908 and 1950. At one end of the scale Republicans came to win, usually without contest, a block of seats; at the other end of the scale, the number of seats that went to the Democrats by default increased. The proportion of districts clustered about the 50-50 point declined. Whether the direct primary was the cause of it all, a point to be weighed shortly, a sharp change occurred in the period 1908-1950.

A word needs to be interpolated about the rationale for the comparison of two distributions so far separated in time. The

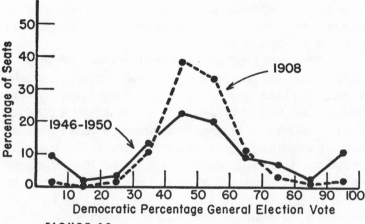

FIGURE 18

Decline in Party Competition Under the Primary: Distribution of Missouri House Districts, 1908 and 1946-48-50 Combined, According to Percentage Division of General Election Vote on Representatives

assumption is that informal habits of political action—the activity of organizational cliques, the loyalty of electors to party symbols, and so forth—are altered only gradually, if at all, by such matters as primary procedures. Patterns of political action have a very considerable durability. If this is true, the effects of the direct primary procedure on political practice become visible only after a political generation or so, not after an election or two. It is, of course, perilous to assume that the two distributions at 1908 and 1946-50 represent observations of two points in a

long-term straight-line trend. Such examination as was made of
the intervening period suggests that the change represented by
Figure 18 is secular.[9]

The broadened dispersion of Missouri districts between
1908 and 1948 shown in Figure 18 flows chiefly from the failure
of parties to put forward candidates in some districts, principally
districts in which their chances for victory are low. It seems quite
clear on the whole that if the parties nominated candidates in
these districts they would poll about the same proportion of the
popular vote as do the party candidates for President and for
governor in the same areas.

What seems to have happened is not so much that districts have become safer for one party or another in their popular
vote but that candidates have been put up less frequently when
the party can look forward to fairly certain defeat. A check on
this proposition may be made by comparing a party's presidential vote with its legislative votes in the districts with legislative
candidates. This relationship is shown for the 1948 Massachusetts election in Table 26. Although some divergence exists between the division of the vote for President and for legislator,
even with the Massachusetts office-bloc ballot a fairly close
agreement exists between the votes for the two offices. A similar
analysis of the 1948 Missouri election, in which the party-
column ballot was used, revealed an even closer matching of
party division of the vote for governor and for legislator in those
districts in which both parties had legislative nominees.

The broadened dispersion of legislative districts, such as
is recorded in Figure 18, flows primarily from a failure to put up

[9] The difference between the two Missouri distributions is accounted for in large measure by the growth in the number of seats uncontested at the general election. From 1908 to 1916 between 2 and 4 per
cent of the house seats went by default at each election. In 1918 a sharp
rise in the proportion of uncontested seats occurred and then the proportion of seats won by default settled down to a new plateau between 5 and
10 per cent of the total. In 1938, another abrupt upturn in the percentage
of uncontested seats took place—to a peak of slightly over 30 per cent—
and again the level settled down to another plateau in the neighborhood
of 20 per cent.

candidates rather than from a tendency of the voters to give legislative candidates a markedly different proportion of the vote than they accord to the party's candidates for higher office. An atrophy of party leadership manifests itself in many districts in a

TABLE 26

Relationship Between Partisan Division of Vote for President and for Legislative Candidates in Massachusetts Single-Member Districts, 1948

DISTRICT'S DEMOCRATIC PRESIDENTIAL PERCENTAGE 1948	NUMBER OF DISTRICTS[a]	DISTRICTS WITH NO		DISTRICTS WITH LEGISLATIVE CONTEST, MEAN DEMOCRATIC PERCENTAGE OF POPULAR VOTE ON LEGISLATOR
		DEMOCRATIC LEGISLATIVE CANDIDATE	REPUBLICAN LEGISLATIVE CANDIDATE	
10-19	1	1	0	
20-29	4	4	0	
30-39	15	7	0	39
40-49	27	13	1	41
50-59	15	0	1	59
60-69	12	0	1	65
70-79	15	0	6	67
80-90	7	0	6	73

[a] *Only 96 of Massachusetts' 240 House members are chosen from single-member districts.*

failure to put forward candidates. This state of affairs exists not only in districts overwhelmingly attached to one party or another but also in districts in which minority legislative candidates would poll quite respectable votes and even on some occasions have a chance to win. The chances are also that the districts that show up in this analysis—those without enough of a party apparatus to turn up a candidate—differ only in degree of party decay from other districts in which the party has a self-appointed candidate. If so, our indicators detect only a part of the disintegration of party that has occurred.

Another check on the question of whether voter desertion or organizational atrophy underlies the widening dispersion of legislative districts may be made by considering the data re-

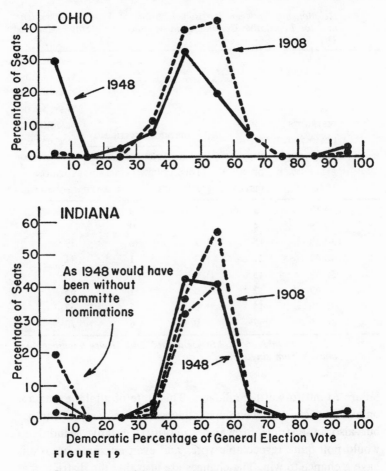

FIGURE 19

Pre-Primary and Post-Primary Contrasts: Distribution of Single-Member House Districts, 1908 and 1948, Ohio and Indiana, According to Party Division of District General Election Vote for Representative

corded in Figure 19 concerning the single-member districts of Ohio and Indiana for 1908 and 1948. The distributions for these states are of considerable interest because they suggest an entirely unexpected clue to the nature of the relation between primary and party organization. They give us a lead toward a solution of our broad problem. The contrast between the 1908 and 1948 Ohio distributions resembles that previously shown to exist between similarly separated Missouri distributions. The Ohio distribution, however, curled up only at the Republican end of the spectrum which reflects in part a difference between the party systems of Ohio and Missouri. On the other hand, the Indiana distribution changed comparatively little between 1908 and 1948. It flattened out somewhat but in 1948 a large proportion of the districts remained in the 60-40 range in general election vote (83.1 per cent against 93.2 per cent in 1908), i. e., they were carried by a ratio of 3 to 2 or less. Figure 19 also provides a minimum measure of the effect of party organization in maintaining the 1948 Indiana distribution close to that of 1908. Shown there is the form the 1948 Indiana distribution would have taken if one regarded as uncontested those districts in which the nominee was named by party committee rather than by primary.[10]

The contrasts between the Indiana and Ohio patterns suggest a reformulation of our notions about the bearing of primary procedures on the vitality of informal party groups and cliques. Indiana nominates its state legislative candidates by direct primary; its candidates for governor, United States Senator, and other statewide offices, by state convention. Ohio, on the contrary, nominates for state as well as for local offices by direct primary, although it uses conventions to draft platforms. The necessities of state nominating convention operation may stimulate the maintenance in all localities of party leadership cliques with at least the capacity to round up delegates to the state con-

---

[10] Undoubtedly in both states there occurred nominations by primary which resulted from draft or designation by party committee. The Indiana procedure segregates at least some of such nominations.

vention. A delegate from a county 20 per cent Democratic weighs as heavily as one from a county 80 per cent Democratic. Thus stimulated, the activity of party cliques may carry over into the recruitment of legislative candidates. On the other hand, similar external forces may not sustain the same degree of inner-core activity in all districts when a state nominates for state office by direct primary.[11] The hypothesis, thus, might become that the atrophy of local or district party cliques derives not solely from local factors but more significantly from the erosion of the organizational superstructure that once linked local minorities to central points of power within the state. Or, conversely, that local minority cliques once gained vitality from their linkage with state leadership and from the functions they performed vis-à-vis that leadership.[12]

If the primaries so far dissected are representative, minority party cliques in sure legislative districts have tended to decay since the introduction of the direct primary. The vexing problem is how to establish whether the primary had anything to do with that development. From the beginnings of the primary to the present a variety of other factors have been operative, all of which might be supposed to have had some effect on the system of informal groupings which make up a "party."

If party atrophy in legislative constituencies is associated with statewide and local nomination by primary, the same sort of local decay of leadership cliques would not occur in states that retain the convention system for both state and local nominations. Since the use of the primary is so widespread, comparative

[11] If this theory is correct, the 1908 and 1948 distributions of New York legislative districts should resemble those of Indiana, for New York also nominates for important statewide offices by convention. Although the 1948 New York distribution curls up somewhat at the extremes of the scale of party strength, this turns out to be the result of dual nominations of the same candidates by both parties, mainly in the Bronx, presumably by interparty negotiation. The New York data, hence, conform to expectation.

[12] Compare, on the national scene, the historic reasons for being of Republican "machines" in the southern states: to control national convention delegations and to dispense patronage. Or, consider the role of Democratic organizations in the northern New England states.

experience from convention states is scarce. Connecticut, although it adopted a modified version of the primary in 1955, remained a more or less simon-pure convention state until that time. Its record may be laid alongside the data thus far presented. Figure 20 shows the distribution of Connecticut legisla-

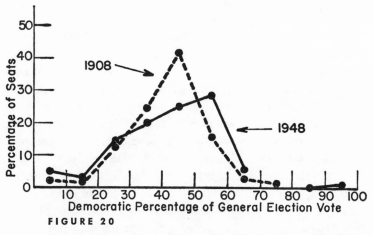

FIGURE 20

Sustained Party Competition for Legislative Seats: Distribution of Connecticut House Seats According to Party Division of District General Election Vote for Representative, 1908 and 1948

tive seats according to the party division of the general election vote in 1908 and 1948. While the 1948 distribution, in comparison with 1908, flattens out a bit, it does so only in parallel with the shift in general party complexion of the districts as measured by their presidential vote.[13] Moreover, the proportion of seats in the 40-60 range in 1948 differs very little from that of 1908. If attention is centered on the districts carried by one or the other party by default, striking differences appear between Connecticut and Indiana and the other states on which data have been presented. The proportions of seats uncontested at the general election were as follows:

[13] That is, a pair of distributions of the Connecticut districts according to their presidential vote in 1908 and 1948 resembles the distributions according to legislative vote shown in Figure 20.

	1908	1948
Connecticut, all seats	2.4%	4.8%
Indiana, all seats	1.0	5.0
Indiana, single-member districts	1.4	7.6
Ohio, all seats	1.8	18.5
Ohio, single-member districts	2.6	32.1
Missouri, all seats	1.4	21.4

In these contrasts, the Connecticut distributions reflect the least movement of districts into the uncontested category. In Indiana, which retains the state nominating convention but uses the primary for local nominations, the rise in the proportion of uncontested seats has been comparatively small. On the other hand, in those states in which both state and local candidates are nominated by primary, sharp rises have occurred in the proportions of seats won without general election contest.[14]

In the absence of contrary explanations for these different tendencies, they could be attributed to the effects of the direct primary and, perhaps more particularly, to the statewide primary with its reduction of the necessity for the maintenance of going local party cliques in all counties for the operation of the state nominating convention. The problem then becomes one of whether an explanation other than the institutional one can be found for the differences in behavior of Connecticut and the full-fledged primary states. A genuinely rigorous demonstration of the association between primary procedures and organizational decay

[14] The 1948 Connecticut figure reflects in part the fact that in some rural towns the Democrats could muster only one candidate when two seats in the house were to be filled. Comparable New York figures for the two years are zero and 13.3 per cent. The uncontested 1948 seats were principally the result of dual nominations. If it is assumed that without the availability of this nomination procedure such seats would have been contested, 0.7 per cent of the 1948 seats went by default. In 1908 in Massachusetts 19 per cent of the single-member-district seats went by default to one party or another. By 1948 this percentage had increased to 42. Data on the presidential vote by legislative district are not available for 1908 to permit a check on the question whether a marked realignment of partisan division may have had some bearing on the decline of party competition for legislative seats. In Iowa in 1908, 1.9 per cent of the seats of the lower house were uncontested at the general election; in 1948, 31 per cent went by default.

requires the exclusion of all other explanations of the differing behavior of the two types of states. This step, it ought to be made most explicit, represents the crucial stage of the analysis. If it is conceded that interparty competition occurs quite generally when statewide nominating conventions are employed and considerably less generally when both state and local nominations are made by primary, the question remains whether some factor other than nominating procedure accounts for the differences. Since no means exists to determine whether all the other possibilities have been excluded, findings based on such reasoning must remain provisional.

An alternative explanation of the growth in the numbers of districts in which only one party puts up a candidate could be that a long-run partisan realignment has created many more districts in which the minority cause is hopeless. Perhaps in our primary states the movement of population and the shifts in partisan loyalties have created many more solidly one-party districts. Meanwhile, in the convention states the demographic trends may not have been such as to destroy the bases for party competition in many districts.

While population movement has occurred and partisan realignment has taken place, these factors do not seem to explain the occurrence of many uncontested legislative races. At any rate, among districts with like divisions of the presidential vote a much higher proportion is now uncontested in state legislative elections than was the case earlier. Illustrative are the following comparisons of the incidence of election by default in single-member districts in Ohio in 1908 and 1948:

DEMOCRATIC PERCENTAGE PRESIDENTIAL VOTE	1908 DISTRICTS		1948 DISTRICTS	
	# TOTAL	% UNCON-TESTED	# TOTAL	% UNCON-TESTED
30-34	3	33	2	100
35-39	12	0	11	67
40-44	14	0	26	38
45-49	19	0	23	13

Thus, in this array of districts, in only one did the Democrats fail to run a candidate in 1908, a district with less than 35 per cent of its presidential vote Democratic. In 1948 in a goodly number of districts with a stronger Democratic presidential vote, Democrats allowed the legislative seats to go by default to Republican candidates.[15]

In Missouri the figures show a similar contrast between 1908 and 1948. Districts that in 1908 had competing Democratic and Republican legislative candidates frequently had only a single candidate in 1948, although the division of their presidential vote at the two points in time was similar. The conclusion seems clear that if there were enough of a party organization in each district to bestir itself to put up a candidate and to campaign a bit, the current distributions of legislative districts according to the division of the popular legislative vote would more nearly resemble the distributions according to presidential strength in the districts.

Several other explanations, in addition to nominating practices, could be offered for the differences between 1908 and 1948 legislative distributions. Thus the introduction of the popular election of United States Senators may have eliminated centers of state leadership that took steps to assure that a legislative candidate ran in almost every district. While this constitutional change probably was of significance for the organization of state politics, had it been controlling, the Connecticut party organization would have atrophied in a manner similar to the state organizations in states using the direct primary. Another explanation, and one more difficult to cope with, is the theory that the

[15] As might be expected, in parallel with the decline of party competition for legislative posts an increasing proportion of county offices has come to be filled without contest between opposing party candidates. The changes in the proportions of county offices filled by default in those Ohio counties with the indicated percentages of presidential vote Democratic in 1908 and 1944 are as follows:

PER CENT DEMOCRATIC	COUNTY OFFICES FILLED BY DEFAULT	
	1908	1944
35-39	17%	53%
40-44	10	37
45-49	3	28

informal structure of the Connecticut party system has always had a strength exceeding that of the other states with which it has been compared. Otherwise the Connecticut organization would not have been capable of preventing the imposition of a mandatory direct primary system while other state organizations succumbed to the demand for reform. Unless the retention of the convention system alone be regarded as proof, the supposition would be extremely difficult to test.[16] Another possibility is that over the past forty years those groups disposed to seek office and those groups able to support office-seekers have gravitated toward the Republican party. No one is left, so the argument goes, to run for office in many districts under the Democratic banner even though there may be a good many Democratic voters left. If this were the explanation of the tendency in the primary states, the same sort of trend would also probably exist and be felt in Connecticut. It is also possible that if such a movement of leadership strata has occurred, it may have been, especially among office seekers, at least in part a consequence of the primary system itself.[17]

[16] The Connecticut convention system is said to have persisted in part because of the fact that delegates in the Republican state convention have been apportioned in the same manner as the members of the lower legislative house. The small towns, greatly overrepresented, would lose advantage by the adoption of the statewide primary.

[17] While the governments of American states are notable for their surface similarities, even the most cursory examination unearths persistent peculiarities in their informal political organization and practice. The basic question here comes down to whether some feature of Connecticut, independent and separate from the convention procedure, operates to maintain an informal political order different from that of the primary states. One reader suggests a variation on the demographic theory tested in the text, viz., that the changing demography of the primary states oriented the rural districts toward antimetropolitanism. Given a degree of independence between national politics and state legislative politics, that sentiment of antimetropolitanism reflects itself in a lack of party competition for legislative seats in these districts even though they may have a substantial minority vote in gubernatorial and presidential elections. In Connecticut, on the other hand, the demographic fact of a sprinkling of smaller cities rather than a dominant metropolis or two has not provided the conditions for so high a degree of antimetropolitanism. The hypothesis is difficult to test. If it were correct, the Indiana and New York 1908-1948 distributions should behave as do those of Missouri and Ohio, but they do not.

3. *Popular Nominations: Influences on Majorities and Minorities*

The data make it difficult to reject the hypothesis that the creation by direct primary legislation of new channels to power, more readily accessible and less readily monopolized than antecedent procedures, operates over the long run to modify the nature of the informal structure of party leadership in biparty systems. The inferences about the effects on informal party structure have, to be sure, been based largely on the indirect evidence of the presence, absence, or performance of candidates. That evidence deserves weight on the principle that where there are no bear tracks there are no bear. Yet the conclusions should be limited to the type of situation examined and perhaps even to the specific cases studied.

1. The transfer, to considerable extent, of the actual popular choice to the majority party primary probably has brought a basic change in the role and structure of the inner party leadership within the majority party in such legislative districts. Such a conclusion must rest on the assumption that in pre-primary days inner party cliques had a relatively free hand in nominations. That state of affairs must be contrasted with the genuine competition for popular favor that appears at majority party primaries, although the level and regularity with which it is sustained differ from district to district with factors such as closeness of the general election vote. The data tell little about the workings of party cliques within majority districts, other than that if or when they exist they do not ordinarily operate without at least occasional serious challenge. Related questions on which the data throw no light are whether the shift from competition between candidates of parties to that between candidates within parties brings with it alterations in the nature of the issues of campaigns, in the conduct of campaigns, in the relation of legislators to their party group in the legislature, in the nature of the choice presented to the electorate, and so forth.

2. The direct primary leaves a clearer trail in its ef-

fects on the minority party. Over the long run there seems to be associated with the primary a tendency for the district party cliques and leadership in the minority party to atrophy. The comparative analysis suggests that a critical factor underlying this drying up of local leadership is not the local primary alone but the combination of the local primary with the alterations in the structure and place of state leadership involved in the abandonment of the state nominating convention. This special case of organizational atrophy may be subsumed under the more general proposition that institutional decay follows deprivation of function.[18] The loss of the biennial responsibility of going to the state convention to take a hand in the important business of selecting the statewide candidates left the leaders of district minorities with very little to do.

3. These two broad effects combined alter the nature of political competitors, if not the character of the process of political competition itself. The transfer of actual choice to majority primaries, to the extent that it occurs, affects the monopoly of opposition enjoyed by the minority party, which, Schattschneider asserts, "is the most important asset of the second party." [19] The function of opposition comes to be carried out in considerable measure by candidates within the majority party primary. If carried to its extreme, this process would destroy the minority.[20] More commonly what has happened is that the atrophy of leadership of the minority party leaves it less well equipped to perform the function of governance at critical moments when it is willy-nilly swept into office.

[18] Institutions are hard to kill but survival bereft of function tends to be associated with a metamorphosis of mission, as when an ancient and honorable volunteer fire company lives on to sponsor an annual ball and to appear in festive costume on ceremonial occasions.

[19] E. E. Schattschneider, *Party Government* (New York, 1942), p. 82.

[20] One is puzzled why in small constituencies forces set in motion by the primary do not draw practically all voters into the primary of one or the other of the parties at least for local purposes. The organizing influence of gubernatorial and presidential politics may maintain a bipolarization that has its effects in a modicum of party identification vis-à-vis local candidates even in the smallest constituencies.

4. Prudence dictates some hedge about the method of analysis and the interpretations that flow from it. Given the complexity of the sort of political phenomena with which we are concerned, it would be a wise conjecture that the institutional variable is only one of a bundle of factors or causes explicative of the contrasts that appear in different states and in the same state at different times. Variations in the proportions of these unidentified variables might even on occasion produce results that diverge from those in the states examined here and thereby lead to the identification of factors significant but not perceived in the situations examined here. An increase, for example, in the effort devoted to the development and maintenance of a state-wide integrated party system might offset institutional depressants of party life that operate when such effort remains more or less constant.

Chapter 7

Party and Plural Executive:
The Lottery of the Long Ballot

Among political systems of the world the governmental structure of the typical American state is a curiosity. The popular election of the governor accords, of course, with the presidential pattern, but the election also of several lesser executive and administrative officers adds a feature which is paralleled in few, if any, governmental units of comparable size and importance. The selection by popular vote of such officers as attorney-general, comptroller, treasurer, auditor, and secretary of state is a vestigial survival of Jacksonian democracy. In its inception the practice represented a departure from the custom dating from colonial times of designation of these officers by the legislature. The popular choice of minor executive officers first took root in the states of the West in the 1830's.[1] In the East the Jacksonian formula of popular election gained attractiveness from the supposition that it would cure abuses associated with legislative choice of these officials. The position of the legislature as an electoral body gave it powerful leverage in the extraction of patronage from executive officers.[2]

[1] A. N. Holcombe, *State Government in the United States* (New York: Macmillan, 1916), pp. 89-92.
[2] New York, for example, by its constitutional revision of 1846 sought to eradicate the abuses of the Albany Regency by transferring from the legislature to the electorate the power to choose minor officials.

The new system of popular election, however, had its own set of side effects. Along with related actions, it created a multi-headed leadership of state government consisting of officers each constitutionally independent of the governor and under no legal compulsion to collaborate, either with the governor or among themselves, in the achievement of state policies. For forty years the architects of orderliness in state governmental structure have struggled to reform this ungainly apparatus.[3] In this endeavor they have achieved a considerable success. Minor state elective offices have become both less numerous and relatively far less important in the whole range of state operations; the great expansion of state functions of recent decades has occurred mainly in departments headed by appointees of the governor. Nevertheless, the anachronistic multiple executive remains and becomes at times a block to effective administration; at others, a haven for incompetence; and, on occasion, a means for obstructing the evident majority will.

The immediate object is not an examination of the administrative consequences of the independence of popularly elected minor offices. The purpose is, rather, to ascertain how the party system has adapted itself to the tasks imposed upon it by the existence of a large number of offices to be filled by the vote of the people of the entire state. In the more exuberant elaborations of its role, the American party system is credited with the function of imposing an informal order and coherence upon an unintegrated governmental structure. The ties of party loyalty and the compulsions of common cause, so the supposition goes, induce extralegal collaboration among legally independent officials in the prosecution of the public business. We need not worry about formal organization of government; the necessities of the party cause will compel the politicians to work together. While this sort of informal unifying influence does prevail to some extent,

---

—New York Bureau of Municipal Research, *The Constitution and Government of the State of New York, An Appraisal* (New York: 1915), pp. 30-31.

[3] See Leslie Lipson, *The American Governor* (Chicago: University of Chicago Press, 1939).

its existence requires the election of both governor and minor officers of the same party. That type of electoral result, in turn, demands of the voters a habit of choice in terms of party rather than of individuals and of the parties a capacity to put forward slates of candidates of a character to justify adherence to that habit.

1. Fate of the Party Ticket: Extent of Split Election Results

The electorate evidently does not work on the theory that it should employ the cohesive element of party to unify an unintegrated state administrative apparatus. In fact, governor and minor state officers often wear different party labels. An examination of the extent to which a single party fails to carry its entire slate into office and the circumstances associated with this sort of split control will give some insight into the role of party in relation to state government.

In about one-half of the elections in which a governor goes into office by a narrow popular margin, candidates of the opposition party win some or all of the minor state offices. At least, this ratio of split results prevails in the states here analyzed. The narrower the popular margin by which a governor wins office, the greater is the probability that the opposition will carry some or all of the races for minor statewide offices. Conversely, the wider the gubernatorial margin, the greater is the likelihood that all the winners of the minor office races will be, at least nominally, affiliated with the governor's party. All these conclusions are underpinned by the data in Table 27, which shows, for nine states for the period 1900-1952, the relation between the outcome of gubernatorial elections and of simultaneous elections of minor officials chosen by statewide vote. Most of the states whose records are analyzed in the table often have had, especially since 1930, fairly close party competition. Hence, extension of the table's coverage to all states would doubtless show larger proportions of governors winning elections by wide margins, with concurrent victories by all their running mates.

The relations between the closeness of party competition and the completeness of party control of the multiple executive, shown in Table 27, have droll consequences for the doctrine of party accountability for the conduct of administration. In an even larger proportion of elections than is indicated by the table, which gives inadequate representation to the sure states, Republican and Democratic, the dominant party is rarely threatened in its possession of both the governorship and all minor offices. It is when parties face the weakest opposition that they are likely to be least cohesive and, hence, to have the least capacity

TABLE 27

Relation Between Size of Gubernatorial Pluralities and Outcomes of Simultaneous Elections of Minor States Officials in Nine States, 1900-1952[a]

PER CENT 2-PARTY VOTE FOR GOVERNOR	NUM- BER OF GUBER- NATO- RIAL ELEC- TIONS	RESULTS OF SIMULTANEOUS ELECTIONS OF MINOR OFFICERS					
		ALL FROM GOVERNOR'S PARTY		ALL FROM OPPOSITION PARTY		DIVIDED BETWEEN PARTIES	
		#	%	#	%	#	%
50.1-52.4	58	32	55.2	12	20.7	14	24.1
52.5-54.9	49	30	61.2	5	10.2	14	28.6
55.0-57.4	40	35	87.5	0	0.0	5	12.5
57.5-59.9	23	23	100.0	0	0.0	0	0.0
60.0-62.4	18	18	100.0	0	0.0	0	0.0
62.5-64.9	8	8	100.0	0	0.0	0	0.0

[a] *The states covered are Illinois, Indiana, Iowa, Massachusetts, Michigan, Missouri, Ohio, Rhode Island, Wisconsin. The table rests on an analysis of all statewide offices including, when chosen on a party ticket, judicial offices, but excluding presidential electors and United States Senators. Most common were officers such as lieutenant-governor, comptroller, treasurer, and attorney-general, all being the more or less standard basic equipment of American state government. The other officers were most diverse in title and ranged from state geologist to university regent.*

to tie together the work of the scattered agencies of government. No doubt the widest variety prevails in actual practice among the states in which one party is dominant. Examples are common in which a minor office comes to be held on something of an informal career basis by a man who becomes so well known that he wins the primary readily and his victory in the general election is only a formality. At another extreme, in Louisiana Democratic factions designate slates of candidates for all statewide offices in the primary and voters seem to support factional slates about as consistently as voters in two-party states support party tickets in the general elections. In any case, whatever order and coherence develops within the administration in one-party situations must rest on some factor other than the tie of party. When one party holds both governorship and minor offices without effective challenge, the incentives for collaboration among fellow partisans are not apt to be strong.

When parties compete most nearly on even terms, the impulses toward cohesion within the party leadership are most exigent. Competition induces discipline in warfare against the common enemy. Yet it is precisely under these circumstances of the highest party discipline that some or all of the minor offices are most likely to be held by the party in opposition to the governor. Some, or even all, of the minor offices are beyond the integrating power of the governor's party, whether that influence be beneficial or otherwise. In short, a party in unchallenged control of all executive posts is apt to be too weak to impose an order over the independent offices. When party bonds become strong enough to have meaning, a single party often is unable to place its nominees into all the offices.

Incidentally, under conditions of close party competition a multiplicity of elective offices sets in motion forces which, under some circumstances, may offset the compulsions toward unity within the party leadership. When elections are closely contested and the results are in doubt, the individual candidate may be tempted to differentiate himself from the ticket in the public eye. The option of differentiation is no doubt open more frequently to senatorial and gubernatorial candidates than to candidates for lesser state office, although some holders of minor posts succeed in establishing their names advantageously in the public mind. The frequency of division of statewide posts between parties in close elections, as it appears in Table 27, reflects to some extent the effects upon party fortunes of this consequence of the governmental structure for individual candidate behavior.

2. Determinants of Deviations from Party Regularity

Often the division of the various elective officers between different parties is attributed to a more or less rational estimate by the electorate of the relative qualifications of individual candidates without respect to their party affiliation. To charge the electorate with the task of screening the long list of obscure candidates for obscure offices places upon it a trying chore. Yet instances may be cited in which an individual candidate has managed to achieve such notoriety for incompetence that the good voters threw him out of office while returning all his fellow partisans to the statehouse. And in other instances minor officeholders gain a reputation, sometimes deserved, for doing a passable job and the electorate rewards them by re-election as it sweeps out of office all the rest of the party's slate.

While a theory of fine electoral discrimination accounts in part for the splitting of governorship and minor executive offices between the parties, other factors are more frequently responsible. Various uniformities of behavior exist which suggest broader explanations. Some further analysis of the data of Table 27 will lead to more inclusive explanations of deviations from party regularity.

Republican gubernatorial candidates happen to go into office with a full complement of Republican minor officers much more frequently than Democratic gubernatorial candidates manage to carry their slates to victory with them. This difference prevails consistently at different margins of gubernatorial popular victory, but it is most marked in the closer gubernatorial races.

In the states and elections covered by the analysis reported in Table 28 about five out of six Republicans winning the governorship by a narrow margin (50.1 to 52.4) carried the entire Republican minor office ticket with them. On the other hand, only about one out of five Democrats with comparable margins of victory had the same good fortune. As the size of the gubernatorial plurality increases, the relative advantage of Republican over Democratic governors in this respect declines.[4]

The easy explanation of the greater Republican success in putting its candidates into minor office along with its governors would be that the GOP on the average offered better men and the electorate responded accordingly. A better, and more general, guess might be that under the conditions of American politics the lesser of the two major parties, whether it be Republican or Democratic, encounters exceptional difficulty in carrying a full slate into office. How may this hypothesis be tested? The states analyzed in Table 28 were, with an exception or so, "normally Republican," or they moved during the period covered by the table from that status to one in which their politics became more competitive. What would be the results of minor-office races in "normally Democratic" states, enough of whose voters became sufficiently exasperated to elect a Republican governor? Although in most of the South the memory of no man runneth to the

---

[4] The election of some minor officers for terms shorter than that of the governor, or at times other than that of the gubernatorial election, introduces another complicating factor. An analysis was made of the elections in those states of our group (Illinois, Indiana, Michigan, Missouri) that elect some or all minor offices in off years, that is, in years when no gubernatorial elections are held. At some elections governors carried into office at the time of their election all their party's minor-office slate. In only about two-thirds of the immediately following off-year elections did the governor's party elect all its candidates for minor office. Of those elections in which minor offices filled simultaneously with the governorship were divided between the parties, about one-half were followed by an off-year sweep by the governor's party of all minor offices. Republican governors who went into office with their entire ticket had to work relatively less frequently with opposition minor officers chosen at the next off year than did Democrats who had been elected with a full slate of their own party. Similarly, Republicans had a better chance to convert an on-year defeat or division of the minor slate into a clean sweep at the off year.

time when a Republican governor was chosen, the evidence such as it is, suggests that if states in that area began to elect Republican governors now and then, these governors would not uniformly carry their fellow Republicans into minor office.

The evidence consists of bits of experience from several border states, which may be regarded as "normally Democratic." Republican candidates won the Maryland governorship in 1912, 1934, 1950, and 1954, but all the minor officers elected simultaneously were Democrats. In 1927 Kentucky elected a Republican governor but filled the eight minor offices with Democrats; in 1943, however, the Republican gubernatorial candidate took into office with him seven of his party's eight minor-office candidates. In 1910 and 1912 Tennessee elected a Republican governor along with a Democratic railroad commissioner, the only other statewide elective officer. In 1920 the Republican candidate for governor of Tennessee won by a comfortable margin of 43,000 votes while the Republican railroad commissioner edged into office by a plurality of only 1300 votes.

TABLE 28

Proportions of Gubernatorial Elections, in Relation to Division of Popular Vote, Accompanied by Sweeps of All Minor State Offices by Candidates of Governor's Party: Nine States, 1900-1952[a]

PER CENT 2-PARTY VOTE FOR GOVERNOR	REPUBLICANS			DEMOCRATS		
	NUMBER OF GOVERNORS	MINOR-OFFICE SWEEPS		NUMBER OF GOVERNORS	MINOR-OFFICE SWEEPS	
		#	%		#	%
50.1-52.4	31	26	83.9	27	6	22.2
52.5-54.9	26	21	80.8	23	9	39.1
55.0-57.4	25	23	92.0	15	12	80.0
57.5-59.9	18	18	100.0	5	5	100.0
60.0-62.4	12	12	100.0	6	6	100.0
62.5-64.9	8	8	100.0	0	—	—

[a] *The coverage of states is identical with that of Table 27.*

Some common misfortune evidently is shared by Democratic candidates for minor office in states that have been more or less normally Republican when Democratic gubernatorial candidates win and by Republican candidates for minor office in Democratic states that happen to elect Republican governors. Whether any single source of misfortune leads to these similar results may be doubted, but the facts suggest some partial explanations. The special role of the governor in our politics accounts in part for the divergence between results of elections of governors and elections of other officials. The prominence of the governor in the field of public attention and the tendency of popular discontent and hope to center upon him often make candidates for that office either weaker or stronger than the general strength of their party, if such a generalized party following may be supposed to exist. Crusades tend to form behind personalities, not parties. Similarly, scorn and disfavor more easily find a focus on the governor than on the party slate as a whole. Consequently the gubernatorial vote has a relatively mercurial quality.

Closely associated with this position of the governor is the popular conception of party. The average voter's conception of party is difficult to surmise, but from the data it is clear enough that the electorate has only a weak conception of party as an instrument for the accomplishment of broad social ends through the collaboration of officers of government. If voters by and large had such notions, they would vote differently. When they wanted to throw the rascals out, they would throw all of them out and thereby give them greater incentive among themselves to restrain their rascality.

Some verification of these propositions comes from another analysis of the data. Tables 27 and 28 conceal some sharp differences over the decades in the capacity of gubernatorial candidates to carry their running mates into office with them in the states analyzed. Democratic candidates for governor have become more successful in carrying their entire slate with them while Republican gubernatorial candidates have become less so. The contrasts between the periods 1900-1920 and 1922-1952 emerge from the details in Table 29.

Before commenting on these contrasts, which will provide a clue toward the explanation of split election results, it is in order to note that the data of Table 29 have a bearing on the suggestion that the position of special prominence of gubernatorial candidates helps to account for divided control of the multiple executive. In the period 1900-1920 the characteristic deviation from straight-party voting seemed to be the election of a Democratic governor along with a complete slate of Republican minor officers. Some of these instances occurred in 1910 and 1912 and were often associated with the Progressive-Standpat rift among the Republicans. Others, however, illustrate our remarks about the capacity of individuals to attract popular followings not transferable to their party associates. The tabulation includes, for example, Massachusetts' election of W. S. Douglas, Brockton shoe manufacturer, he of reform inclinations and a famed mustache, as Democratic governor in 1904 along with Republicans for other offices. In the same cell of the table falls the 1904 election in Missouri of the Democratic candidate, J. W. Folk, who had gained national attention by his prosecutions of boodling in St. Louis, and the simultaneous defeat of the remainder of the Democratic state ticket.[5] Mr. Folk's exploits had given currency to the belief that he was the only honest Democrat active in Missouri politics.

Evidently in one type of situation, which was more common earlier but still arises from time to time, a crusader or an appealing figure could build a strength in excess of that of his party and win the governorship, a lone Democratic victor surrounded by triumphant Republicans. In the later period a Democratic gubernatorial candidate, although he might win by the same margin that a Democratic governor polled in the earlier decades, had a far better chance to go into office with all or some of his partisan running mates. The converse of this change on the Democratic side was an increase in the later period of the fre-

---

[5] The present generation, I find, is unfamiliar with the term boodling: roughly, it denoted graft on a heroic scale.

quency with which Republican governors failed to bring their entire slate into office on their coattails.[6]

These changes over time suggest that in these states a

TABLE 29

Governors and Minor State Officers in Nine States: Contrasts Between 1900-1920 and 1922-1952 in Success of Governor in Carrying His Party Candidates for Minor Statewide Posts into Office with Him[a]

			NUMBER OF ELECTIONS WITH MINOR OFFICES—		
PER CENT 2-PARTY VOTE FOR GOVERNOR	PERIOD	NUM-BER OF ELEC-TIONS	ALL TO GOVER-NOR'S PARTY	ALL TO OPPOSI-TION PARTY	DIVIDED BETWEEN PARTIES
Republican					
55-59	1900-20	26	26	0	0
	1922-52	17	15	0	2
50-54	1900-20	28	27	1	0
	1922-52	29	20	1	8
Democratic					
50-54	1900-20	18	2	12	4
	1922-52	32	13	3	16
55-59	1900-20	3	2	0	1
	1922-52	17	15	0	2

[a] *This table analyzes the same elections as does Table 27. Doubts may be raised about the interpretations based on this table because it includes elections at which the same party was continued in control of the governorship as well as those at which this office changed hands. The latter type of election might be supposed to provide the better test of the capacity of a party to carry its slate. Another analysis of 15 states restricted to elections at which the governorship changed from one party to another shows the same sort of relationships that appear in this table.*

[b] A factor that may have some bearing on the differences between the two periods is that in the second period the full consequences of the direct primary began to be felt. Because of the vagaries of the direct primary, a larger number of odd characters stimulative of electoral discrimination, may turn up on the general election ballot. Recent instances doubtless occur to most readers of persons who, by accident of name, manage to obtain the primary nomination and are regarded by all hands as a drag on the ticket.

shift in the underlying balance of power between the parties has occurred. Earlier the Democrats could muster enough strength to carry a governor's race now and then. Later they developed a more generalized sort of strength that enabled them to compete on more even terms for all statewide offices. Gubernatorial victories alone may come from circumstances quite peculiar to the individual and the situation, but a victory for the entire slate indicates a deeper permeation of the electorate by an attachment to the party. When this deeper attachment divides the electorate close to the 50-50 mark, the circumstances are such that split election results occur more frequently. What seems actually to exist in the case of a party gaining in strength over the long term is something of a set of strata of party attachment paralleling the ladder of officialdom. By growth to one point a party may carry the governorship. Another step upward in party strength brings to effectiveness another layer of support adequate to carry some of the minor offices. Further consolidation of party position raises to the point of effectiveness electoral strata sufficiently attached to the party label to carry the entire slate into office.[7]

Another check on our interpretation of the behavior of the electorate when confronted by a multiplicity of candidates for executive office develops from the notion that perhaps over the past half century voting independence has gradually grown among the voters. That idea turns out, on examination of the

[7] It might be supposed that the splitting of minor offices between the parties is largely a function of the advantage enjoyed by incumbents whose names have become recognizable by the electorate. While incumbency is an element, the advantages associated with it account for only a part of the phenomenon. The point is illustrated by an analysis of the sixteen elections from 1922-52, noted in Table 29, in which Democratic governors won by 50-54.9 per cent of the vote but whose election was accompanied by a split of the minor offices. Of the nine Democratic incumbent minor officers seeking re-election, 89 per cent were returned, a ratio that might be expected in "Democratic" years. The Democratic non-incumbent candidates managed to win 28 per cent of the 29 races against incumbent Republican candidates. Of the 31 contests unembarrassed by incumbency on either side, Democrats won 48 per cent. Thus, when the factor of incumbency is squeezed out the minor offices were divided about half and half, a result resembling that which would have occurred had the choices been determined by a series of tosses of a coin.

data, not to fit the complexities of the realities. Perhaps the ties of voter to party have become weaker, but the test applied produces results more consistent with the general interpretations already advanced than with the supposition of a gradual elevation of the capacity of the electorate to discriminate among candidates.

If the factors conducive to straight-ticket voting have been in a long-term decline, the dispersion of the total votes cast for candidates on a party slate would probably have undergone a parallel increase.[8] A test of this supposed relationship appears in the graphs in Figure 21 which present changes in the index of dispersion of votes for candidates on the Republican and Democratic slates in Massachusetts and Missouri for half a century. An explanation of the arithmetic underlying the index may be in order. The basic figures for the index are the votes polled by each of a party's candidates at an election. The average vote per candidate is then figured for each party. The difference between the vote of each candidate and the average for all is obtained. Then the average deviation from the mean for all candidates may be calculated. For example, on the average eight Democratic candidates polled 100,000 votes each. Their actual individual vote ranged perhaps from 90,000 to 110,000. On the average they deviated, say, 5,000 from the mean of 100,000. The index of deviation then becomes, in effect, 5 per cent, which would be relatively the same dispersion as in another situation in which the average vote was 200,000 with an average deviation of 10,000.

With this explanation in mind, examine the graphs in Figure 21. Note that the Massachusetts Republican graph reflects a gradually increasing relative spread of the vote for Re-

---

[8] This expectation has implicit within it the assumption that the frequency of stimulus or occasion for splitting tickets had either remained constant or perhaps had also increased. A decline in "party loyalty" would not be reflected in the indicated measure—vote dispersion —if the occasion for or the inducement to split tickets declined in frequency or in force. Presumably, without provocation to split tickets the weakest sort of party loyalty might result in similar votes for all the candidates on the ticket.

publican candidates.[9] To this graph a straight line has been fitted by the method of least squares, not with the suggestion that the underlying change should be regarded as linear but to indicate more sharply the direction of change. While the Massachusetts Republican graph shows a clear trend, the Democratic series is erratic especially in its earlier years.

The Massachusetts Democratic curve really reflects the sorts of differences earlier noted in contrasting the periods 1900-1920 and 1922-1952. In the earlier period extremely sharp

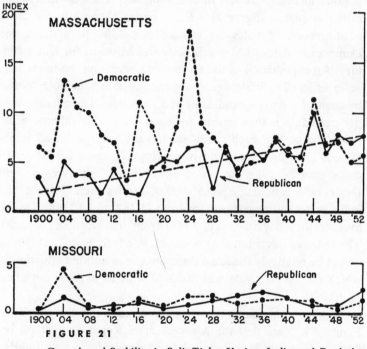

FIGURE 21

Growth and Stability in Split-Ticket Voting: Indices of Deviation of Absolute Votes for Statewide Republican and Democratic Candidates in Massachusetts and Missouri, 1900-1952

[9] The presidential and senatorial votes are included in the computations as well as those for governor and other statewide officers. It might be supposed that a widening spread between presidential and other votes accounted for the trend, but a computation which excluded presidential and senatorial votes produced about the same trend line.

fluctuations occur in the Democratic index. The peaks usually occur at years when a Democratic gubernatorial candidate ran far ahead of his colleagues; that margin produced a high index of dispersion. In later years the Republican and Democratic dispersion curves fluctuate roughly together; one becomes almost a reflection of the other; the parties are competing on fairly even terms although neither is able to muster its full strength for all its slate. Presumably if general Democratic strength continued to grow, the party's index of dispersion would decline in reflection of a capacity to deliver about the same vote to all candidates after the fashion of the behavior of the Republican curve in the earlier period covered by the graph.[10]

The tendencies in the other states analyzed—Wisconsin, Iowa, and Ohio—resemble the record of Massachusetts, as it appears in Figure 21, and apparently reflect similar underlying changes in the relative positions of the parties. In Missouri a radically different sort of pattern in vote dispersion appears, as Figure 21 shows. The Missouri index shows no long-term trend but remains relatively stable over the entire period. A peak occurs in 1904 in the election mentioned earlier involving Governor Folk but otherwise a high degree of straight-ticket voting seems to be the normal practice. Missouri has maintained a fairly close party competition over a long period. All candidates, in comparison with other states at least, receive about the same vote, although the division of the electorate is from time to time so near the 50-50 point that a slight net splitting of tickets can and does give the governorship to one party and minor offices to another. The contrasts in vote dispersion between Massachusetts and Missouri may be attributable in some measure to the difference in ballot forms, office bloc and party column. Since the ballot form in Massachusetts remained the same over

[10] The reader with arithmetical insight may raise the question whether the trend in the Massachusetts Republican index series might not be due to a tendency for an increasing proportion of voters to fail to mark the ballot for minor offices, which would spread the votes for candidates over a wider range. In fact, the Massachusetts data show a fairly stable ratio of total minor office vote to total gubernatorial vote.

the entire period, the trend in the Massachusetts series can not be plausibly charged to the ballot form.[11]

3. Consequences of the Divisibility of the Executive

It is possible to regard with considerable equanimity the oddity of state governmental systems that permit control of governor and minor offices to be divided between the parties. Most minor elective administrative officers are entrusted with minor responsibilities, and most of the time states manage to get along well enough despite the eccentricity of their constitutional arrangements. Yet governmental mechanisms should be designed for the exceptional situation, the time of trial, rather than for untroubled days, and it is precisely in the exceptional situation that the prevailing arrangements manifest their potential consequences. And they gain significance also as a part of a larger constellation of institutional forms, each of which contributes to the same broad results.

In the large a multiplicity of independent elective offices

[11] In an attempt to measure the effect of ballot form, my research assistant, Mr. H. D. Price hit upon an interesting incidental consequence of ballot form. The office-bloc ballot evidently handicaps the minor-office candidates of the party whose adherents include the larger proportion of poorly educated voters. Massachusetts in 1888 adopted the Australian ballot in the office-bloc form to replace, effective with the election of 1889, ballots provided privately by parties.—*Acts and Resolves,* 1888, ch. 436. With the election of 1889 the Democratic minor-office vote dropped sharply in relation to the Democratic gubernatorial vote, whereas the Republican minor candidates continued to poll about as large a vote as the head of their ticket. The average minor-office vote as a percentage of the gubernatorial vote for each of the parties follows for a series of elections:

Year	1885	1886	1887	1888	1889	1890	1891
Republican	100.2	100.2	102.4	103.0	103.4	99.8	101.1
Democratic	100.7	100.0	97.3	97.6	89.2	90.0	88.6

While factors other than ballot form doubtless contributed to this spread between the vote on minor office and on governor, the timing of the appearance of the spread strongly points to the ballot reform as differential in its partisan incidence over the short-run at least. However, in the period 1930-1950 the difference between the parties in the spread between gubernatorial and minor-office votes had disappeared. By this time the differences in educational level of Republican and Democratic partisans had sharply declined.

obstructs party government and thereby obstructs popular government. Our inspection of the data suggests that party competition for public favor should not be considered so much as a struggle election after election with a real probability on each occasion of an overturn of the party in power. Rather a pair of types of situations have been identified of a different character from the common stereotype of a struggle of continuing uncertainty. These patterns of action, as the electorate gropes for expression, need to be kept in mind in assessing the effect of the system on popular government.

In one of these types of situations the general prospect is for one party to remain in control save for most infrequent victories by the opposition. On occasion a drive for reform, an urgent demand for action, or some other special set of circumstances agitates the electorate. Sufficient support is centered on a gubernatorial candidate to put him into office, but so poorly articulated is the system that the crusader finds himself obstructed by his minor-office associates of the opposition or by an opposition legislature.[12]

In a second type of situation the multiplicity of executive offices tends to retard a long-term shift of the balance of power between the two parties. The lesser party evidently tends to gain first the governorship and perhaps a part of the minor offices and only slowly to build up sufficient strength to capture all the offices. At such times, control by the old majority of minor posts may become of new and special importance both in providing a base for partisan in-fighting and a source of sustenance for the faithful.[13] This possibility of holding power points within the government may well retard the rise of a party long in a minority position. It often also provides opportunity by

[12] Illustrative were the relations between Democratic Governor Culbert L. Olson, of California, and his Republican attorney-general, Earl Warren. See R. E. Burke, *Olson's New Deal for California* (Berkeley: University of California Press, 1953), pp. 71-72, 105, 194-99.

[13] For example, in Michigan in 1954 the Republican members of the state administrative board (which consists of the governor and the principal elective state officials) volunteered to serve as a "truth team" to oppose Democratic Governor Mennen Williams' bid for re-election.

which the older majority, through its control of a gerrymandered legislature, may frustrate a governor of an emergent party by the assignment of administrative powers to elective officers not in partisan alliance with the governor.[14] In a sense, under the prevailing procedures a party can win an election without winning working-control of the government. And at times a party may in fact lose an election without losing control of the government. That so bizarre a system is tolerated must be indicative of a rather low-temperature politics in the states.

The two classes of situations that have been described do not, of course, cover all instances of divided control. Nor has the discussion treated all the practical problems associated with such a division. The possibility, for example, of the election of a lieutenant-governor of the party in opposition to the governor creates a special type of problem in the event of a succession to the governorship or when the lieutenant-governor is called upon to act temporarily for the governor. In proposing that the New York governor and lieutenant-governor be jointly elected, as are the President and Vice-President, Governor Thomas E. Dewey in 1953 observed that the election of a governor and lieutenant-governor "politically opposed to each other involves serious problems. As a practical matter the Governor must encounter difficulty in leaving the State even for a short period and on

---

[14] Thus, in 1941 the Indiana Republican legislature sought to deprive Democratic Governor Schricker of power by the transfer of responsibilities to the Republican lieutenant-governor and to various boards not under gubernatorial direction. The state supreme court held the action void as an attempt to "usurp functions which are normally and generally understood to be the functions of a Governor, and vest them in minor administrative officers." See R. F. Patterson, *The Office of Lieutenant-Governor in the United States* (University of South Dakota, Governmental Research Bureau, Report No. 13, 1944), p. 12. An institutional gadget that gives more directly the power to a gerrymandered legislature to frustrate the general sentiment is the election of minor executive officers by the legislature. The consequence is virtually assignment to one party by constitutional law of the right to fill these offices. Among the states in which the legislature elects some or all such officers are Maine, New Hampshire, Maryland, and Tennessee. The problem created for party government by these arrangements is suggested by the election in Maine in 1954 of Democrat Edmund S. Muskie as governor along with a Republican legislature which chose the minor executive officers.

pressing public business. This has created the greatest embar-
rassment in other states, to the damage of public confidence in
government and the injury of the public interest." Governor
Dewey's proposal makes more sense in New York, with its convention nominating system not dissimilar in its operation from
the national conventions, than it would in those direct primary
states in which the designation of the nominee for the second
place on the ticket may be a most fortuitous process.

The architecture of the executive branch of state governments has incidental effects on the recruitment of top party
leadership. Given the factors that permit candidate differentiation, those minor officers whose names become widely known
by their appearance on drivers' licenses or other such docu-
ments of general distribution at times are able to poll a mighty
vote to overcome swings against their party. Such officers, even
when they are only most moderately endowed, often begin to
picture themselves as statesmen or great tribunes of the people
and become formidable, even successful, aspirants for senatorial
or gubernatorial nominations. While examples are numerous,
mention of the candidacy of Joseph Ferguson, former Democratic state auditor of Ohio, against Robert A. Taft, for the
Senate in 1950 will give concreteness to the general observations.[15]

The existence of a multiplicity of statewide elective offices tends to introduce divisions into party leadership. Presumably the maintenance of a modicum of collaboration within the
ranks of party leadership is an essential of party government.
Yet a multiplicity of elective offices creates incentives for politicians to assay the role of the lone wolf. The design of governmental mechanism, if party government is a desideratum,

[15] The same set of facts may be used to justify the existence of
minor statewide elective offices as a means for the recruitment and development of leaders. In practice, according to the findings of Joseph A.
Schlesinger, the degree to which such offices are stepping-stones to the
governorship differs greatly among the states. Of those governors who
have advanced from minor statewide elective office, about three-fourths
have come from the lieutenant-governorship and often after service in the
legislature. See his *The Emergence of Political Leadership: A Case Study*

should be calculated to induce politicians to labor in common cause and to compel them to accept common risks of responsibility.[16]

In its total effect, the institutional ensemble of which the elective minor offices are a part complicates and obstructs popular decision. While the existence of independent minor elective offices makes difficult the enforcement of "party accountability" and the exercise of "party responsibility," perhaps the greater significance rests in the obstruction of popular decision by making difficult clear-cut choices of alternative governing groups. In serene days, to be sure, a governor of one party may co-exist quite peacefully with minor officers of another, but often divided administrations occur in times of dissatisfaction and turmoil when it is fairly clear that the prevailing sentiment is toward a change of direction. The institutional arrangement under analysis evidently conspires to make difficult the accomplishment of that change through the party system.

---

of American Governors (MSS Dissertation, Yale University, 1954). From a larger view, it might well be preferable to encourage recruitment of leadership from the legislature. Insofar as the institutional situation may influence routes of advancement, elimination of minor elective offices might have that effect.

[16] On a priori grounds one may develop enthusiasm for ballot forms that stimulate straight-ticket voting on the assumption that one sour apple might induce the voter to take the simplest course and throw out the entire barrel. Party leadership then would exert itself to present a slate of more nearly uniform quality. If and when leadership cliques have such an inclination, they are mightily handicapped by the direct primary which, on occasion, produces most extraordinary nominees. A classic example is provided by the nomination by Massachusetts Democrats in 1954 of John Kennedy as their candidate for state treasurer. Kennedy, a most minor clerical employee of a safety razor company, happened to have the same name as the junior United States Senator, and the name Kennedy is powerful medicine in Massachusetts politics. Kennedy won the primary nomination in a contest against the aspirant endorsed by the Democratic pre-primary convention. The Democratic State Committee swallowed its astonishment and in its campaign literature characterized Mr. Kennedy's political success as "typically American." Mr. Kennedy, it was said, had caught the "imagination and interest" of his fellow citizens and his election would "afford proof that in Massachusetts democracy works and that Americans invariably draw their best talent for leadership from the rank and file of the people." Mr. Kennedy won.

Chapter 8

Electoral Foundations of State Parties

For decades American state governments have supported a flourishing profession of experts on the design and construction of governmental apparatus. In the main, these specialists in their diagnoses and recommendations have not gone far beyond the forms and procedures of the administrative structure of state government, a matter admittedly worthy of attention. Yet such a definition of mission excluded from attention some of the more fundamental issues of popular government. All the problems of the party system—the recruitment of leaders, the maintenance of responsiveness and responsibility, the assurance of opportunity for popular choice—have been in the main outside the domain of the experts on state government.

In their disinclination to tackle such matters the experts have undoubtedly been prudent and perhaps even wise; for those who would construct or remodel political systems must deal with the most immalleable materials. The party system of a state—or whatever set of practices fulfills the purposes of a party system—is not the creation of a day. Its form bears the imprint of events long past and its practices are often dictated by customs of long-forgotten origin. Further, the form and orientation of the parties reflect differing modes of life among the peoples of the state, powerful in their capacity to project their image upon the political system and stubborn in their resistance to change. Party systems evolve; they are not made. The form and character of political systems reflect the pattern of the heritage through which they are extruded into the present, as well as the insistent determinism of the environment from which they draw their strength at the moment.

Such observations should serve adequately to discourage all save the most hardy persons from concerning themselves with the institutions of popular government. Yet political systems do evolve and adapt themselves to new necessities, not from some inner instinct for survival, but from the application of ingenuity and effort by men. To suggest what the would-be reconstructor of political leadership would encounter, as well as to indicate something of the nature of the party systems in the states, a few of the recurring characteristics of the American state parties may be explored. The description of the political system of a single state in all its ramifications would require a volume. The object at this point is only to attempt to identify a few aspects of the social foundations of parties and to suggest some of their significance for the form and nature of political leadership. Earlier chapters have dealt chiefly with the institutions and procedures through which the forces of politics operate. At times those chapters may have conveyed the impression that forms and practices existed quite independently of their social setting. Here the focus will be on types of electoral groupings that act through the institutional forms of state politics.

1. *Accidents of Birth and Migration*

Modern popular political parties, in contrast with party systems composed of squabbling factions of notables, rest on foundations of support by groups of voters. The composition, the interests, the passions, and the aspirations of these blocs of voters tend to fix the style of politics and the policy orientations of the leadership echelons of the parties. Whether leaders manipulate their followers or only attempt to anticipate their movements and keep a few steps ahead of them is a question gravely disputed by the philosophers. Whatever the answer, if any, may be, the character of the groupings that exist within the electorate profoundly conditions the form and nature of political leadership.

While the partisan divisions of voters on questions of state politics by and large parallel the cleavages in presidential voting, the proportions of the components of the political mixture within each state differ in greater or lesser degree from the proportions in the nation as a whole. The peculiar combination of ingredients within each state contributes to the conformance or divergence of the pattern of the state from that of the nation as a whole.

Among the elements that make up state electorates are some strange sorts of blocs of voters, groups that exist for reasons not clearly associated with the political issues of the day. These blocs of voters, some Republican, some Democratic, were deposited by two great streams of westward migration, that from New England and the northeastern states, and that from the states of the South. The westward travelers carried their partisan loyalties with them and the paths they followed can even today be traced on the maps of party voting. The areas of southern settlement appear as regions of relatively strong Democratic attachment while loyal Republicans continue to inhabit the territories taken up by their Whig and Federalist forebears. The steady impact of the political events of a century has, of course, gradually worn down the ancient deposits of party loyalty. The partisan lines between the descendants of the southerners and of the New Englanders becomes more and more blurred, yet they remain to provide one of the ingredients of the politics of some of the states. As migration reached the Rockies and the Pacific the streams of settlement became mixed. Migrants to these areas doubtless brought their politics with them but areas of Democratic settlement are not often sharply separated from areas of Republican settlement. If the old loyalties persist, they are hidden from easy view.

The significance of the traditional partisan loyalties tempered by the Civil War remains most notable, of course, in the party systems of the states of the Solid South. The upper New England states are the Republican counterparts of the Solid South, although in these states the old-time Republicanism has been diluted by immigration and by the cleavages introduced by industrialization. In the Border States and in the states of the Old Northwest where the streams of sectional migration met, the patterns of partisan loyalty deposited by these streams can still be identified although their practical significance in the total configuration of forces in state politics varies considerably from place to place. In Indiana, the areas of settlement from the South, generally in the southern part of the state, continue to constitute an important element of the Democratic party of the state while the northern rural counties, peopled more largely from the Northeast, remain in the main Republican strongholds.[1] In Missouri, outside the cities the principal areas of Republican and Democratic inclination may be traced back to the days of settlement. The "Little Dixie" counties, along the northern banks of the Missouri, were settled early by southerners and along with the Delta counties, peopled more recently by southern cotton growers, constitute important elements in the Democratic party of the state. On the other hand, the Ozark counties, with their population drawn from the Republican hill counties of Tennessee and Kentucky, and the counties of the northwestern part of the state, with a population drawn from Iowa and other such states, provide a bloc of rural support for the Republican party of the state.[2]

The contribution of transplanted partisan attachments to the construction of the party system of a new state finds neat exemplification in the comparatively recently settled state of

[1] The question has been explored intensively by Frank Munger, *Two-Party Politics in the State of Indiana* (MSS dissertation, Harvard University, 1955).

[2] These relationships have been traced through in detail by John Fenton, *The Political Dynamics of the Border States* (MSS dissertation, Harvard University, 1955).

Oklahoma. Withheld in the main from settlement until the 1890's, it was pressed upon from the North by the westward stream of people of Republican persuasion. Across its southern boundaries people of Democratic inclination eyed its undeveloped acres. In 1889, 1891, and 1892 heavy population movements into the lands that now make up the state of Oklahoma occurred. In 1890 the combined population of Oklahoma Territory and Indian Territory was 270,000; by 1900 it had reached 790,000. In another ten years it mounted to 1,660,000.

The newcomers brought with them the political attachments of the sections from which they had come. Kansas made a heavy contribution to the early influx from the North. A severe drouth in western Kansas in 1887 stimulated movement from the Kansas plains across the border to the new lands of Oklahoma. From the South, Texans and other southerners made their way into the southern part of the state. When the lands in the center of the state were opened the two streams of migration, from North and South, met.[3]

The political precipitate of the process of settlement of the state appears in the pattern of partisan division in Oklahoma today. While the Republican party has never won the governorship of the state, it polls a substantial vote, a vote drawn in large measure from those areas that became Republican by the settlement of Republican farmers from Kansas and elsewhere. The concentration of Republicans in the northern half of the state and of Democrats in the southern half shows up clearly in the map in Figure 22, which indicates the division of the gubernatorial vote, by counties, in the 1946 race between Democrat Roy J. Turner and Republican Olney F. Flynn. The mechanisms that perpetuate such a pattern of politics doubtless involve more than a simple inheritance of partisan loyalties. Different types of agriculture dominate the two parts of the state. The existence of a cotton economy in the southern half of the state doubtless contributes to the maintenance of a

[3] See Edwin C. McReynolds, *Oklahoma: A History of the Sooner State* (Norman: University of Oklahoma Press, 1954).

community of interest and attitude between the southern Okla-homans and the older South. The north central and northwest-ern sections of the state are devoted in large degree to wheat farming as are the lands of Kansas to the north. The traditional Republicanism of the northern half of the state has also been re-enforced more recently by new recruits from the petroleum industry.

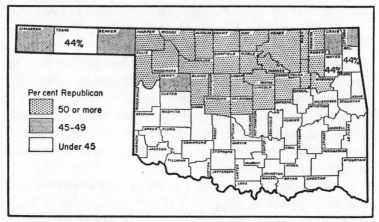

FIGURE 22

Partisan Patterns Left by Streams of Settlement: Republican Per-centages of Oklahoma Gubernatorial Vote, 1946

Insofar as a Democratic-Republican cleavage exists in Oklahoma it rests in rather high degree on the traditional and inherited vote which persists roughly in the pattern laid down by the movement of settlement. In the older states the tradi-tional patterns have become both somewhat obscure and less important as an element in the total state political situation in which they occur. Illinois is an illustrative case which both indi-cates a degree of persistence of the traditional pattern and the manner of its modification by later developments.

Two streams of population movement contributed to the early settlement of Illinois. From New England, New York, and the East, newcomers arrived by way of the Erie Canal and the Great Lakes and occupied northern Illinois. From Kentucky, Tennessee, and other states of the South, new arrivals came to people the southern half of the state. In the disputes of the years before the Civil War both northerners and southerners generally sympathized with their folks back home. When the war came sentiment in Illinois was divided North against South in a miniature of the nation as a whole. The outbreak of hostilities brought talk in southern Illinois Democratic journals of a division of the state to permit the southern counties to join their brethren in the Confederacy. After all, Cairo, the chief city of Egypt, as the southern tip of the state had come to be called, was further south than Richmond. Though there was no open rebellion, southern Illinois supplied some volunteers for the Confederate armies and was a center of Copperhead activities.[4]

Today the popular conception of Illinois politics is that of Democratic and metropolitan Chicago arrayed against a rural, Republican downstate. Yet Illinois outside of Chicago is not all of the same piece politically. The rural areas of the state show varying proportions of Democratic strength, and these variations in partisan division are roughly related to the sectional origins of settlement. Democrats are more numerous in the southern-settled counties of the state while Republicans have their greatest strength in the north. Only a few southern counties regularly return Democratic majorities, but a shift of a few percentage points in a good Democratic year makes many of these counties Democratic. In contrast, the rural counties of the northern half of the state remain staunchly Republican even when adversity is the lot of Republicans almost everywhere.

These relationships turn up clearly in the maps in Figure 23. The first map outlines roughly the areas of southern and nonsouthern settlement within the state.[5] The two other

[4] A. C. Cole, *The Era of the Civil War: 1848-1870* (Centennial History of Illinois, Vol. III, Springfield: 1919), p. 302.

[5] The data on which the map is based are not entirely satisfactory indicators of sectional origin. The map is based on the proportions of county population born in Kentucky, Missouri, Tennessee, and Virginia

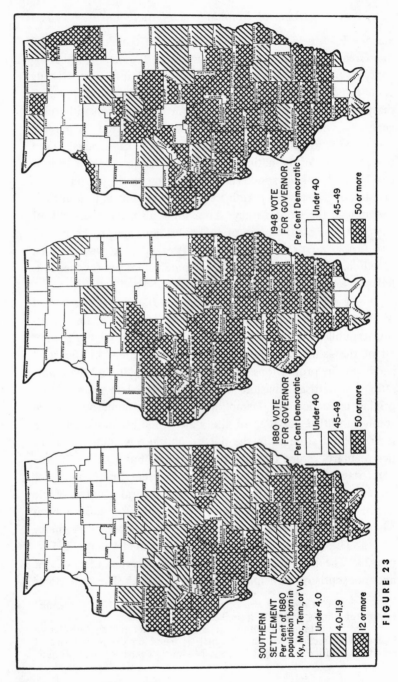

SOUTHERN
SETTLEMENT
Per cent of 1880
population born in
Ky, Mo., Tenn., or Va.

☐ Under 4.0
▨ 4.0–11.9
▩ 12 or more

1880 VOTE
FOR GOVERNOR
Per Cent Democratic

☐ Under 40
▨ 45–49
▩ 50 or more

1948 VOTE
FOR GOVERNOR
Per Cent Democratic

☐ Under 40
▨ 45–49
▩ 50 or more

FIGURE 23

Residue of Traditional Voting: Areas of Southern Settlement in Illinois and Vote for Governor in 1880 and 1948

maps in the figure show the distribution of counties of heavy Democratic strength and of those of Republican inclination over the state. One indicates the pattern of voting in the gubernatorial election of 1880 (Republican S. M. Cullom versus Democrat Lyman Trumbull) and the other shows the voting in the gubernatorial election of 1948 (Republican Dwight Green versus Democrat Adlai Stevenson). In both elections the correlation between the centers of rural Republican and Democratic strength and the pattern of settlement appears clearly enough.[6]

The map of the 1948 vote makes obvious the modifications that the original sectional pattern has undergone. The growth of the industrial cities and the parallel growth of the Democratic vote in these cities make the rural Democrats definitely a junior partner in the Democratic party. In 1948 about 60 per cent of the Democratic vote of the state came from Chicago's Cook County in contrast with 14 per cent in 1880.[7] Similarly, the Illinois industrial counties across the river from St. Louis have become centers of Democratic strength of greater weight in the following of the party than might be inferred from

---

as reported by the census of 1880. The census thus records the presence in a county of the survivors of the early wave of settlement and of late-comers. It is probably safe to assume, however, that the areas so identified were generally the places in which southern settlers tended to concentrate.

[6] It is an amusing indoor sport to search out possible explanations for the departures from such patterns as those appearing in the maps in Figure 23. Note, for example, Edwards County, a staunch Republican county, in southeastern Illinois. Its county seat, Albion, was founded in 1818 as part of an English colony. The colonists, anti-slavery in sentiment, consisted generally of persons who could be regarded as well off and well educated, at least in comparison with their neighbors. The counties at the southern tip of the state, strongly Republican in both 1880 and 1948 despite their southern heritage, formed part of the congressional district represented before the War by John A. Logan, of Williamson County, "the little Egyptian giant." A fire-eating southern sympathizer before the War, "Black Jack" Logan reversed himself to become a general in the Union Army, the darling of the Grand Army of the Republic, and Republican boss of the state in the generation following the Civil War.—Cole, *op. cit.*, pp. 279, 327-328, 396.

[7] Over the same period the proportion of the Republican gubernatorial vote from Cook County increased from 17 per cent to 50 per cent.

the map alone. While maps such as those in Figure 23 accurately record variations in the division of party strength from county to county, they can easily be misconstrued if it is forgotten that population density differs widely from county to county.

Most of the states in which the traditional rural vote, with the roots of its partisan orientation in the Civil War period, bulks large in the electorate are definitely one-party states, either in the South or in upper New England. In such states the relatively high degree of partisan homogeneity throws the political conflict back into the primaries of the dominant party and the nature of the significant political cleavages must be sought along lines other than party lines, insofar as state politics is concerned, the traditional vote is nominal rather than controlling. The traditional vote of Civil War origin plays a different role in those two-party states in which it remains sufficiently large to affect materially the tone of the politics of the state. Sectional conflict between agricultural regions with a commodity, rather than a class, orientation has contributed to the peculiar nature of the party battle in national politics. In those states in which distinctions between predominantly rural areas —distinctions based largely but not entirely on ancestry—play a role, the party system tends to share some of the characteristics of the national party system. The Indiana Democratic party, for example, draws its leadership from the lawyer-merchant-farmer classes of the areas of southern settlement as well as from the leaders of the new urban industrial classes. On the whole, the older elements of the party generate a conservative contribution to the leadership of the party. Similarly, the "Little Dixie" element of the Democratic party of Missouri serves to moderate the newer urban sectors of the party. In West Virginia, the so-called "Bourbon Counties," one-time areas of slavery, vie for position in the Democratic party with the coal miners. To a lesser degree in other states, such as Ohio and Pennsylvania, patches of rural Democracy survive to fly the banner of Jefferson in combination with the new urban and industrial elements of the party.

The strand of rural and small-town politics contributes a special color and tone to the American political system. Over considerable areas even yet such a politics is predominantly a one-party politics which is reflective of a highly integrated community life with a powerful capacity to induce conformity. In those areas party as such often has no meaning as a combination to fight the opposition. It is rather an expression, continued from generation to generation, of the consensus of a more or less undivided community or at least of a majority in such overwhelming command that it is unaware of any challenge to its position. Banker, merchant, farmer, lawyer, clerk, and workman alike bear in this community the Republican label and in that the Democratic. The politics of the locality is a politics of personality and of administration rather than a politics of issues. The issues have long been settled and the outcome embodied in a durable equilibrium of power and status within the community. Only when these centers, some Democratic, others Republican, meet in the politics of state or nation does an awareness of partisan difference develop. When they do meet, the substantive issues, insofar as there are substantive issues, tend to be conflicts of interests associated with territory rather than with class. Over the long pull the significance of this type of politics has been on the decline, yet it remains as an element of considerable importance in the politics of some states and it remains in sufficient quantity to give a distinctive quality even to national politics.

2. *Variation from Bipolarization Toward Political Homogeneity*

The patterns of partisan loyalties deposited by the flow of westward settlement, though modified by the erosion of passing events, remain as an element of the electoral foundations of the party system in some of the states. The heritage of the diverse origins of western settlement, however, persists most perceptibly in rural areas and has come almost everywhere to be matched, or more often, outweighed in significance by other characteristics determinative of the nature of the political system. The gradual induction into the political order of the newer European immigrants, who settled principally in the cities, added new dimensions to the bases of the state political systems. To this modification of the old order was added those changes produced by vast internal migrations from South to North, from country to city, from city to suburb.

In the demographic patterns of the states are to be found the raw materials with which politicians work in the construction of party systems. Conflicts of politics arise between country and city, between farm and factory, between rich and poor, between Protestant and Catholic, between early arrivals and recent immigrants, between descendants of the South and of the North. From such materials party systems are fashioned. The proportions and distribution of all these ingredients of political systems vary from state to state and those variations account in part for the differences in the political organization and practice of states. Other elements of variation are introduced by the contrasting political histories, traditions, and experiences of states which differ more than is commonly supposed to be the case.

In terms of the politically relevant characteristics of their population, states could be arranged along a scale from the maximum degree of political homogeneity to the highest degree of diversity. To carry out that exercise with exactness would be an involved task, but from the most limited observation it becomes evident that some states practice their politics on a rather low level of tension. They may have spirited contests for office, usually within the primary of the dominant party, but the minority party is too small to challenge effectively the more or less homogeneous majority. One-partyism, as measured by formal attachment to a single party, is by no means a satisfactory indicator of political homogeneity for within southern one-party states from time to time deep and abiding cleavages make themselves manifest in the primary vote.

If one arranged the states on the homogeneity-diversity scale the point would be reached at which political groups would be divided by deep and lasting differences, within, to be sure, the general framework of consensus on constitutional fundamentals. As politically significant diversity develops in the proper proportions it tends, outside a few rather peculiar one-party states, to reflect itself in a more evenly matched, more continuous, and often more spirited contest between the major parties. Diversity does not, of course, invariably lead to political dualism. It may well lead to a multiplicity of politically distinctive groups, yet on the American scene these groupings tend to be concealed through their consolidation within one or the other of the major parties.

In the popular lore of American politics great store is placed on two-party competition as a means for assuring to the electorate a choice between governing groups and, at least from time to time, a choice between broad philosophies of government. In national politics the two-party scheme rests on a foundation unique to the national scene; within the states, a variety of foundations for two-party competition exist and they differ greatly in the degree to which they provide support for such competition. It seems clear that a pair of conditions must be met if a dual organization of parties is to prevail within a state. First, within the electorate itself two major groups must exist with each possessed of the capacity to maintain a corps of political leaders. Such groups are, of course, the product of an interaction between the issues of politics and the characteristics of the people. Second, a substantial similarity should prevail between the divisions created among the people of a state by the issues of both national and state politics. If the issues of national politics, for example, tend most strongly to unite the people of a state, divisions on questions of state politics may be pushed back into the primaries of the state's major party in national affairs.[8]

The cleavage between metropolitan residents and rural

[8] This is essentially the argument of Chapter 2.

and small-town dwellers has become a most significant foundation for dual systems of state politics.[9] In large measure the issues of national politics of recent decades have re-enforced the
rivalry between metropolis and country over control of state
government. Metropolitanism and ruralism, of course, are broad
and deceptive terms that mask other differences that are probably more influential politically than is the fact that some people live in the city and others in the country. Nevertheless, the
urban-rural difference makes a convenient peg on which to
hang a discussion of factors that go into the make-up of some
types of state party systems.

    Cities and the Structure of State Politics.   Every newspa-
per reader knows that the great cities tend to be Democratic
strongholds while the small towns and the country are the hab-
itat of Republicans. This bit of political folklore contains a large
grain of truth, but it conceals as much as it reveals. The differences between metropolitan people and the outstaters form an
enduring basis for party competition but their impact on the
organization of state politics varies considerably from state to
state. Nor do people divide nearly so sharply along metropolitan
and nonmetropolitan lines as is often supposed.

    The metropolitan and nonmetropolitan basis for the or-
ganization of state politics appears most sharply in those states
in which a single great metropolis seems to dominate the state.
Under such conditions a bipolarization of attitudes may tend to
develop. The outstate has its anxieties about metropolitan domination, while the metropolis complains of the brakes on progress
wielded by the rural element within the state government. New
York, Illinois, and Michigan are states of the unimetropolitan
type. Each state contains, of course, centers other than the major
city which would rate as metropolitan in Kansas. Yet within
their own commonwealths the pre-eminence of New York City,
of Chicago, or of Detroit is hardly challenged. The sheer size of
these cities, not only in population but also in the industrial,

    [9] It is evident that the lively dualism of the Rocky Mountain
states has a different sort of foundation.

financial, and commercial affairs of their states, contributes a distinctive quality to the political systems of their respective states.

It may be said that the New York Democratic party is a party of New York City; the Illinois Republican party, a party of downstate Illinois; or that the Michigan Democratic party is a party of Detroit. The belief that such descriptions are correct may be widespread within these states and as popular beliefs they may be of genuine political significance. Yet such descriptions obviously overstate the reality. It would be more nearly correct to say that the center of gravity of the Illinois Democratic party rests in Chicago; that Michigan's Republican party leans especially heavily on outstate Michigan; and that upstaters have a powerful but not always decisive voice in the New York Republican party. In each of these states Democrats, to win the governorship, must draw heavily on the nonmetropolitan vote. Nor can Republicans carry a gubernatorial election without substantial metropolitan support.

These observations gain support by inspection of the ways in which the metropolitan and nonmetropolitan voters of these states divide. While the Democrats lead in the metropolitan centers and the Republicans are ahead in the nonmetropolitan areas, each party draws a large proportion of the total vote in the opposition stronghold. The partisan divisions of the popular vote for governor in recent elections within the principal city and within the remainder of the state were as follows:

	% DEMOCRATIC	% REPUBLICAN
New York City, 1950	53	47
Upstate	36	64
Cook County, 1952	52	48
Downstate	42	58
Wayne County, 1952	62	38
Outstate	42	58

These figures indicate the divisions within the metropolis and elsewhere but they provide no indication of how large the metropolitan vote bulks in the total state Democratic vote or of what proportion of the Republican vote comes from the non-metropolitan areas. Whether the leadership of a party looks to the city (or to the country) for 90 per cent or for only 10 per cent of its votes would presumably be a most significant indicator of the character of the party. In fact, no such extreme situation exists, but there are differences of lesser degree. In New York a Democratic candidate for governor receives about six out of ten of his votes from New York City while a Republican candidate must look to upstate for about six out of ten of his popular votes. Illinois Democratic candidates receive about six out of ten votes from Chicago while Republican candidates poll about one-half of their votes in Chicago and one-half downstate. Michigan Republicans, in recent elections, have been especially dependent upon the outstate vote. About 70 per cent of their vote has come from outside Detroit's Wayne County. Mr. Mennen Williams has drawn about half his votes from Wayne County. The exact figures are as follows:

		% FROM CITY		% FROM OUTSTATE	
		D	R	D	R
New York,	1946	64	42	36	58
	1950	57	40	43	60
	1954	57	30	43	70
Illinois,	1948	62	50	38	50
	1952	58	49	42	51
Michigan,	1948	48	31	52	69
	1952	48	29	52	71

The metropolitan-outstate cleavage tends to appear much more sharply in the legislative representation of the two parties than in the popular vote for governor. The fact that New York Democratic legislators consist overwhelmingly of New York City legislators and that New York Republican legislators are mainly upstaters doubtless helps create an exaggerated image of the state's politics as one of metropolis versus upstate. The same fact generates other problems for governors, both Democratic and

Republican, as well as problems in the management of statewide party affairs. The proportions of Democratic and Republican members of lower houses from the metropolis and from elsewhere in New York, Illinois, and Michigan are as follows:

		% FROM CITY		% FROM OUTSTATE	
		D	R	D	R
New York,	1950	90	11	10	89
Illinois,	1948	46	28	54	72
	1952	49	28	51	72
Michigan,	1948	67	2	33	98
	1952	74	3	26	97
	1954	70	3	30	97

The election of a large proportion of Democratic legislators from the cities and an excessive share of the Republican legislators from the smaller cities and rural counties results in part from the effects inherent in systems of geographical representation as well as from the manner in which the district lines are drawn. These effects, as may be noted from the figures above, are offset in Illinois by a system of cumulative voting in multi-membered districts. The Illinois system guarantees a substantial downstate Democratic representation and assures a goodly number of Chicago seats to the Republicans. Even so, downstate Republicans are predominant in the Republican group in the Illinois lower house.[10]

In the unimetropolitan states each party tends to be oriented toward the center of its greatest strength. Yet the cleavage between metropolis and outstate is not clear-cut. To win statewide elections each party must not only muster a maximum strength on its home grounds but must attract substantial support in opposition territory. Gubernatorial candidates must carry the

[10] With representation according to districts carried, rather than under the prevailing cumulative voting system, the 1952 Illinois election would have resulted in a Democratic legislative group with 87 per cent of its members from Cook County and a Republican group with 83 per cent of its members from downstate. On the Illinois arrangements generally, see George S. Blair, "The Case for Cumulative Voting in Illinois," *Northwestern University Law Review*, 47 (1952), pp. 344-357.

brunt of the task of bridging this gap for a large proportion of the office-holding echelons of the party leadership, legislators and local government officials, usually spring from the areas most strongly attached to the candidate's party, be it Republican or Democratic.[11]

In another group of states cross-currents are introduced into the pattern of metropolitan-outstate politics by the existence of pairs of metropolitan centers. In these bimetropolitan states rivalries between great urban agglomerations cut across and modify the simpler city-upstate cleavage of the unimetropolitan state. Examples of such states are California with its pair of urban concentrations around Los Angeles and San Francisco Bay, the latter itself divided between the principal cities of San Francisco and Oakland, Pennsylvania with Philadelphia and Pittsburgh, and Missouri with its St. Louis and Kansas City. With the exception of California, in these states the broad differences in metropolitan and nonmetropolitan political loyalties already identified tend to prevail. The divisions of recent gubernatorial votes in the combined metropolitan centers and in the remainder of the states were:

	% DEMOCRATIC	% REPUBLICAN
St. Louis-Kansas City, 1952	58	42
Rest of Missouri	50	50
Philadelphia-Allegheny County, 1950	54	46
Rest of Pennsylvania	46	54
Los Angeles-San Francisco-Alameda County, 1954	44	56
Remainder of California	42	58
Minneapolis-St. Paul, 1952	50	50
Rest of Minnesota	41	59

[11] In addition to the unimetropolitan states mentioned in the text several other states have somewhat similar patterns of politics although usually the population of the metropolis accounts for a smaller proportion of the total popular vote of the state. Colorado and Denver, Wisconsin and Milwaukee, Maryland and Baltimore are instances in point. Massachusetts might be classified with these states, but Boston must share position with a number of other cities of goodly size.

In the bimetropolitan states the metropolitan vote constitutes a substantial proportion of the following of the Democratic party. Yet in none of the states listed do the major parties differ quite so sharply in the sources of their support as they do in the unimetropolitan states. The figures, comparable with those presented earlier for other states, on the proportions of party gubernatorial vote drawn from metropolitan and nonmetropolitan populations are as follows:

		% FROM CITIES		% FROM OUTSTATE	
		D	R	D	R
Missouri,	1948	39	32	61	68
	1952	38	31	62	69
Pennsylvania,	1946	44	39	56	61
	1950	42	35	58	65
California,	1954	56	54	44	46
Minnesota,	1948	37	32	63	68
	1952	41	33	59	67

An inflation of urbanism within the Democratic legislative group and of ruralism within the Republican group, similar to that noted earlier for the unimetropolitan states, appears also in some of these states. Of the Democratic members of the Pennsylvania lower house elected in 1950, 54 per cent came from Philadelphia and Pittsburgh. On the other hand, 83 per cent of the Republicans came from outside these two centers. In 1950 Los Angeles County and San Francisco furnished two-thirds of the Democratic members of the California lower house.

The practical effects of the existence of a pair of metropolitan centers upon the organization of the politics of a state are generally to introduce lines of cleavage that cut across the simple metropolitan-rural division, although the degree and form of this criss-crossing vary from place to place and time to time. The rivalry of Los Angeles and the San Francisco Bay area in California politics is legendary. At one time within the Democratic party this took the form of wrangles between a conservative southern wing of the party and a more liberal northern wing.

In the Democratic party of Missouri, St. Louis and Kansas City leaders have vied for supremacy. In its hey-day the Pendergast organization of Kansas City called the turn. Some of the epic struggles within the Pennsylvania Republican party have been between political and financial interests based on Philadelphia and Pittsburgh. Minneapolis and St. Paul tend to move in opposite directions in Minnesota politics. The Irish Catholics of St. Paul give strength to its Democratic party while in Minneapolis a Scandinavian and Lutheran leadership pulls the city toward Republicanism.[12]

Although the states do not fall neatly into these types of metropolitan-rural patterns, another general sort of population distribution exists with its peculiar bearing on problems of state party organization. In the multimetropolitan state a handful of urban centers contain a large proportion of the vote. Instead of one or two major metropolitan concentrations, the urban vote is dispersed among a half dozen or so centers. Ohio and Connecticut may be placed in this general category, although marked differences exist between them. Cleveland's Cuyahoga County polls a huge vote but it by no means dominates the state. Connecticut's major centers are neither so large nor so varied in size as are those of Ohio.

When the urban centers of these states are grouped the familiar metropolitan-rural differences emerge. Eight urban counties of Ohio's 88 counties are grouped for comparison with the remainder of the state and six of Connecticut's more populous towns are grouped for contrast with the remainder of that state.[13] The divisions of the vote in the two sorts of territory in

[12] Roman Catholics, as reported by the 1936 *Census of Religious Bodies,* amounted to 29.8 per cent of the estimated population of Ramsey County (St. Paul) and only 13.3 per cent of the population of Hennepin County. In the 1948 gubernatorial election Ramsey was 57 per cent Democratic; Hennepin, 54 per cent Republican.

[13] The Ohio counties grouped are: Cuyahoga (Cleveland), Franklin (Columbus), Hamilton (Cincinnati), Lucas (Toledo), Mahoning (Youngstown), Montgomery (Dayton), Stark (Canton-Massillon), and Summit (Akron). The Connecticut towns grouped are: Bridgeport, Hartford, New Britain, New Haven, Stamford, Waterbury.

these states in recent gubernatorial elections have been as follows:

	% DEMOCRATIC	% REPUBLICAN
Metropolitan Ohio, 1952	59	41
Nonmetropolitan	52	48
Metropolitan Connecticut, 1952	58	42
Nonmetropolitan	44	56

In the 1954 Ohio elections, 62 per cent of the Democratic members of the lower house of the legislature came from the metropolitan counties. On the other hand, 72 per cent of the Republican legislators came from the nonmetropolitan counties, a proportion markedly higher than the nonmetropolitan contribution to the vote of the Republican candidate for governor. In Connecticut's senate chosen in 1952, the metropolitan towns elected 71 per cent of the entire Democratic group; the nonmetropolitan towns elected 82 per cent of the Republican group.

Metropolitan concentration probably makes for special difficulties in the organization and prosecution of a statewide politics. The effects tend generally to differ for Republicans and Democrats. Even in states with a single metropolitan center Democratic leadership, because of its metropolitan insularity and often because of the satiation of the rewards of metropolitan politics, falters in the development of programs and candidates with an effective statewide appeal. Multiplication of the number of urban concentrations serves to increase the practical problems of formation of leadership coalitions in support of statewide candidates and of collaboration in the maneuvers of politics. The state Republican parties, although hampered by the weight of their rural followings, tend to operate with the advantage of leadership elements dispersed throughout the state. They have, to be sure, large aggregates of voters in particular centers but urban leaders without majorities on their home grounds are apt to be more nearly as one among equals in the councils of state leadership than are those who command the control of metropolitan governments. Probably the organization and maintenance of a statewide politics—the focus of public attitudes on state questions and the organization of a state-wide party leadership —is a radically different problem in a state of relatively small political units, varying not so much in size, than in a state with huge concentrations of population and tremendous variation in the population of the basic units of political organization.

To some extent these differences in the partisan orientations of metropolis and upstate mask differences of national origin, confessional contrasts, and differences in ways of making a living. Yet these differences, like the partisan differences, are blurred. If a ready and feasible way were available to make the necessary systematic observations, it probably would be found that outside the major cities an antimetropolitanism, quite independent of the supposed occupational and class determinants of political attitude, exerts its effect on partisan alignments in state politics. Within the major cities a similar sort of localism against the outstaters may have an influence but probably a lesser one. At any rate the readily identifiable differences between metropolitan and nonmetropolitan populations are not invariably sharp, a state of affairs that is in part a consequence of the manner in which they have been defined for the purposes of this discussion. Fairly marked differences prevailed in the proportions of population foreign-born or of foreign-born or mixed parentage in 1930, an indicator of the relative importance of more recent types of immigration in the two populations. The percentages are as follows:

	METROPOLITAN	NONMETROPOLITAN
Illinois	63%	27%
Michigan	57	41
New York	73	46
Pennsylvania	51	32
Missouri	30	10

	METROPOLITAN	NONMETROPOLITAN
California	40	34
Ohio	40	18
Connecticut	71	60

Somewhat similar contrasts in religious affiliation prevailed at the time of the 1936 census of religious bodies. The figures, with reported church membership as a percentage of the estimated 1936 population, are:

	% CATHOLIC		% JEWISH	
	METRO-POLITAN	NONMETRO-POLITAN	METRO-POLITAN	NONMETRO-POLITAN
Illinois	25	12	9	0.3
Michigan	21	13	5	0.3
New York	21	26	28	2.8
Pennsylvania	29	20	11	2.1
Missouri	19	7	5	0.7
California	14	16	4	0.5
Ohio	20	10	5	0.2

The available occupational and economic statistics provide no simple and adequate measure of politically significant differences between metropolitan and nonmetropolitan populations, at least as we have defined those groups. Yet some simple contrasts, perhaps politically significant, may be shown to exist between the metropolitan and nonmetropolitan groups. The proportion of self-employed (a category ranging from owner-operators of factories, through farm operators, the professionals, independent merchants, to the peddlers) in the nonmetropolitan areas exceeds that in the metropolis. Similarly, the proportions of dwellings owner-occupied tends to be considerably higher in the nonmetropolitan sections of our states. The contention is not that these characteristics are determinative of political attitude; it is rather that the rate of incidence of these characteristics probably serves as an index of complex combinations of characteristics associated with partisan differentiations. For the record the contrasts on these points between the metropolitan and non-metropolitan populations, as defined earlier, were in 1950 as follows:

	% OF EMPLOYED SELF-EMPLOYED		% OF OCCUPIED DWELLING UNITS OWNER-OCCUPIED	
	MET.	NONMET.	MET.	NONMET.
Illinois	8	20	37	64
Michigan	7	17	58	73
New York	11	14	19	60
Pennsylvania	8	12	54	62
Missouri	8	31	42	67
California	10	27	51	58
Connecticut	8	12	32	62
Ohio	7	19	57	67

These broad differences in the composition of metropolitan and nonmetropolitan peoples underlie the differences between the major parties in most of those states in which the metropolitan-rural cleavage achieves political significance.[14] The divisions between the parties within the electorate do not, to be sure, follow exactly the lines between the recent immigrant and the older generations, the lines between Roman Catholic and Protestant, or the lines between wage earner and others. The coincidence of political cleavage and social cleavage is far from complete and local peculiarities of partisan alignment are legion. Yet the broad correlations do prevail.

These characteristics of party composition affect fundamentally the nature of the party systems of these states and, indeed, color American national politics. The relatively strong

[14] The gross data on the composition of metropolitan and non-metropolitan populations are, of course, not in a form to demonstrate connections between social characteristics and party affiliation. Those associations have been established, however, by a large number of detailed analyses of voting behavior. Yet even the aggregate characteristics shown in the tables are suggestive. Consider, for example, the fairly consistent similarities between California metropolitan and nonmetropolitan populations, in contrast with the wider differences between these populations in other states, and the deviate character of the California party system.

political dualism of the metropolitan-rural states derives vitality from the abiding, though sometimes subtle, differences between the followers of Republicanism and the cohorts of the Democracy. The separate psychological worlds of religions, the gulf in the understandings and in the ways of life of those of different national origin, and the separateness of manual worker and the white-collar and professional classes have formed lasting foundations for competition between political parties. A politics built upon such foundations becomes devoted peculiarly to the question of who is to rule, although from time to time great policy questions come to the fore to re-enforce—and occasionally to weaken—the partisan loyalties that may have had their origins fundamentally on nonpolicy grounds.

While the social characteristics—religious, economic class, national origins—of party groupings can be differentiated, it seems fairly clear that as partisan groupings develop they come to have an existence quite independent of the affiliations of their members with other social groups. The Republican inclinations of Protestants in the North and the Democratic leanings of Catholics fortunately do not depend on the current existence of lively substantive issues dividing them as Protestants and Catholics. Among nonterritorially defined groups, as among the northerners and southerners with partisan loyalties inherited from the Civil War, a process of acquisition and perpetuation of partisan loyalties operates. Irish Catholic immigrants in the eastern cities did not become Democratic because of any inherent consanguinity between Democracy and Irish Catholicism. They merely chanced to move into situations in which, in the main, Democratic machines welcomed—and perhaps at times exploited— them. On the other hand, the opposition rarely cultivated and often deliberately excluded them.[15] From time to time events

[15] The Republican machine of Philadelphia, unlike its counterparts in Providence and Boston, cultivated the Irish. Although the Republican loyalties of the Philadelphia Irish were sorely strained by the 1928 candidacy of Al Smith, the organization managed by heroic efforts to hold their support fairly well. See J. T. Salter, *Boss Rule: Portraits in City Politics* (New York: McGraw-Hill, 1935), pp. 102, 158-159.

hardened their partisan loyalties. The campaigns of the American Protective Association, the APA, in the 1890's with its anti-Catholic program and with its collaboration with the Republican party was such an event. The campaign of Al Smith for the Presidency in 1928 renewed and strengthened the old loyalties. Group and family affiliations came to be fixed and perpetuated. And the Irish, too, traveled West and carried their politics with them. As they moved across the continent—to dig canals, to lay railroads, to build cities—clusters of Irish Catholics became prominent in Democratic circles in place after place across the country. And so it is for both Republican and Democratic parties. This group, that group, often for fortuitous reasons, becomes allied with one party or the other. Accretion after accretion becomes amalgamated into the party group which has an impressive capacity to perpetuate itself across the generations.[16]

Factors in a More Homogeneous Politics. Although the processes of urbanization have radically changed the face of the land, in some states the ingredients of metropolitanism and nonmetropolitanism and their associated political characteristics exist in such unbalanced proportions that the minority party is extraordinarily weak. In such states the population is far from homogeneous and far from lacking in internal political differences, but the balances are such that the majority controls with only occasional serious challenge. In South Dakota, Kansas, and Iowa, for example, the Democratic party rarely captures the governorship.[17] Over the long pull, the Democrats of Nebraska have been a more formidable threat to Republican dominance than have their partisan brethren in the other three states, but the Ne-

---

[16] David Hume commented long ago about, to be sure, a somewhat different situation: "Nothing is more usual than to see parties, which have begun upon a real difference, continue even after that difference is lost. When men are once enlisted on opposite sides, they contract an affection to the persons with whom they are united, and an animosity against their antagonists: and these passions they often transmit to their posterity."—"Of Parties in General" in *Essays, Literary, Moral, and Political* (London: Ward, Lock, and Tyler, n. d.), p. 37.

[17] Of the 24 gubernatorial elections beginning with the election of 1908, Iowa Democratic candidates won three. The same rate of Democratic victory prevailed in Kansas over the same period.

braska Democratic party has been in murky eclipse since 1940.[18] In all these states the elements of the population on which the Democratic party builds in other states are comparatively small proportions of the whole and are inadequate as bases for a party competition, both close and sustained, for control of the state government. The political pot, rather, boils up at widely separated intervals. Dissatisfaction usually works itself out through the internal conflicts of the Republican party, but on occasion Democratic candidates win the governorship. Deviation from Republicanism seems to be more a matter associated with recurrent agrarian distress than with the continuing differences of deeply rooted concentrations of Democratic and Republican strength.[19]

For those who wish to speculate about their significance, comparisons of a few population proportions, apparently politically relevant, in these bulwarks of Republicanism and in a pair of two-party states are set out below:

	IOWA	KANSAS	NEB.	ILLINOIS	N.Y.
Mean Democratic % of Gubernatorial Vote, 1908-1952	42.4	43.2	41.8	49.1	51.5
% of Lower House Legislative Seats Democratic, 1940-52[20]	13.6	14.9		46.4	37.6
% Population in Cities over 100,000	6.8	8.8	18.9	45.6	62.4
% Foreign Born or of Foreign-Born or Mixed Parentage, 1930	30.4	18.0	34.8	45.8	61.0

[18] For concise accounts of the principal political episodes in Nebraska's recent history, see James C. Olson, *History of Nebraska* (Lincoln: University of Nebraska Press, 1955).

[19] See J. A. Neprash, *The Brookhart Campaigns in Iowa, 1920-1926* (New York: Columbia University Press, 1932); H. F. Gosnell, *Grass Roots Politics* (Washington: American Council on Public Affairs, 1942), ch. 5.

[20] Nebraska's legislature is chosen on a nonpartisan ballot.

	IOWA	KANSAS	NEB.	ILLINOIS	N.Y.
% Population					
Catholic, 1936	11.7	8.6	11.5	18.6	23.4
% of Employed Self-					
Employed, 1950	39.5	36.1	41.2	19.3	17.9

These gross figures do not bring out some politically relevant characteristics of the population of these states. The foreign born and the population of foreign-born or of mixed parentage differed in the one-party and two-party states. Thus the newer population of Nebraska, which in 1930 constituted a quite large proportion of the total, included large German and Scandinavian components. Germans, from the impact of Democratic national policy in World Wars I and II, have developed a coolness toward Democratic candidates. Scandinavians, too, tend toward Republicanism.

A feature of the demography of these states that bears on the nature of their party systems is the relative uniformity of the geographical distribution of both the Republican majority and the Democratic minority. Almost every county has a Republican majority and in almost every county the Democrats find themselves consistently in the minority. The consequence is that Republicans virtually monopolize local government offices and can thereby support a corps of professional leaders as well as a reservoir of potential candidates for state office. Democrats, on the other hand, are almost always without nonfederal public employment. With 40 per cent of the total state vote more irregularly distributed geographically the minority party would have a source of support for leadership through local office, a means of training in practical politics, as well as a greater attraction to young persons interested in the public service. A larger contingent of professionals would probably give somewhat more vitality to the state party organizations. The leanness of the Democratic local strength in Kansas, Iowa, Nebraska, and South Dakota may be inferred from Table 30, which shows the distribution of the counties of these states according to the percentages of their vote for the Democratic candidates for governor in 1950. In only about 10 per cent of the counties did the Democratic gubernatorial candidate draw more than 50 per cent of the vote, and the chances are that the showings of the local tickets were even less impressive.

These cursory probings into the factors underlying the

TABLE 30

Distribution of Counties of Kansas, Iowa, South Dakota, and Nebraska According to Democratic Percentage of Two-Party Vote for Governor in Each County, 1950

DEMOCRATIC PERCENTAGE OF VOTE	KANSAS	IOWA	SOUTH DAKOTA	NEBRASKA	TOTAL COUN-TIES
10-19	0	0	2	0	2
20-29	0	7	5	5	17
30-39	32	46	25	23	126
40-49	62	41	29	48	180
50-59	11	3	5	14	33
60-69	0	2	1	3	6
80-89	0	0	1 ª	0	1
	105	99	68	93	365

ª *This was the unorganized County of Armstrong, six of whose seven votes were Democratic.*

politics of Kansas, Nebraska, and Iowa have been directed more toward an exposition of a general notion about factors bearing on the structure of state party systems than toward an outline of the specific facts concerning these states. The statistical facts show some relatively sharp differences between the population composition of these states and that of those states that more regularly conduct politics through a two-party competition. In a sense these midwestern states approach more closely a homogeneity than do Illinois and New York. Yet the objective char-

acteristics of the population do not automatically create particular types of political systems or practices. The tendency for
the politics of these midwestern states to be one of Republican
dominance reflects the exertion of corps of Republican leaders
whose efforts have been facilitated by the historical heritage of
their peoples and by the accidents of the impact of Democratic
national policies upon elements of their populations, as well as
by the relative weakness of the sources for the support and maintenance of a competing Democratic leadership. The addition of
a variety of influences produces a political system radically different, at least in the structure of competition, from that which
exists in the two-party states.

3. *Electoral Groupings and the Coincidence and Divergence of State and National Cleavages*

The sorts of electoral foundations of Democratic and
Republican parties that have been differentiated are formed, at
least in their origins, by the impact of political conflict and by
the divisive effects of political issues. No law of political behavior makes an urban Negro a Democrat. Nor is there any
imperative of political action to dictate that an Ohioan whose
ancestors came from Connecticut should be a Republican. Partisan groupings are molded by the matrix of political alternatives
and they tend to maintain and perpetuate the forms so acquired
until pressures build up to alter them.

The electoral groupings that exist within individual states
are profoundly affected by the impact of national issues and by
the alternatives fixed by the competition of national political
leadership. Current national issues—and the cumulative residual
effects of past national conflicts—may push a state's local politics toward a Republican or Democratic one-partyism or they
may so divide the electorate of a state that it is closely competitive between the parties in both national and state affairs.

The relation of the effects of state and national politics

on the basic electoral groupings within individual states is a relatively uncomplicated matter so long as the cleavages of state and national politics generally coincide. When those cleavages diverge, some of the oddities of American state politics develop. In states with a politics based fundamentally on metropolitan and nonmetropolitan foundations the issues of state and national politics since 1932 have roughly coincided in their impact. On the other hand, the southern states provide examples of states in which the cleavages of national and state issues have, most of the time, radically diverged with significant consequences for the organization of state politics.

Although detailed proof of the proposition would be a laborious task, it seems probable that within most states that have even the semblance of a party system national and state cleavages roughly coincide. The consequence is that the hard core of the Republican party in national politics and in state politics of such states is composed of about the same people. Similarly the die-hard Democrats in state and national politics are the same people except perhaps in the South. These groups, moreover, have a rather high stability of composition over considerable periods of time. Furthermore, it is doubtful that the competitive manipulations of party leaderships can establish hard cores of party followers for the local politics of such states that differ radically in composition from the groups of faithful national partisans, at least save in the most exceptional circumstances.

Within individual states the character of the political system depends to a considerable extent on the relative sizes of these groups of die-hard partisans. In some states that ratio is such as to make the outlook for the weaker party hopeless. In close states, however, a major component of state political strategy is to contrive a division of the electorate on state questions somewhat different from that which occurs on national issues. State leaders may not often be able to create durable electoral groupings different from those that exist for national purposes. Nevertheless they can and do form groupings of the moment which, at least on their margins, differ from the groupings within the state for national purposes. In California, for example, Governor Warren, by the prosecution of policies that appeared dangerously like the New Deal to his midwestern Republican colleagues, managed to hold a Republican majority within the state despite the state's national Democratic inclination. Or in New Jersey, Republican Governor Driscoll succeeded in accomplishing a similar end by means not fundamentally dissimilar.

In Ohio Democratic Governor Frank Lausche has practiced a style of politics that has split the state's electorate in state elections somewhat differently than have national issues. His personal politics, more or less independent of the state Democratic party, such as it is, has enabled him to cut into the support of Republican gubernatorial candidates especially heavily in those areas strongly committed to Republicanism nationally. A bland, conservative, and highly moral candidate, not lacking in the appeal of a friendly and dignified showmanship yet not given to the pyrotechnics that arouse the anxieties of men of substance, he has run far ahead of Democratic presidential candidates in Republican neighborhoods. On the other hand, not addicted to the polemics of rabble repression of the right-wing Ohio Republican, he has managed quite well to hold the support of those groups committed to Democratic presidential candidates, a feat facilitated by the fact that such classes of voters have had little or no alternative in state politics. An analysis that demonstrates these observations about Lausche's pulling power among the staunch Republican groups as well as his capacity to hold the support of the heavily Democratic areas appears in Table 31. From the right-hand column of the table it may be seen that Lausche's lead over Truman in 1948 increased as the Republican percentage of the presidential vote increased from precinct to precinct.[21]

---

[21] The adept at arithmetic will, of course, note that this increasing margin from area to area would appear if, say, five per cent of all Republicans everywhere split their tickets for the benefit of Lausche. The

Attempts, such as that by Mr. Lausche, to split a state's
electorate in a slightly different way on state questions from the

TABLE 31

*Frank Lausche and the Republicans: Lausche's 1948 Margin
Over Truman Related to Division of Presidential Vote in
Cuyahoga County Precincts*[a]

RANGE OF PRECINCTS IN DEMOCRATIC PERCENTAGE OF PRESIDENTIAL VOTE	NUMBER OF PRECINCTS	MEAN DEMOCRATIC PRESIDENTIAL PERCENTAGE IN PRECINCTS (1)	MEAN PERCENTAGE FOR LAUSCHE IN PRECINCTS (2)	(2) MINUS (1)
0-9	2	6.9	26.4	19.5
10-19	8	15.8	34.9	19.1
20-29	21	24.5	40.3	15.8
30-39	24	35.2	47.8	12.6
40-49	22	45.1	55.9	10.8
50-59	44	55.2	59.6	4.4
60-69	53	64.5	66.1	1.6
70-79	48	73.8	72.9	− 0.9
80-89	14	83.4	84.3	0.9

[a] *The analysis is based on a sample of the voting units,
usually precincts, in Cuyahoga County. The sample consists of
every fifth unit as listed in Ohio* Election Statistics.

division on national questions and thereby to win the state are
common in close states. Yet such variations are marginal and

---

margins in this table have a wider range than would occur with a uniform degree of ticket-splitting among all types of Republicans. The figures
give no measure of total ticket-splitting but they suggest that a minimum
of 20 per cent of the presidential Republicans in neighborhoods with
Republican pluralities split their tickets for the benefit of Lausche. In
Democratic precincts a far smaller proportion of Republicans crossed
the line for the benefit of Lausche. The phenomenon shown by the table
to exist in Cleveland has been found elsewhere in Ohio by Marc Gertner
in his study of Lausche, *The Man Who Walks Alone* (MSS, Harvard
College honors thesis, 1954).

do not reflect sharp differences in the composition of the hard core of partisans of either party even though they may determine the outcome of particular elections. When, however, the deep cleavages of national politics happen to diverge sharply from the durable lines of division within state politics, the effect upon the organization of state politics is rather drastic. Such a deviation is uncommon, but when it does occur the results are striking.

North Dakota provides an illustration of a sharp divergence in the impacts of state and national politics upon the electorate of a state. The long-standing cleavage in state politics has been along economic lines, a split that manifested itself in state politics long before the New Deal sharpened this division in national voting. Under the leadership of the Non-Partisan League a movement for state enterprise captured the state, under the Republican banner, and also aroused the most bitter and uncompromising opposition both from within and from outside the boundaries of the state. In the primaries of the Republican party the battles between the conservatives and the NPL have on the whole found the voters of the poorer farming counties, principally in the western two-thirds of the state, casting NPL majorities while the more fertile farming counties of the eastern part of the state record high proportions of their vote for the conservative candidates, who in recent years have run under the auspices of the Republican Organizing Committee. Most of the time the Democrats, a relatively conservative bloc in state politics, have played a minor role.

The foreign-policy issues of national politics came to divide the voters of the state in a different manner than did the early sharp economic cleavages over the question of state socialism. The NPL draws heavy support from the so-called Volga Germans of the state who happen also to be concentrated mainly in marginal agricultural areas. Enterprising railroad promoters sold both transportation from Bremen to Bismarck and semi-arid lands in North Dakota to Volga Germans. The baptism of political fire undergone by the NPL at the time of World War I hardened the loyalties of the followers of the League. Its leaders attacked the war as an adventure fostered by the plutocracy while its enemies assailed the League as both socialistic and disloyal.[22]

As the Democratic party nationally came to be associated with a policy of alliance with Britain and France against Germany, the national Republicanism of North Dakota was re-enforced. At the time of World War I Scandinavians, who seem to lean somewhat more toward the anti-NPL wing of the Republican party in state affairs, tended to share the foreign policy impulses of their fellow North Dakotans of German origin.[23] the events leading up to World War II again activated the foreign-policy question and deprived the national Democrats of their depression-born gains in the state.[24] Despite the fact that the impact of national issues drove Republicans of varied ethnic origins toward loyalty to the national ticket, the NPL and anti-NPL groups fought bitterly for control of the government of the state and came to form fairly well-crystallized competing electoral groups with organizational apparatus much like that of a political party.

The upshot of all these developments is that the traditional lines of cleavage on state questions by no means coincide with the impulses toward unity and division generated by the

[22] Samuel Lubell has a brief account of the matter in *The Future of American Politics* (New York: Harper, 1952), ch. 7. For the full story, see R. L. Morlan, *Political Prairie Fire: The Nonpartisan League, 1915-1922* (Minneapolis: University of Minnesota Press, 1955).

[23] Wilson carried the state in 1916 but in 1920 Cox, the Democratic candidate, drew only 18.9 per cent of the vote and in no county won as much as one-third of the vote. The 1920 decline in Democratic strength was least in those counties with the smallest proportions of population of German origin.

[24] In 1936 Roosevelt carried all save five counties, four of which were centers of German population. In 1940 the nine counties with the sharpest drop in Democratic presidential percentage from 1936 (a mean decline of 35.6 percentage points for the nine counties) were counties that had had in 1930 a mean percentage of 54 per cent population of German or Volga German origin. The 10 counties with the least decline in Democratic presidential percentage, 1936-40, had on the average a German population of 6.7 per cent in 1930.

issues of national politics. Both the followers of the NPL and its enemies could come to the support of the national Republican party on foreign policy grounds. Yet the inherited economic division on state policy kept them more or less at each other's throats in state politics. The anti-NPL bloc, most recently styled the Republican Organizing Committee, finds it most distasteful to support an NPL-Republican nominee for state office. The NPL bloc, despite its tradition of economic liberalism, remains ordinarily unattracted by Democratic candidates, either national or state.[25]

The effects of the criss-crossing of state and national cleavages are to complicate the politics of the state and, incidentally, to provide a striking illustration of the difficulty of maintaining a state party system independent of the national parties. Non-Partisan Leaguers and regular Republicans fight out their battles in the Republican primaries, but the losers are rarely happy about the outcome of the primary and on occasion take an appeal in the general election. The career of the late John Moses, a Democrat and a beneficiary of the internecine struggles of the Republicans, gives clues to the broad characteristics of the total state situation. In Moses's first race for the governorship in 1936 he polled only 29 per cent of the total vote. William Langer, NPL leader, had been nosed out in the Republican primary but ran as an independent. He managed to carry enough of his NPL followers out of the party to give him the governorship with 36 per cent of the total vote in a three-way race. In 1938, the NPL candidate won the Republican nomination and the conservative wing of the Republican party discovered great virtue in Moses, who won as a Democrat with substantial support from anti-NPL Republicans.[26] In 1940 and

---

[25] The conflict works itself out in national politics through the looseness of the national system. Senator William Langer, a Non-Partisan Leaguer, has voted with the Democrats on domestic economic questions and usually with the isolationist Republican wing on foreign-policy roll calls.

[26] The total Republican primary vote was 173,000; the general election vote for the NPL-Republican candidate was 101,000.

1942 NPL candidates again won the Republican nomination and Moses again drew sufficient support from conservative Republicans to carry the elections. Moses was no New Dealer; a conservative Democrat, he supported measures acceptable to most businessmen and conservative Republicans.

In the Republican primaries beginning in 1944 and running through 1952 candidates sponsored by the Republican Organizing Committee won the Republican nominations. Under such circumstances, conservative Republicans had no reason to bolt to the Democrats. Nor did the Democratic state candidates have much appeal for the NPL voters many of whom, in harmony with what might be expected from their ethnic origins, reacted negatively to the Democratic label whether worn by a state or national candidate. In 1944, the defeated NPL candidate ran as an independent but polled only 19 per cent of the total gubernatorial vote. This showing perhaps discouraged the NPL. At any rate in the following general elections it did not run independent candidates against the regular Republican nominee.

It is clearly difficult to maintain a state politics organized differently from national politics within the state. The Roosevelt-Truman policies on domestic matters, especially on agriculture, had great appeal to the old Leaguers who found little in Republican national economic policy to relish, although they may have had memories of the fact that Democrats waged a couple of wars against the Fatherland. The conflicting tugs on the League followers have been made manifest in recent years by the advocacy by a League faction of union with the Democrats. In fact, in 1952 four of the five members of the NPL executive committee supported Adlai Stevenson for President.[27]

In a sense, North Dakota has had a three-party system: the NPL, the ROC, and the Democrats. Most of the time the numerical balance among these "parties" has been such that the

[27] Paul David and others, *Presidential Nominating Politics in 1952*, vol. IV, p. 243.

choice of state officials could be settled by primary fights between the two Republican parties. Yet on occasion the Republican primary outcome is not accepted as determinative. One of
the Republican factions may then run an independent candidate
in the general election to make the campaign a three-way race,
a situation which has arisen rather frequently in North Dakota
to the advantage at times of the Democratic candidate.[28] Under
some circumstances the defeated Republican faction may aid the
Democratic candidate in the general election campaign, a type
of party perfidy of which the right-wing Republicans have been
principally guilty.[29]

4. Corps of Party Leadership and Their Electoral Roots

In the preceding discussions the term political party has
been employed without precise definition, a convenient failing
not uncommon in the literature on the subject. In reality, when
the observer of politics in the American states attempts to look
at parties he may, confronted by a phenomenon both nebulous
and complex, despair of formulating a single definition that
fits the realities everywhere. Yet some crude identifications of
the components of political parties may be made which are
applicable after a fashion in all the states.

[28] Independent candidates polled substantial votes in the gubernatorial races of 1936 and 1944 and in the senatorial races of 1938, 1940,
1944, and 1946. The frequency of independent candidacies by men defeated in the primaries has stimulated those who thought they had something to gain by the maneuver to tinker with the election laws. In 1939
the legislature established a rule that a candidate defeated at the primary
would be ineligible to run for the same office at the general election. The
state supreme court later held this law inapplicable to federal office.—
State ex rel. *Sundfor v. Thorson,* 72 N. D. 246 (1942). In 1945 the legislature acted to exclude the names of defeated primary candidates from the
general election ballot. If such persons run as independents, they must run
as write-in candidates.

[29] In 1928, however, the Democratic gubernatorial candidate
withdrew after the primary and was replaced as the candidate by the
Leaguer who had been defeated in the Republican primary. This "Democratic" candidate in the year of Al Smith polled 43 per cent of the vote
in North Dakota, perhaps not a bad showing all things considered.

On the American scene a basic element of a political party consists of that group within the electorate which ordinarily supports its candidates. Both Democratic and Republican groups include a relatively hard core of partisans who stick with the party candidates through thick and thin. The strength of partisan attachments within the electorate ranges from very strong to quite weak. On the fringes of the electoral group are persons readily swayed from the nominal party attachments and usually with a low level of interest in politics. It seems quite evident that the size of the electoral groups concerned with the affairs of states is considerably smaller than those brought to the polls by presidential elections.[30]

The factors that enter into the formation of groupings of strong partisans are by no means solely the issues of the moment. The impact of great crises brings accretions and losses to party groups. The accidents by which particular groups were once excluded from the ruling cliques left residues of loyalty to the party of the outs of the time. Great leaders arouse enthusiasms that are translated into loyalties to the party generally. The identification of a party with individual or class interest adds another type of adherent. However partisanship may be created, a complex of factors operates to maintain it, although from time to time the blows of great events bring considerable realignment. In any case, complex processes extended through time construct and maintain groups of voters, each of which generally prefers to see its own govern rather than the representatives of the other group.

To be differentiated from the electoral element of the party, although closely associated with it, is the party's leadership corps. While a great deal of information has been assembled about the composition of the electoral followings of the parties, the character and structure of the leadership corps are matters about which reliable data are scant. The leadership echelons of party include, of course, persons in positions of official leadership in the party—committeemen, city and county

---

[30] Refer to Table 1, p. 16.

chairmen, state chairmen, and the like—as well as individuals of power through informal status among the bigwigs of the party. Included are candidates, successful and unsuccessful, and would-be candidates for posts from constable to governor. The structure of relationship among all these individuals differs, of course, enormously from party to party and from state to state. In some instances lines of communication and consultation knit together a considerable number of these individuals scattered over a state into a relatively cohesive group concerned with affairs of the party. In other instances only the loosest and most infrequent links of communication tie together individuals who have in common roles of leadership and partisan affiliation.

Obviously, the quality, character, skill, and capacity to act of the leadership corps associated with an electoral grouping profoundly affect not only the fortunes of the party but the nature of the governing process as well. In turn, the characteristics of the leadership corps are mightily influenced by the nature of the electoral grouping from which it springs. The bulk of the leadership echelon, if one includes the base as well as the summit, tends to resemble in many respects the electoral mass which gives it birth. The capacity of an electoral grouping to maximize its political potentiality depends in large measure on its capacity to support a leadership echelon skilled in the arts of politics and able to devote its time and energies to political endeavor.

In states with the rudiments of a two-party system striking differences exist in the characteristics of the leadership corps of the major parties and those differences are closely associated with contrasts in the composition of the Republican and Democratic electoral groupings. The capacity of a state to develop and maintain a two-party politics depends not only on the existence of separate electoral groupings but upon the capacity of each of these groups to support a leadership corps. On the whole, outside the South the Republican group has far greater resources for the support of leadership as well as a far larger reservoir of persons with leadership skills on which to draw. Well-connected lawyers, businessmen with time and money to devote to politics, and, perhaps to a lesser extent, persons with skill in professional politics gravitate in greater degree to the Republican party than to the Democratic. By the secondary network of economic relations within their own group—legal retainers, insurance commissions, real estate transactions, and the like—the business community within the Republican party can sustain a class whose time and energies may be dedicated principally to the practice of politics.

The Democratic party, on the other hand, enjoys the handicaps in recruiting leadership created by its position as a party devoted in principle to mass causes. By and large it must depend on somewhat different classes of individuals to man its leadership echelons. Nor is the mass of the party ordinarily able, through the unplanned economic relations that develop, to sustain a leadership with the leisure to devote its efforts to public affairs. Democrats can draw upon the professions—open as they are to young men of talent whatever their social origin—for leadership, yet in many jurisdictions a young lawyer with Democratic political ambitions is likely to have to spend a good deal of time in the police courts in earning his livelihood. The contribution of workers, numerous in the Democratic ranks, to the party leadership echelons is limited by the fact that such men cannot afford to devote their time to politics. More and more, however, such men are assuming positions in the Democratic hierarchy as a sideline to jobs as union employees or officials. To some degree, unions have moved into the role of financial support of Democratic leadership that business has long occupied with respect to the Republican party.

These contrasts in the composition of Republican and Democratic leadership are most marked in those states in which the Democratic party has a metropolitan base and the Republican party a nonmetropolitan center of gravity. When remnants of the rural Democracy of Copperhead lineage happen to be allied with the new urban Democracy, they contribute a leadership sector by no means unlike the average run of rural Republicans, merchants, lawyers, leading farmers—the political elite of the rural and small town community.

These contrasting characterizations of Democratic and Republican leadership echelons—probably annoying to Democrats and Republicans alike—need to be buttressed by facts. Unfortunately all the facts necessary for a completely satisfactory description of the party elites are not readily available. Yet we do have some data about the members of most state legislatures. Doubtless Republican legislators do not constitute a representative sample of all those persons who would be categorized as among the Republican influentials in a state. Nor are the Democratic legislators a cross-section of the big and little brass of the Democratic party. The chances are that the differences between these two groups are wider than those between the entire leadership corps of the two parties. Nevertheless, some quite simple analyses of the occupational differences between Democratic and Republican legislators point to problems of fundamental importance in the party system.

An analysis of the occupational composition of the Republican and Democratic groups in the Michigan lower legislative house in recent sessions, which appears in Table 32 bears on our general observations.[31] Several sharp contrasts in the composition of the two groups of legislators may be seen from the table. The business and managerial classes contribute far more heavily to the Republicans than to the Democrats.[32] Moreover,

[31] This and the succeeding analyses were suggested by a similar tabulation of the membership of the Indiana legislature reported by Munger, *op. cit.*

[32] In the main the categories in the table correspond to those employed by the Census Bureau in its reports on the labor force. The professional group corresponds to the "Professional, technical, and kindred workers" of the census and includes such occupations as accountants, engineers, funeral directors, and chiropractors along with law, medicine, education, and religion. The business-managerial group corresponds roughly to "Managers, officials, and proprietors, excluding farm"; sales-clerical to the two groups "Clerical and kindred workers" and "Sales workers." The manual workers item lumps together the census categories of "Craftsmen, foremen and kindred workers," "Operatives and kindred workers," and "Service workers, except private household." Two principal

among those Democrats classified as business or managerial were goodly numbers of persons engaged in the liquor business and in enterprises of opportunity such as advertising or industrial relations counselling. On the other hand, on the Democratic side were to be found most legislators who could be classified as manual workers. The title of this category is a bit deceptive, for it also includes persons who identified themselves

TABLE 32

Democratic and Republican Contrasts in Michigan: Occupational Distribution of Democrats and Republicans Serving in Lower House of Michigan Legislature in Sessions of 1945, 1947, 1949, and 1951[a]

	DEMOCRATS		REPUBLICANS	
OCCUPATIONAL CATEGORY	#	%	#	%
Professional	15	22.4	35	24.1
Business-Managerial	18	26.9	63	43.4
Farmer	0	0.0	24	16.6
Sales-Clerical	6	8.9	3	2.1
Manual Worker	18	26.9	1	0.7
Local Government Official	6	8.9	7	4.8
Retired and unidentified	4	6.0	12	8.3
Total	67	100.0	145	100.0

[a] *Based on information in the* Michigan Manual. *Each individual legislator was included in the tabulation only once although he may have served for more than one session.*

departures from the census categories were made to separate out politically relevant groups. The census groups labor union officials with "Managers, Officials, and Proprietors." They are here grouped with manual workers. Those persons reporting themselves as employees of local governmental units have been classified not according to their reported occupation but in the special category of local government official. Those who have perused the legislative manuals know well that some legislators report their occupations too vaguely to permit exact categorization. Many state representatives thus report "Insurance and Real Estate," an honored and ancient political calling, as the source of their livelihood. Where no further information was given, such individuals have been classified with the business-managerial group although the census would probably pay no deference to their legislative status and throw many of them in among the "Sales workers."

as trade union officials. Ten legislators, all Democrats, indicated in their biographical data that they were trade union officials. No Republican member claimed such a connection. The farmer component of the Republican group, one out of six, reflects the outstate concentration of strength of the Republican party in Michigan.

The analysis of the membership of the Pennsylvania lower house in Table 33 reveals contrasts between Democratic

TABLE 33

Democratic and Republican Contrasts in Pennsylvania: Occupational Distribution of Democrats and Republicans Serving in Lower House of Pennsylvania Legislature in Sessions of 1945, 1947, 1949, and 1951[a]

	DEMOCRATS		REPUBLICANS	
OCCUPATIONAL CATEGORY	#	%	#	%
Professional	48	28.9	70	28.1
Business-Managerial	27	16.3	114	45.8
Farmer	10	6.0	17	6.8
Sales-Clerical	22	13.3	18	7.2
Manual Workers	35	21.1	7	2.8
Local Government Office	18	10.8	18	7.2
Unidentified	6	3.6	5	2.0
Total	166	100.0	249	100.0

[a] *Compiled from biographical data reported in the* Pennsylvania Manual.

and Republican groups quite similar to those that have prevailed in Michigan. About one-fourth of each legislative group in Pennsylvania was drawn from those occupations classified as professional. Doubtless if all the relevant data were available rather different status and connections would be found to exist for the Democratic and Republican professional groups. In Pennsylvania the business-managerial category accounted for almost one-half of the Republican legislators but only about one-sixth

of the Democratic group. Again manual workers and union officials bulked much larger in the Democratic group than among
the Republicans. In both parties small groups of legislators were
local government officials. Local government offices are not un-
commonly employed to support state legislators, especially in
metropolitan centers. Although more Democrats held such posts
than Republicans, the difference between the party legislative
groups in this respect was not large.

The composition of the Massachusetts legislative groups
both resembles and differs from those of Michigan and Pennsylvania. As in the other states, both Democratic and Republican
groups in Massachusetts have about the same proportions of
persons classified as professionals. Doubtless differences between these professional groups exist that are not revealed by the
bare biographical data.[33] The business-managerial group accounts for about four out of ten Republican legislators, a much
larger proportion than for the Democrats. Among the Republicans of this category were to be found manufacturers, business
executives, and persons in finance. The Democratic group ran
more to small retail merchants, real estate and insurance men,
contractors, and the like. The most notable difference between
Massachusetts and the other states rests on the fact that the
manual worker group is relatively small within the Democratic
group and the sales-clerical group is quite large. About one out
of five Democratic legislators reports a clerical or sales occupation, jobs rather low down the business scale. Republicans draw
proportionately only about a third as many legislators from this
occupational category. Impressionistic evidence also suggests
that the Massachusetts political division tends to be a class
division modified by a religious division—or perhaps a cleavage
along religious lines modified by the pull of a class division.
Insofar as the evidence goes, the legislative groups reflect this
complication.[34]

[33] Of the Democratic lawyers, 46 per cent had their training in
night law schools; of the Republican lawyers, 32 per cent.

[34] Massachusetts legislators do not report religious affiliations in
their biographical data but often indicate fraternal connections. Of the

The close communion and correspondence of the leadership corps of the parties with their respective electoral bases fixes some of the fundamental conditions for the conduct of politics in the American states. While to a degree the electoral groupings are a product of the manipulation of leadership, per-

TABLE 34

Democratic and Republican Contrasts in Massachusetts: Occupational Distribution of Democrats and Republicans Serving in Lower House of Massachusetts Legislature in Sessions of 1945, 1947, 1949, and 1951[a]

OCCUPATIONAL CATEGORY	DEMOCRATS		REPUBLICANS	
	#	%	#	%
Professional	85	39.9	80	34.3
Business-Managerial	49	23.0	94	40.3
Sales-Clerical	47	22.1	16	6.9
Manual Workers	13	6.1	5	2.1
Farmers	1	0.5	16	6.9
Local Government	7	3.3	3	1.3
Unidentified	11	5.2	19	8.2
Total	213	100.0	233	100.0

[a] *Compiled from biographical data in* Public Officers of the Commonwealth of Massachusetts, *a biennial publication of the General Court.*

haps the differing leadership groups are more a product of the differing groups within the electorate. To the extent that this is the case, the maintenance of competing party hierarchies depends on the capacity of the major electoral groups to generate and support elements of political leadership.

Even the simple analyses of Michigan, Pennsylvania, and Massachusetts reveal marked contrasts between the leadership

---

Democratic members of the lower house whose religion could be inferred, 93 per cent were Roman Catholics; 11 per cent of the Republicans were of that faith. However, 24 per cent of the Democrats and 43 per cent of the Republicans reported nothing to indicate religious connections, if any.

levels and suggest inferences about the relative strength of the parties on the leadership levels. Both parties, if the legislators constitute anything approaching a representative sample of their middle levels of leadership, have leadership corps oriented toward the solid core of their electoral groupings. In the generation of top-level and statewide leadership each party thus has the problem of grooming and developing men with the earmarks of spokesmen for the party as a whole rather than the traits of partiality and particularity of the bedrock elements of the electoral following.[35] Beyond this—and here the data are most scant—in the typical nonsouthern state the Republicans have a much larger supply of middle-level influentials than do the Democrats.[36] The odds ought to be high that large numbers of middle-level leaders will include more persons with the requisites for statewide leadership than will a smaller group.

The chances are that over forty or fifty years a change of considerable significance has occurred in the leadership echelons of the Democratic party, especially in the older industrial states. Larger and larger numbers of young men from groups traditionally associated with that party have moved into the professions and into business and some of them have developed an interest in political leadership. From the same groups there have emerged more men with both sufficient wealth and interest to aid in the support of the party.[37] More strikingly, in some states the closer affiliation of the unions with the Democratic party has provided a new source of leadership with financial

[35] This problem may well be aggravated by the differentials in participation in the nominating process. Consider in this connection the matters dealt with on pp. 152-65.

[36] In Elmira, New York, Berelson and his associates found that 80 per cent of what they called "the occupational elite" were Republicans. About three-fourths of the officers of clubs were Republicans. Their report on the political leadership of Elmira is most instructive. See *Voting* (Chicago: University of Chicago Press, 1954), chap. 8.

[37] An analysis of Massachusetts party finance shows striking differences in the occupational pursuits of those supporting the Democratic and Republican parties, differences congruent with what might be expected from our knowledge of the composition of the underlying electoral groups. See H. D. Price, "Massachusetts Campaign Finance in 1952," *Public Policy*, VI (1955), pp. 25-46.

support independent of public employment and, hence, with some capacity to assume the risks of a political career.[38] Yet this sort of dependence is not entirely advantageous in American politics. The tendency seems to be to abhor individuals with clear and open identification with special interests or at least to make it difficult for them to achieve leadership of large and diversely composed constituencies.[39] Partial interests more commonly find it advantageous to work through fronts, a custom which gives the lawyer peculiar eligibility as a candidate for elective office.

The emerging relations between the partisan electoral groups and their respective leadership corps may be producing a basic alteration in the conditions of competition between the parties. One of the ancient problems of American state politics has been the fact that the leaders—the organization—of both parties from time to time fall under the influence of fundamentally the same interests in society. The old-time reformers despaired of the party organizations for this reason—among others. In truth, the predatory interests often owned both crowds of professionals. How a mass-based, popular party can manage to own its own politicians will doubtless be a question

[38] William H. Riker has argued that trade union leaders have moved most readily into formal positions of party leadership in those states in which the Democratic organization was moribund at the time of the growth in labor's political interest. Thus in Michigan the labor element in the Democratic party has become especially strong. See his *The CIO in Politics, 1936-1946* (MSS, Ph. D. Dissertation, Harvard University, 1948).

[39] The CIO has, in particular, had its dilemma in adjusting itself to the necessities and traditions of the political system. When its own men, candidates clearly and prominently identified with it, run for office it apparently can muster a maximum campaign strength and enthusiasm. Yet the candidate may, with the wider public, suffer the curse of his affiliation. Or the CIO-PAC may spend generously to support its own in districts where they are either certain to lose or certain to win when the funds could be more wisely spent in hopeful districts in support of a friendly professional politician. See Riker, *op. cit.,* and the cases reported by Fay Calkins, *The CIO and the Democratic Party* (Chicago: University of Chicago Press, 1952). All these growing pains of adjustment to the prevailing political practices are quite like those undergone by Negro groups. See H. D. Price, "The Negro and Florida Politics, 1944-1954," *Journal of Politics,* 17 (1955), pp. 198-220.

perpetually with us. Yet perhaps the development of new lines of career and new sources of support may in some of the states enable the Democratic electoral group to maintain a leadership whose integrity is re-enforced by an independence of financial support. The more formidable and more independent that leadership becomes, the greater would be its assistance to the Republican politicians in persuading its business support to avoid the easy course of regarding its self-interest as the equivalent of the public interest.

Chapter 9

Lines of Action

The objective of these chapters has been analytical rather than prescriptive, but the picture that emerges of American state politics arouses the interest of those concerned about the adequacy of state political institutions to fulfill their developing role. From a study designed as a series of exploratory cross-sections rather than as a comprehensive inventory of the variety of practice among the states, no census of conditions in every state is to be expected. Yet certain problems, some undoubtedly common to all the states, others limited to indeterminate numbers of states, appear quite clearly from our inquiries. These problems, given the definition of the area of investigation, bear on the adequacy and suitability of the systems of political parties and other more or less equivalent informal organizations to meet the demands that are coming to be placed on them.

The conditions revealed by the investigations provoke no hysteria over the condition of the politics of the states, but the studies do lead to questions about our arrangements for popular government that merit the most sober and thorough consideration. Those questions organize themselves around several interconnected broad problems which are, nevertheless, separable for purposes of discussion:

1. Evidently the organization of state politics builds

into the governmental system a more or less purely political factor that contributes to federal centralization. The combination of party system and the structure of representation in most of the states incapacitates the states and diverts demands for political action to Washington. This institutional channeling of political forces is, of course, a far less important component of the drive for centralization than are the economic facts of life. It simply guarantees that states will not be utilized to the limit of their potentiality in the total task of government.

2. The question suggests itself whether the organization of political forces within the states has kept pace with the rapid growth of state responsibilities. In a day when the states did far less, an unstable, weak, even chaotic organization of party perhaps made no great difference. Stability, firmness, competence become more and more important and can find no base for existence in the erratic and atomized politics that characterizes many of the states in varying degrees.

3. The system that has gradually developed places serious obstacles in the path of popular government. In some types of situations and at some times the expression of broad popular mandates becomes practically impossible, in part because of the constitutional system and in part because of the inadequacies of the organization and operation of the party system itself.

4. Over a period of a half century party organizations have seriously deteriorated. Their decay has been associated with the rise of the direct primary system of nomination. The question occurs whether the presuppositions about the nature of popular government underlying the direct primary movement do not require a thorough reconsideration. What lines, if any, may be pursued to create party organizations adequate to the changed circumstances both of the people and of the states? Or are other forms of organization of popular leadership feasible?

1. Rationale and Conditions of Partisanship

A general point of view of the preceding detailed analyses has been that political parties have a positive and useful
function to perform, a proposition that might be regarded as
a truism were it not for the fact that the doctrines and actions
of half a century have operated by and large to depreciate the
role of party and to handicap its work. Yet the broad questions
of governmental principle implicit in the doctrine of party government in its application to the states have not been treated as
an incident to our detailed inquiries. The assumptions of that
doctrine and the problems it raises need to be brought together
and argued with some explicitness. The entire question should
be treated in a tentative spirit. The scholars and publicists have
studied and debated the place of party on the national scene at
great length, but the special problems and considerations bearing
on the question of the role of party in the state governments
have been neglected. In short, the sum of knowledge and reflection on the matter is not imposing; he who speaks dogmatically
on the subject unnecessarily places himself in peril.

A basic proposition, which itself is subject to debate, is
that the problem of popular government is at bottom a problem
of party government. In the hopeful days of the Progressive
movement the heralds of a new day propagated the notion that
political parties were superfluous institutions and that their eradi-
cation would pave the way for government more responsive to
mass sentiment. The weakening of disciplined party hierarchies
would permit the readier emergence of truly popular leaders.
The birth of a more critical attitude within the electorate would
insure meaningful alignments about issues as they arose rather
than divisions reflecting inherited attachments to party labels.

Political parties, however, refuse to die. Some day some-
one may contrive a superior means for the management of
popular government. So far parties, no matter what the obstacles
or discouragements may be, operate in one form or another,
under one title or another. Even in cities with nonpartisan gov-

ernment, groups and associations arise to perform the functions of party. A consolidation of electoral strength must be accomplished to govern; that consolidation is accomplished through some combination of leadership elements capable of gaining majority electoral support, ordinarily against the challenge of some other clique or cliques of persons with the ambition to govern. These elements of a party system may exist in a bewildering variety of combinations and forms. Leadership cliques may be amorphous and transient or tightly structured in a long-continuing existence. The electoral followings arrayed around leadership cliques may be persistent or volatile in their loyalties. Yet party may be found, at least in rudimentary form, in any going democratic society save perhaps the most tranquil or stagnant in which the governing processes are reduced almost solely to habit and tradition.

The elements of party exist, of course, in all the American states although they do not always bear the title of "political party." In some states the reality of party is not found in the entities formally described as Democratic or Republican but in political subsystems within the dominant party of the state. Cliques of leadership operate within the dominant party and vie for the support of the voters within that party's direct primary. On the other hand, in such states as Connecticut, Indiana, and New York party as an institution assumes a considerable reality as a going combination of leadership clique and associated electoral following. A somewhat different, but lively, party rivalry prevails in such states as Colorado, Wyoming, Montana, and Idaho. The determination of the extent to which over the country viable state party systems exist and the extent to which intraparty cliques and factions fill the place of party would not be a small task. It is easy enough to differentiate states according to the character of the customary electoral division between Republicans and Democrats at general elections, but the accumulation of the data to describe the structure of leadership, party and factional, would be enormously difficult. Given that difficulty and the central significance of leadership structures in political systems, the discussion of the state political systems must be based in considerable degree upon impressionistic evidence. About all that the gross data that has been analyzed reveals is that as the closeness of competition between parties declines, competition between intraparty centers of leadership becomes more sustained and assumes more and more the central role in state political systems.

Even if the thinness of the data is conceded, the analyses that have been made point to serious limitations on party in the performance of the functions that need to be carried out if the optimum conditions for popular government are to prevail. One set of limitations arises from the fact that the mechanisms of government of the states generally place severe limitations on the operation of parties. The independence of the executive, the powers given to small minorities by the systems of representation in most state legislatures, and the existence of a multiplicity of statewide elective offices operate both to make collaborative control by party leadership of the government either impossible or difficult and to place upon the electorate quite unnecessarily complicated problems of choice and discrimination. To be sure, the basic system of separation of powers rests upon the doctrine that internal checks within the machinery of government should place limits upon party leadership in the exercise of power. Yet the constitutional structures of the states, partially through the unforeseen and unplanned consequences of changes in the context in which they exist, rather than through deliberate and considered choice, have come to limit and obstruct party far more severely than do the national constitutional arrangements. To a far greater extent than in the national government, the state party systems, through division of control of the branches of the government, compound rather than mitigate the difficulties inherent in the separation of powers. If the states had parties both disciplined and doctrinally opposed, their present constitutional systems could scarcely operate, so frequently would conflict produce stalemate.

The institutional obstructions to party government are

plain enough. Another set of limitations arises from the infirmities of parties themselves. The most apparent, and perhaps the fundamental, incapacity of state parties lies in the frequency with which the leadership corps is fractionalized and lacking in both capacity and organization for action. Some state party organizations, to be sure, have an evident vitality as well as a fairly high degree of coherence. Yet a more common situation is the almost complete absence of a functioning statewide organization. There may be informal cliques that operate by and large in the background. There may be local organizations that exert power. Yet organizations prepared to cope responsibly with statewide matters with a statewide view are the exception. Often party is in a sense a fiction. No finger can be put on any group or clique that has both the power and the inclination to exercise leadership in party affairs or to speak authoritatively for it in any way.

Perhaps the most important function that party leadership needs to perform is the development, grooming, and promotion of candidates for statewide office. Although striking exceptions may be cited, it is in its inadequacy in this role that the most grave shortcoming of party leadership is to be found. To assert that party leadership of many states develops candidates is more an attribution of a duty stated in the textbooks than a description of real activity. The direct primary was, of course, designed to break the party organization's monopoly of this function. In some instances, primary statutes forbade exertion of party organization influence in direct primaries. Even in the absence of such proscription, the primary creates conditions that make it most difficult for party organization to play an effective role in the statewide nominating process. It may well be that the primary by depriving party organization of its most important function has contributed to the atrophy of party organization. However that may be, in the absence of a working party leadership, the function of grooming and promoting candidates goes by default to others. Newspapers, animated by varying motives, may pick up the burden. Private interests, at times with the most dubious aims, may work behind the scenes to build up candidates.[1] The invisibility of such centers of initiative mightily simplifies the task of duping the electorate. In other instances, self-starting individuals with mastery of the arts of haranguing the multitude gain special advantage in the nominating process.

It is a nice, and perplexing, question whether any different results occur when political leadership is exercised by a more or less institutionalized party leadership than when the functions of popular leadership are performed by the more amorphous, complex, and individualized sorts of leadership characteristic, for example, of some one-party states. The question boils down ultimately to whether Joe Doakes, Republican political leader and elective official, will on the average act in one way if he is continuously aware that he acts as a member of a Republican group with both a past and a future and another way if he looks upon himself as a self-made tribune of the people who got where he is under his own power and has but one short life to live. Some plausible hypotheses may be constructed but their verification is another matter. The formalization of roles in party groups and institutions ought in the long run to create fields of influence to move individual behavior toward some concern about the long-run fate of the institution as against shorter-term individual concerns. Collective action should nudge individuals toward a sense of concern for and responsibility about others engaged in the joint enterprise. It may well be that a major consequence of institutional action in general is that role patterns are imposed to restrain somewhat the caprice, as well as the peccadillos, of individual behavior. The mores of collective action may, of course, be the mores of the gang and of the ring as well as the standards of virtuous

[1] For example, in speaking of the 1946 Republican primary to nominate a candidate for attorney-general in California, Arthur Samish, noted lobbyist for brewing and related interests, said: "We decided on Howser because his name sounded like the Fred Houser who had been a great Lieutenant-Governor."—Robert S. Allen, *Our Sovereign State,* pp. 402-413. Howser, nominated with 50.4 per cent of the vote in a five-man primary race, went on to win the general election and to serve a term marked by charges of corruption.

public conduct. In political systems perhaps the mores that build up for leadership groups are fundamentally governed by the necessities of political survival, viz., what the electorate will tolerate or reward.

Although instances of the extravagance and erraticism of individual and factional leadership in highly fluid social situations could be cited at length, the proposition that an institutionalized collective leadership will on the average better promote the public weal than an atomized leadership of individuals must be in high degree an affirmation of faith rather than the confident utterance of a prediction. Indeed, organization of political leadership can be far too effective for the public good. A tightly structured leadership that succeeds in repressing dissent may become a plunderbund. Short of that it may lack daring; it may, perhaps in accord with some universal law of hierarchies, reproduce in its candidates its own dull drabness. It has been contended that party hierarchies have an innate fear of the popular leader who can, by gaining a direct hold on the people, become independent of those on whose shoulders he rose to power.

The prescription of popular political theory for the protection of the public against the abuses and shortcomings of party organization is the maintenance of a pair of competing party hierarchies. The harmony of this prescription with the abstract necessities of popular government may appear to be axiomatic. Yet practice in the American states, as our data have shown, by no means invariably accords with the prescription.

If practice reflects belief, the belief in party competition is by no means universal in the American states. Not only are many states dominated by men bearing the label of a single party, in many of them all sorts of barriers have been erected against the achievement of power by the lesser party. Doubtless among politicians, as among businessmen, some sort of deep urge toward monopoly exists. No matter how ringing their affirmations of faith in the great American two-party system may be, party politicians endlessly devote themselves to the contrivance of ways and means by which the opposition will not have much of a chance. In area after area for long periods power has been thoroughly and completely monopolized. Short of monopoly, the minority may become, not a competitor but a willing acceptor of a secondary role, with limited power and perquisites enjoyed through the indulgence of the majority. At times, however, the evenness of the strength of the contenders creates an equilibrium favorable to a spirit of live-and-let-live. While under some circumstances political warfare may be disruptive of social processes and even indicative of grave illness of the body politic, the problem of American state politics is more one of keeping the politicians fighting among themselves than of avoiding damaging conflict.

The basic proposition that popular government is facilitated by competition between cliques of leaders working as party groups is itself debatable. A contrary view might be that the necessities are quite as well served by individual politicians competing against other individuals for the governorship, for other statewide offices, and for legislative seats in the districts over the state. This latter type of situation is often approached in practice in the American states, although it may be masked by the appearance of collaboration created by a common party label. A candidate for governor gathers about himself a crowd of lieutenants and supporters but he may wage a fight for a nomination sure to lead to election, with little or no association or identification with candidates for other offices. Similarly other persons independently seek nomination or election for legislative posts and carry their respective battles independently. Whatever reality of political leadership collectivity there may be tends to come into being after the election, at least in the extreme sort of situation. In a way this atomization of leadership is encouraged by the forms of American government. If the legislature were charged with some great and dramatic collective action of general public concern—say, the election of the governor—scattered legislative candidates would certainly be united in collective alliance with common aim at the campaigning stage—and legislators would probably become ciphers on the order of the members of the electoral college. Under such circumstances the necessity of competition between identifiable groups of leaders to permit effective popular choice would be glaringly apparent.

Certainly some American states manage to get along with atomized and individualistic systems of political leadership. While competition between individuals serves the wholesome purpose of maintaining a sense of insecurity in the mind of the elective official, it is doubtful that meaningful popular decision is readily feasible except when competition occurs between groups of political leaders allied under a party banner. The practical importance, of course, that the electorate be presented with a choice between visible and identifiable groups of leaders varies from time to time with the character of the issues that stir the public. Yet without such groups the choice presented to the electorate is by no means clear. Moreover, without such groups with some sense of common responsibility for the management of government swings of popular sentiment are apt to be frustrated insofar as they seek to affect the course of governmental action. While differentiation of competing political groups by their party label simplifies matters for the electorate, it has to be recognized that from time to time within the major political party competing cliques develop who come to be identified and differentiated in the public mind about as clearly as if they bore formal party designations.

The weakness of the party system in the states outside the South is principally a weakness of the Democratic party, although the Republican party is a feeble enterprise in some of these states. Witness its condition in Rhode Island. The weakness of the Democratic party, moreover, is more a weakness of its leadership corps than of its electoral following. In state after state Democratic voters record a substantial vote for candidates whose election would do little credit to the state or to the Democratic party. And in state after state Democratic party

tickets appear which though they may have several strong candidates, include many others of the most dubious quality. In a
fine nonpartisan spirit it ought to be pointed out that Republicans put on the ballot their share of dubious candidates, even
perhaps now and then an outright crook. Yet it is not incorrect
to conclude that the Democratic party for a variety of reasons
and, of course, in differing degrees from place to place, does not
have the sort of statewide leadership necessary to maintain a
continuing challenge to Republican leadership. In many states,
thus, the advocate of a two-party competition is thrown into
the position of urging a better organization and manning of the
leadership levels of the Democratic party.

In truth, be the weaker party of a state Republican or
Democratic, the maintenance of an adequate minority party
leadership is for the public good. At least this conclusion is an
unavoidable corollary of the proposition that the existence of a
pair of leadership corps facilitates popular choice and the electoral enforcement of accountability. Whether so arranging the
political institutions that popular action may be effective is for
the public good would undoubtedly be questioned, perhaps sotto
voce, by many. When it has no leadership, when it is presented
with no alternatives, when the governing processes seem hope-
lessly fixed, the capacity of the public to accept, to tolerate, to
regard as inevitable, even to applaud government that governs
for itself and for special interest is monumental. And there are
those who prefer to keep the public in a state of obfuscation.

Quite apart from such philosophical considerations that
go to the foundations of the doctrine of popular government,
some earthy and practical considerations urge the maintenance
of a fairly competent and respectable leadership of the lesser
party in the American states. In most of the states outside the
South the lesser of the two parties consistently polls a substantial proportion of the vote; sooner or later its candidates win
at least the major state offices; those victories are certain to
come often as incidents of shifts of sentiment about national
issues rather than through considered action on state questions

and candidates. The weaker party is thrown into power without much regard for what it has to offer.

The idea of competition between parties carries with it, of course, the corollary of a considerably higher degree of unity within the levels of party leadership than prevails in perhaps most of the American state parties, although some state parties have a far greater unity of outlook than exists in their national counterparts. When the question of party unity arises, professional students of government often become involved in a warm debate on a side issue, viz., the question whether American parties can and should be reconstructed in the image of the British party system. Discussion of that question must, in the nature of things, be bootless. Given the constitutional machinery which they must operate, the parties of the American states can never be of the British sort. Given the electoral foundations of our parties they will inevitably be somewhat loosely articulated at their leadership levels, although the electoral foundations for disciplined and competing parties exist in much more clear-cut form in the larger industrial states than they do in the nation as a whole.[2]

The case for conscious and deliberate development of the strength of party hierarchies within the states gains strength not from any abstract yearning for a situation in which all Republican candidates and office-holders take one position and all Democratic candidates and office-holders take an exactly opposite position on policy questions. When issues that involve

[2] A good deal of the discussion of party unity and discipline has been conducted in a political vacuum. Party unity cannot be readily manufactured. Insofar as the unity of party groups in legislative assemblies is concerned, it seems to result, when it does exist, from a fundamental parallelism of interest among the constituencies represented. Thus on a considerable range of significant policy issues in some state legislatures, a fairly high degree of common attitude exists among Republican legislators and among Democratic legislators, differences in position paralleled by differences in the sorts of constituencies they represent. Yet on large proportions of the more or less administrative questions dealt with by most legislatures the information, involvement, and concern of the constituencies are not great, and party unity in the legislature is not induced by extra-legislative forces. On such questions greater party unity could be manufactured by processes of consultation and leadership.

the cherished interests of many people happen to divide, say, Republicans, the Republican leadership will certainly divide. Yet most questions that state governments decide are, in fact, questions of which few people indeed are aware. Even questions that more or less directly affect the welfare of the mass of the citizenry may be fought out between the immediately affected interests with little public attention, so completely blanketed out of the media of communication are the actions of the state-houses. The more effectively each of the competing corps of political leadership is bound together for common action and mutual defense, presumably the greater is its capacity to maintain for their members a degree of independence from those immediately concerned with public questions. In a sense a state government—executive, legislators, and other influentials— much of the time functions as a jury to settle disputes between powerful contestants over questions which may affect the public but of which most people are scarcely aware. Party organization, when it has a strength and unity of its own, can at least limit tampering with the jury and permit some considered search for the general welfare in these more or less private disputes colored with a public interest.

Beyond policy questions involving great stakes that are settled by the states, most decisions of state governments are of matters on which public information is limited and about which only a romantic would expect many people to be informed or to have much of an opinion one way or another. State politics is peculiarly a politics of administration. Perhaps the only way in which any sort of electoral verdict can be rendered is by some relatively clear identification of the crowd responsible for running things which may be thrown out of office if it loses the favor of the majority. Yet, as the foregoing analyses have made pretty clear, the existence of sets of circumstances that make possible this sort of electoral enforcement of accountability are exceptional in the states. The extraordinary ingenuity of politicians in the contrivance of arrangements to obstruct the popular enforcement of accountability can only excite the profoundest, though reluctant, admiration.[3]

In the catalog of speculations about the functions of parties in popular government we have assigned prominence to that of competition for power and office. Yet perhaps equally significant is the institutionalization of dissent and criticism in the hands of the party of the outs, who may earn their salt if they never gain office or even seriously threaten to do so. Governments commit minor boners; they are guilty of abuses; on occasion they are disastrously wrong. In a viable party system the minority has a vested interest in dissent and in innovation. Often the efficacy of practices of dissent in the American state systems is by no means imposing, a condition of affairs not entirely attributable to the weakness of the leadership of the second party. Dissenters need a forum for the expression of dissent. The legislature, by supposition, provides that forum, yet the average American state legislature, hamstrung in a variety of ways, is ill equipped as a medium for the fulfillment of the basic function of dissent.

2. Emerging Trends and Ranges of Choice

A theoretical position that merits respect, if not complete concurrence, is the view that systems of political leadership, and in particular the informal systems existing as political parties or their equivalents, cannot be shaped by forethought or deliberate planning. Ordinarily they develop gradually, by the cumulation of habits, by the lessons of trial and error, and from the determining context of the society within which they exist. Once they acquire momentum they are maintained by the logic of their own being and are amenable to change, not by

[3] A considerable body of thought has developed concerning the role and place of party in America although it has been focused chiefly on parties in the nation. For a thoughtful analysis, see Austin Ranney, *The Doctrine of Responsible Party Government, Its Origins and Present State* (Urbana: University of Illinois Press, 1954).

resolutions and statutes, but by the same more or less blind process through which they came into being. So deterministic and fatalistic a view may contain too much truth for comfortable contemplation. To the extent that the proposition induces a belief in the futility of human effort, it is re-enforced, in its application to the American states, by the special circumstances that subject their party systems to powerful, and often controlling, external influences.

Despite the elements of persistence and stability in the party systems of the American states, those systems are certain to undergo basic changes during the next fifty years, a span set not to suggest an exact schedule of alteration but to emphasize the proposition that the insensible steps of political evolution cumulate only slowly into institutional transformations. The precise paths of developments in the making cannot be surely mapped by the extrapolation of past trends. Moreover the extent to which the direction of change can be guided is most problematic. Nevertheless, if the form and direction of latent events could be discerned, the exercise of choice would be facilitated within that range of freedom of action between the inevitable and the desirable.

Basic changes that have long been in process are almost certain to alter fundamentally the electoral foundations of our parties. The traditional partisan attachments are wearing away, perhaps to be replaced by new habitual orientations and alignments but nevertheless different ones. The ancient sectional loyalties, burned into our politics by the Civil War and by memories of it, have been weakening in the South, where they have been most notable, but they also are wearing away in the older states of the North. Similarly, the patterns of loyalties within the industrial and metropolitan populations, a product of the peculiar and unprecedented process of the political assimilation and adaptation of great numbers of immigrants, are constantly under pressure and evidences of their erosion appear on every hand.

The jolts that re-arrange partisan alignments within the

electorate seem to be administered more by the issues of national politics than by the conflicts of state politics. Eventually the reshufflings of electors induced by the spirited debates of national politics seep into the affairs of states and localities and create new groupings of electors with a potential impact on state politics. The shape of these new alignments will depend, of course, on the kinds of issues that arise and the skill of politicians in exploiting those issues. Yet it is possible that the groupings that develop will have a more immediate relevance to the questions of the day than do traditional alignments with a close kinship to long past, even dead, issues.

The impact of the emerging electoral realignments on state politics will, to be sure, vary from state to state. It is possible, of course, to conceive of great issues that might stamp a new pattern of sectional one-partyism upon the nation. Given the marked tendencies away from economic homogeneity in most of the states, the more probable line of development is toward the creation within most of the states of electoral foundations less favorable to dominance by a single party. If this comes about, it will, of course, lay the basis for changes of the most profound significance in both state and national politics.[4]

[4] The great one-party sections have furnished a basic ingredient in the two-party system nationally. The existence of areas from which a party could not be uprooted has assured the minority an independent base for existence even though it lost control of the Presidency and the federal administrative apparatus. It can be contended with some plausibility that the national party system might be weakened or altered by the development of more evenly balanced systems of state politics. Such an expectation rests on the assumption that the existence of closely competitive states and congressional districts would permit almost complete elimination of minority representation in the House and Senate by a slight swing in electoral sentiment. Yet it seems almost inevitable that large numbers of congressional districts will, short of a political revolution, always be rather strongly committed to whichever party is in the minority nationally. The probability seems to be that the lines that divide districts tending Republican and those tending Democratic will come more and more to be fixed by factors other than sectional differentiation. It may, indeed, be possible to maintain a second party without one-party havens of refuge for minority legislators. Indiana, for example, has maintained an extremely close party competition with frequent alternations in power over a long period, although shifts in power reduce the minority legislative representation to an extremely small legislative bloc.

While the broad trends that affect the electorate and alter the raw materials with which politicians have to work can be discerned at least in their broad outlines with some assurance, there is another element of political party far more difficult to cope with. What has been happening to the leadership corps of the parties? Has their composition been changing? What have been the tendencies with respect to their bases of support and the interests to which they are immediately attached? Guesses may be hazarded about what the trends have been, but their projection would be a hazardous enterprise. Perhaps a change of major significance has been in the making in the composition of the Democratic leadership echelons in most of the states touched significantly by industrialization. That shift has involved the growing political activation of labor union leaders—and those dependent upon the support of organized labor—and their closer and more complete affiliation with the Democratic party. How far this development will go—even whether it will continue—no one knows. If the tendency should proceed far enough, the results might not be entirely healthy for the Democratic party. Yet it has within it the seeds of far firmer foundations for a second party in many American states as well as the corollary possibility of making less probable the old-time curse of American state politics, the domination of both party leaderships by essentially the same peak interests within society. The drives toward political integration and the means for disciplining the dissenter in American political life are truly formidable, yet islands of safety and independence may be emerging for state party leadership beyond ready control of the traditionally dominant clusters of interests.

The position that strengthening partisanship would promote the public weal is a lonely one. That, however, has been the general drift of the argument, although it has been hedged with qualifications and associated with considerable skepticism about what can be done to construct more effective party systems within the states. Yet the evidence makes it appear that emerging conditions will facilitate, if not automatically produce, alterations of substantial importance in the state political systems. What can be done to exploit and to take advantage of these changing circumstances presents another sort of question. Certainly from the welter of our analyses the moral ought to be clear that conditions and circumstances differ greatly from state to state. Prescriptions of blueprints for application under all sorts of circumstances would be both futile and at times self-defeating. Their feasibility as well as their effects would be of one sort in one place and of another in another.

Speculation about the problems of most states requires that the most reflective consideration be given to the place of the legislature in the governance of the state. Institutional reconstruction may have over the long pull significant secondary influences on informal systems of political leadership. Insofar as tinkering with the formal apparatus of government can have such derivative consequences, the odds are that the legislature is the point with the greatest potential leverage. The metamorphosis of the state legislatures constitutes an odd chapter in the history of popular government. At one time regarded as the symbolic embodiment of the people assembled, the state legislature went into a long decline. Sequences of ill-considered actions, or at least of actions that later turned sour, brought in their train drastic constitutional limitations on the power of legislatures that left them unable, even if they had the wisdom, to cope well with the next crisis that arose. Legislative sessions came to be limited to ridiculously short periods and legislative compensation has never adjusted itself to the fact that government is no longer a responsibility of country squires, obliged by position and enabled by status to spend the legislative sessions pleasantly at the state capitals. The legislature finally came to be regarded as a necessary evil whose sphere of action and influence should, like all evils, be restricted to the narrowest possible range. Its sittings engendered anxieties on all sides and rejoicing was the order of the day when its members finally finished their business,

284 American State Politics: An Introduction

sobered up, and went home. Such caricatures perhaps never entirely fitted the realities; yet legislatures have failed by far to meet the expectation that they would be the heart of democratic government.

A basic reconstruction of state legislatures would give free play to tendencies that could very well in the long run move toward a strengthened party system. That reconstruction would of necessity include removal of many of the state constitutional limitations on the substantive powers of legislatures, the removal of set limits on the length of legislative sessions, and perhaps the general introduction of annual sessions. The compensation of legislators would have to be fixed at a level generous enough so that the representative from Madison County would not begrudge each day spent at the state capital lest he miss a chance to sell an insurance policy to earn a commission sorely needed to feed his family. In some states the overall size of the legislature merits a second thought.[5]

If legislative reorganization is to affect the party system, new systems of apportionment of representation must be an element of legislative reform in most states. Yet proposals for broad legislative reconstruction would most probably founder on the rock of stubborn opposition to reform of the geography of representation—and of power. At the moment it is a safe prediction that any strong move for legislative reapportionment in almost any state would incite most of the chambers of commerce to opposition along with the Farm Bureau Federation and a cluster of allied interests. Whether the existing disposition of the forces of opposition will long prevail is another question. Move-

[5] In 23 states the ratio of members of the lower house to population is one to 20,000 or less. In only eight states does each member of the lower house speak, on the average, for 50,000 or more citizens. The average size of upper house constituencies varies much more widely. In 11 states it is under 25,000; in another 11 it is over 100,000; in 17 it ranges between 50,000 and 100,000. In all it requires 8,847 persons to man the American state legislatures, a number probably somewhat in excess of the supply of competent personnel available at the going rates for this kind of work.

ments of population since World War II have tended in many states to create areas of Republican underrepresentation, especially in the suburbs, to match metropolitan areas of Democratic underrepresentation. Circumstances are building up which could bring a realignment of the forces on the question of legislative apportionment, although the odds are that legislative malapportionment will be with us for a long time.

What could be expected from a thoroughgoing legislative reconstruction which included all the components that have been outlined? The consequences for the party system in some situations might be absolutely nil. In others tendencies exist which would be given room for their more complete fulfillment. Thus the battery of changes would make probable a larger representation of the minority party within the legislature. A more adequate compensation—a far more adequate compensation— would certainly widen the range of persons amenable to persuasion to serve in the legislature, a matter of the utmost importance for the perennial outs who, in most states, from the nature of the partisan differentials in the sources of leadership recruitment, tend to be especially dependent on their earnings from politics for a livelihood. A role of somewhat greater importance and prestige for the legislature in the total governmental process should also have its consequences in the attraction of personnel. In all these matters, mere constitutional and statutory changes do not of course in themselves have such consequences; they would merely create opportunity, perhaps provide some incentive. And in their bearing on the workings of the party system the full effects, if any, would develop over perhaps decades rather than an election or two.

In its effects on the party system and on political leadership, the most important consequence that could be hoped for from legislative reconstruction would be the more adequate support of a substantial bloc of party leaders and more especially the support of a minority with a better opportunity to play effectively a role of dissent and criticism. A legislature with a position more nearly comparable to that of Congress would give the minority both a forum and a means of support for many of its principal leaders. Whether all concerned would make the most of their opportunities would, of course, be something else again.[6]

A thorough overhauling of the state legislature would, of course, have consequences far beyond those upon the state party systems. In most states the place of the legislature merits the most thorough reconsideration on grounds quite independent of those mentioned in this discussion.[7] Yet legislative reconstruction could provide support for sectors of the leadership of both parties, it could enable the minority to perform more effectively its role in the governing process, and it might give the opposition a platform from which to carry on its more general role of criticism. Even so, there would remain a problem in the organization of party leadership, the solution to which, if any, is most elusive. That is the problem of the organization of party leadership outside the government.

Commonly the formal organs of state party leadership consist of central committees or executive committees represent-

[6] An interesting tack on the problem of nurturing a functioning minority has been attempted in Puerto Rico. The overwhelming majorities in the legislature won by the Popular party came to concern even the leaders of that party. The 1952 constitution provides, under certain conditions, for an increase of minority representation over and above the number of seats won through the ordinary electoral procedures. See Constitution, Art. III, sec. 7. The Illinois system of cumulative voting assures the minority of a larger representation than would be produced by plurality elections in the same set of districts. The Illinois system, however, has been associated with malapportionment of representation. In effect, each party has had within its legislative group a bloc of members from districts in which the party's candidates could never, or rarely, win if simple single-member districts were the rule.

[7] The resistance in many states to proposals for more sensible organization of the executive and administrative machinery may rest in part on the fact that the legislature is not in session much of the time to keep an eye on the governor and other executive officers. The absence of an effective legislature to exercise a countervailing surveillance may reenforce the general anxieties about executive power. Of course, the long-term tendency has been to fortify the position of the governor, a trend that has strengthened one important center of political leadership within the state.

ative in one way or another of electoral districts of the state. Often the members are chosen by popular vote at the time of the party primaries, although rarely is the level of voter-interest in these choices much more than nominal. The committees are virtually self-designated. While no census of the status of the state central committees is available, the general impression that most of them are virtually dead is probably not far wrong. A few have continuing staffs active in the business of the party. Others have an avid concern about the spoils of politics and present, for that reason alone, an appearance of internal cohesion and strength.

The proposition seems axiomatic that if party as party is to fulfill its role, a more effective organization of its leadership is in order. That can come about probably only through the initiative of leaders within the parties and then probably only through informal action rather than through legislative prescription of party organization. Probably the infirmity of party organization derives in part from the fact that the formal party organs tend to be manned in fairly high degree by those leadership elements concerned with the chores of campaigning and election-day work, a group whose contribution to the success of the party may have been great at one time but has become often more fictional than real. In some way other elements, and often more dynamic elements, of the leadership echelons could perhaps be brought into the formal apparatus of party leadership. The elder statesmen, the major contributors to party funds, the egg-heads—Republican advertising men and Democratic academicians—, spokesmen for interests associated with the party, and other types of party influentials might very well be worked into the formal organs of party leadership in one way or another.

An enlivened, more representative, and active party organization could easily earn its keep by searching out, encouraging, and financing likely candidates for elective offices ranging all the way from legislative seats to the governorship. It remains a serious question whether party organization can exist and function effectively in the promotion of candidates if it must work through the pure form of the statewide direct primary, save perhaps under the most exceptional circumstances.[8] In those states overwhelmingly committed to the candidates of one party or another, the direct primary will probably long remain the unchallenged mode of nomination. In those states with normally close electoral divisions between the parties, however, the process of nominating candidates for statewide office would be worth a responsible reconsideration. It is in such states, of course, that the convention system retains a few footholds, and it is in such states that experiments with variations on the direct primary, such as the pre-primary convention have been most notable.[9] Our analyses indicate that it is in the closer states that warm competition for primary nominations occurs least frequently, a fact that probably reflects informal consultation and agreement on candidates among the elements of party leadership although such action may not be taken through party assemblies or conventions. Any sort of reorganization of nominating procedures and practices will, of course, be of no avail unless it is accompanied by the development of party organizations better equipped to take the lead in the recruitment and promotion of candidates. The two lines of action are, in a sense, intertwined. Wide-open primaries tend both to shatter party organization and to leave it without much of anything to do. In the absence of working party organization or its equivalent, the direct primary often produces almost unbelievable sorts of nominations. And, to be sure, the recruitment of candidates for elective office must over-

---

[8] The observations about the direct primary should be restricted to the statewide primary. The problem of sifting out likely prospects for statewide office differs rather radically from the problem of choice in smaller constituencies. No matter what size the constituency may be, there is a problem in recruiting candidates for elective office. Yet rather different questions arise, which have not been explored here, with respect to the formal methods of nomination in small one-party electoral units.

[9] A committee of the National Municipal League has supported a proposal for pre-primary endorsement of candidates by party organizations acting through committees or conferences. See National Municipal League, *A Model Direct Primary System* (1951).

come many obstacles other than those fixed by nominating procedures.[10]

While general modes and lines of action that might be followed to reinvigorate the state party systems can be contrived readily enough, a more fundamental problem exists in the problem of harnessing human energies to the machinery of party. The preachings of several generations have diverted quantities of civic energy away from partisan activities. The systematic depreciation of partisanship perhaps both depresses impulses to community leadership as well as pushes activity into nonpartisan channels. However that may be, the party system, which lies at the heart of the governing process, often is left by default in a weakened position. The evangel who wishes to strengthen states in the governing process needs to work out ways and means to bring to the service of party a larger share of the energies and abilities of the potential resources of leadership.

[10] See the discussion by Mayor Joseph S. Clark, Jr., of Philadelphia, "Wanted: Better Politicians," *Atlantic Monthly,* August, 1955.

Index